H.F. Parker

Constance Aylmar

A story of the seventeenth century

H.F. Parker

Constance Aylmar
A story of the seventeenth century

ISBN/EAN: 9783744748216

Printed in Europe, USA, Canada, Australia, Japan

Cover: Foto ©ninafisch / pixelio.de

More available books at **www.hansebooks.com**

CONSTANCE AYLMER.

A STORY OF THE

SEVENTEENTH CENTURY.

By H. F. P.

NEW YORK:
CHARLES SCRIBNER & COMPANY.
1869.

CONSTANCE AYLMER.

I.

In the great family room of Burgomaster Zwaller's house, in New Amsterdam, were two guests whose arrival from the Old World was an event of interest in the gossipy little town. One was an elderly woman, portly and pillowy in figure; the other a young girl whose sweetness and grace were more impressive, even, than the delicacy and refinement of her features. Dame Zwaller's interest in the latter was heightened by the fact that she had lost both father and mother, and had just ventured across the sea to accept a home with her father's favorite sister, to whose care he had commended her—Lady Deborah Moody, of Long Island.

Sitting in the bright firelight, on the opposite side of the wide hearth, was Burgomaster Zwaller; his large red nose and folded chin showing how well he loved good cheer, and his kind voice and smile winning now, as always, the good will of strangers. A red skull-cap, a plaited cue, a short, loose jacket, and frieze short-clothes, conspired to make his rotund figure as broad as it was long.

The adornments of the room in which this master of the house sat, were no less quaint than himself.

The floor was white as new pine, and sanded in hieroglyphical figures, which the English girl was in constant danger of brushing out with the long sweep of her dress. The whitewashed walls were zigzagged with a dye as blue as Dame Zwaller's new stockings. A dresser stood at one end of the room, every shelf of which was filled with rows of shining dishes and polished pewter cups. The uppermost displayed a set of Delft china, used only on state occasions. It had long been the provoker of many envious and ill-natured speeches at the expense of the proud housewife. A tall clock, pictured with the sun and moon, majestically ticked in the corner, and a spinning-wheel stood idle before the narrow window. Over the door two rifles were crossed, within ready reach; and above the high mantel hung a huge bow, which had been obtained from an Indian chief for a string of buttons. Two pewter candle-holders, as bright as silver, shone upon the mantel, and sundry small doors, fastened by wooden buttons, varied the bareness of the great chimney wall, besides serving as hiding-places for whatever was uncouth in the neat dame's eyes. Two iron-bound chests, one of which contained the burgomaster's papers and books (the contents of the other, even Vrow Van Weil, who came once a week to gossip, could not find out), together with several broad-seated oak chairs, and a claw-footed table, curiously carved, completed the furniture of the family room of the finest house in New Amsterdam, except the Governor's.

Tall Dame Zwaller, who presided here with broom

and brush, continually went to and fro, busy with household cares. A bunch of keys jingled at her side, and a pair of scissors swung from her apron-strings. Her voice was nervous and decisive in the frequent commands given to old black Mabel or young Minxey, whose round of laborious scouring and polishing knew no end. The voice softened when it spoke to plump, apple-cheeked Barbara, the only and most precious daughter. She was a happy soul, like her father, not seeing at all the vital need of making a shining sun of every pewter cup, or of pursuing spiders to the death, or of devoting all the spare moments of her life to knitting long stockings. She sat now by her father, demure and pretty, with her dark hair nearly hidden under a close-fitting, blue, quilted cap, and her round form snugly laced in a red bodice. The short petticoat disdained to hide the goodly size of her foot, of which she neither thought or cared, so long as the Holland shoe fitted well. One felt inclined to pinch her ruddy, round cheeks, or squeeze her plump, dimpled hands, as if she were a child, only for the tell-tale ring on her finger. She said little as she sat there, stealing glances of profound admiration at the youthful stranger, Constance Aylmer, who seemed to her to have glided out of one of the old legends so often told by the fireside. But a sudden knock startled her, and, hastening to open the door, a frank, manly voice saluted her, which brought the burgomaster to a quick and hearty welcome of the bachelor son of his excellent friend, Lady Moody.

"Is this the same Constance I left romping on the

lawn at Atherton Hall?" asked Sir Henry with some surprise, as he dropped Mynheer's hand, and met his newly-arrived cousin.

"The very same," she said, as his kind arms enfolded her.

"You thought my slow coming a cold welcome, did you not?" he asked. "We cannot speed here at will in a post-coach. It is no small journey from Gravesend to New Amsterdam, as you will soon find. Good-day to you, Dame Zwaller!" he continued, turning to her, who had come in at the sound of his voice. "Thank you for housing my bird!"

"This is Mistress Primley, my chaperone across the Atlantic," said Constance, smiling, and leading him toward her matronly companion, whose eyes had been fixed upon him with interest since his entrance. Mistress Primley courtesied with the dignity of a duchess, but even her cap-ribbons fluttered at the grateful thanks bestowed upon her for her attention to his cousin, during the tedious voyage.

"Lady Moody will come herself to thank you," concluded he, as they sat down by the blazing fire to talk of friends, of the voyage, and of the novelties and hardships that awaited the newly-arrived.

"I am glad you had so fair a voyage, my cousin; but why did you not rough it in the wind, rather than pale your cheeks in the cabin? How did it happen, Mistress Primley?"

"It is unseemly for ladies to spoil their complexions," she replied. "Besides, I feared she would catch cold in the spray, or that a wave might wash her overboard; or that the wind would blow her away, or what not. She was safer by me in the cabin."

"Did you never go on deck?" Sir Henry asked, turning to Constance with a look of mingled surprise and merriment.

"Rarely," she replied, playfully. "Mistress Primley was much distressed lest the rigging should fall and crush me. Indeed, I feared lest I should not behold the sea at all, but my dread of your laughter and my desire to see if the good ship sliced the waves as daintily as you promised, made me over rule her wishes sometimes."

"Mistress Primley," said Sir Henry gravely, "did you mean to roll Constance like a bug in a nut-shell from the Old World to the New, so that she might never be able to find her way back again?"

"I will give your lordship a better reason. There was a certain Lord Percy on board, who took delight in wild tales of the colonies, and insisted that your cousin was to be buried alive among the boors of Long Island, or scalped by the savages. She sat, one day, upon a coil of ropes while he was thus discoursing, and—you see those long curls falling from her temples—he lifted them, circled a dirk-knife round her head, and said, 'This is the way they would rob you of your silken hair!' How did I know but this nobleman, who may or may not be a real lord, (shrugging her shoulders,) might carry the precious child off in the ship's boat? I think he would have the heart for it."

Mistress Primley leaned back in her chair and

drew a deep sigh of relief that her charge was safely here. The burgomaster looked silently at the fire, and thought upon this Lord Percy, whose arrival had already been discussed at the Stadt Huys, and who was established in state at Metje Wessel's Inn. Sir Henry turned inquiringly to Constance, and noticed that her paleness had given place to roses almost as intense as Barbara's.

"Did he offer no apology for his rudeness?" he sternly asked.

"Yes," replied Constance, bowing her head with evident wish to drop the subject. Happily for her, Dame Zwaller announced supper, and, when that was over, the busy housewife drew the spinning-wheel from its corner, and accompanied the chit-chat of her guests with its musical buzz. Mistress Primley brought out her unfailing knitting and industriously clicked her needles, till the tall clock tolled eight. This was the signal for Minxey to come with Bible and taper, and stand behind the burgomaster's chair while he read. An hour afterward, the glowing pine knot was smothered in ashes, the room was deserted, the wheel was still, the cat lay curled upon its cushion and slept softly. Of all in the house, only the curious clock was wide awake.

In spite of the soothing stillness, Constance did not rest well. Her dreams were peopled with impish Minxeys darting arrows at her, Dutch dames twisting her curls into a cue, and Lord Percy smiling and whispering at her side, then oddly perching upon the chimney top and screeching, "te whit, te whoo."

This awoke her. She lay listening a long time to the doleful cry of a real owl who was amusing himself with the echo of his croak, instead of hiding his crooked nose under his wing, as any respectable bird ought to do at that time of night. At last, she espied the first gleam of dawn through the little window opening just beneath the peak of the gable, and too high for her to reach even on tip-toe. At the earliest stir of the household, she presented herself, much to their surprise. Her explanation at breakfast of her early awakening created a round of laughter. Mistress Primley shook her head and looked grave.

"It is a warning. May nothing happen!"

Sir Henry thought this croak as dismal as the owl's hoot. As soon as the curds and new milk had received ample justice, he hastened to prepare for his departure to Gravesend.

Dame Zwaller bade Constance good-by at the gate. Her heart had gone out warmly toward the artless young girl. With real regret at the parting, she earnestly pressed her to spend the coming holiday under her roof. The burgomaster and Mistress Primley went with her to the landing, where Cornelius Dircksen, the ferryman, waited to row them across to Breuklyn. He had ample time for the extra pull, as his regular trips occurred but twice a day, to transport the farmers with their cabbages to market.

Mistress Primley shed tears at the loss of her *protegée*, whom she declared she loved as her own child. She watched the boat as long as she could distinguish Constance.

1*

"What if the boot should upset! Do you think it will, Mynheer?" Her tears flowed afresh at the thought. But Mynheer reminded her that the ferryman was a strong man and a wonderful swimmer, so that he might easily put Constance high and dry in his hat and float her ashore. This was a great consolation. Mistress Primley was content now to leave off straining her eyes in gazing after the boat through her tears, and went back to the house praising Constance all the way.

II.

Gravesend, in its fourteenth year, was a small village surrounded by high palisades. Its streets radiated from a common centre where stood the Town house, the pump and the whipping-post. The best of the houses were double, with long, sloping thatched roofs, and huge chimney-stacks which admitted as much light as the very small windows.

A little beyond the village, and also enclosed by high palisades, stood a large, irregular stone house called Moody Hall, both on account of the superiority of the building and on account of its occupants. Its possessor, Lady Moody, was one of the patentees of the town. She had come here to enjoy more freedom of opinion than was granted her at Lynn among the Puritans. Ten years later she would have been persecuted there as a Quaker. The people of Gravesend, like herself, were English, with few exceptions, and of the same religious belief. They regarded this Lady-mother with awe as well as affection, and submitted to her judgment all difficulties which could not be otherwise settled.

The house, which the villagers pointed out to strangers with pride, was spacious on the ground-floor, and lighted with deep, narrow windows of diamond-shaped panes. The roof was red-tiled, and curved out in a steep slope beyond the front wall, where it was supported by roughly-hewn columns, and formed a long piazza. Some of these rude columns, and part of the roof, were covered with a luxuriant creeping vine. It was a mass of rich green in summer. Now, early in November, it gleamed scarlet. The floor of the piazza and the entrance-path, were paved with round, smooth pebbles. A settle-bench stood against the wall beneath the windows, and was a cool resting-place in summer. The ponderous double door, with "bull's eyes" in its upper panels, opened into a wide hall. Above the doors leading to side rooms, deers' antlers were fixed, in proof of Sir Henry's skill as a huntsman; and Indian trophies hung upon the walls. The large room on the left had the luxury of silk hangings and richly-carved furniture, which had seen their best days in England. If this room had an air of the world, it was no fault of Lady Moody's now; for these vanities were the relics of her gayer days. It was used only on rare occasions—such as the coming of the Right Honorable Lord and Director-General, Petrus Stuyvesant, whom nobody in Gravesend dared to entertain, or knew so well how to manage as the good mother.

The room opposite this was the home of the house. Here the fire always glowed in winter; deep arm-chairs stood hospitably by the wide hearth; a round work-table, with its orderly basket, occupied an inviting corner; and a library filled the space opposite the windows.

This was to be Constance Aylmer's home. Her

first glimpse of the red-tiled roof above the palisades, as she and Sir Henry wound along the road, alarmed her lest she should feel like a prisoner there.

"Why is it so like a fort?" she asked.

"To protect us from the attacks of Indians," was the reply. "Those palisades did us good service two years gone. We can fight our own battles there without help of soldiers." Constance turned toward him with a frightened look.

"Lord Percy spoke truly, then," said she.

"I hope not, my cousin," was the laughing reply. "There is little fear of the savages now, for my good mother has held a great talk with the chiefs. They know she is the soul of honor, for they have tried her and found her true—just as you will find her every day of her life. In any event, my sweet cousin, your bright locks are safe. Take the word of a gallant bachelor for that."

"Thank you," returned Constance, smiling and reassured. "Tell me more of aunt Deborah. Is she like my mother?"

"Her smile alone may remind you of her—perhaps her voice. For the rest, I can only tell you to think of the personification of purity, of uprightness before God and man, of generosity in soul and purse, of strong feelings under complete control, of tenderest affection, and you have my mother as she seems to me. Not the faintest likeness in me, you perceive," he added, suddenly breaking from the grave tone in which he was speaking. "Here we are. You will soon see for yourself."

Constance was trying to reconcile this character with the image she retained of her aunt since childhood. It was that of an elegant woman, attired in embroidered robes and ruffs, and whose animated face was surmounted by a cloud of powdered hair. With this vision still floating before her, she alighted and hastened along the path, just as the ponderous door swung back. There stood Lady Moody, waiting to welcome her. Constance was chilled with disappointment at the first sight. The placid greeting, the nunnish dress, the lace cap—simple and fresh, hiding with rigor the wealth of hair as if to smother pride in it—the smooth neckerchief, white as snow— all together repelled her, and, instead of throwing her arms around her aunt's neck, as she had all the time unconsciously expected to do, she simply clasped her hand, kissed her gently, and smiled a homesick smile. Then she followed her to the library, where they sat a few moments talking of the journey and of the Zwallers. Lady Moody quickly saw the weary, sad look in the face that had never learned to hide the thoughts behind it, and said with cheerful tenderness,

"Come, my daughter, I will show thee the pretty chamber prepared for thee. When tired of us, thee can steal away, as I remember thee did when a child, and can hide there as thee used to behind thy mother's chair, to work undisturbed." Her face shone with smiling goodness so plainly that Constance forgot the smooth cap and gray gown, and thought, after all, she was not as austere as she at first would have believed. Listening to cheerful talk of the past, she found herself laughing by the time they had climbed the stairway, and was interested to see what the pretty room under the eaves contained. A tent-bed stood there, draped with curtains of blue wool, the finest that had been woven at the Hall. The windows were also curtained with blue. A deep, straight-backed chair, with broad arms, standing by the window, and before it a small round table with supports in tripod-form, and a richly-carved wardrobe of black oak, were the chief objects of the pleasant chamber. Lady Moody threw back the wooden blind.

"Thee can see the bay from this window, and the ships and fishermen's craft as they come in. Thee must be watchful to catch sight of one, for they do not come like flocks of white birds as they used upon the Thames. But do not strain thine eyes now. Lie here and rest, and another time we will see all that will be pleasant to thee here."

Constance was grateful for the thought bestowed upon her comfort, but she still felt too much awed to express it. As soon as left alone, she buried herself in the downy bed and, with her cheeks wet with homesick tears, fell into a deep, dreamless slumber, just such as she needed after her sleepless night and fatiguing journey.

While she slept profoundly under the blue curtains in the little chamber, two persons sat in the library talking of her. Sir Henry, in his restless way, teazed the logs into a brighter flame while speaking, and his friend, Mr. Mordaunt, listened with easy indifference.

"She is a fine horsewoman. Joan of Arc could not have done better to-day."

"Englishwomen are hardy," returned Mr. Mordaunt, wondering if the newly-arrived was a stout spinster. There was a twinkle of mischief in Sir Henry's eye when he added,

"She can tie a stronger mesh than Timon, the weaver, in the house beyond the palisades; and I'll warrant there is not an archer in the New Netherlands can send an arrow straighter to the mark than she!"

"Ah! an Amazonian!" Sir Henry made no reply to this, but abruptly turned the conversation to law matters which had brought Mr. Mordaunt from Virginia. An hour later, Constance came in, fresh and smiling, from her rest. Sir Henry presented her to his friend, feeling intense satisfaction at his unconcealed surprise when he found the stout spinster suddenly transformed into a graceful young girl of delicate beauty. Mr. Mordaunt was not captivated however. He was too accustomed to captivate others to be moved at first sight. His ideal of beauty was the dazzling, piquant style; not at all the gentle loveliness of the one before him. He quickly recovered his self-possession and entered into conversation, which was presently broken by the announcement of tea, but resumed with interest around the table. Tall wax candles shed a soft light over the group, and upon the table laid with such nicety and spread with such bounty as to stimulate the daintiest of appetites.

"I need not ask if thou art refreshed, I see it in

thy countenance," said Lady Moody as she made tea from the bright silver kettle before her. "Thee will make a good pioneer."

"Our friends in England promised that I should wilt under the hardness of this new country," replied Constance. "I am glad you do not discourage me, also."

"I should think one delicately bred would find the transplanting harsh," said Mr. Mordaunt, who sat opposite. "Does not the uncouthness of even New Amsterdam look doleful to your eyes?"

"Oh no," she laughingly answered. "Every thing was so droll and yet so simple there, I took pleasure in it."

"But the villages are rude. You can not shop in Gravesend as in London."

"Nor have I the need here, as there."

"Ah! I see! Novelty holds you charmed. When dangers beset you, I am afraid you will not withstand them so bravely as the loss of refined communities."

"I will not boast my courage before it is tried. In any case, why need I fear, since my brave cousin is here?"

"My services are pledged," said Sir Henry gravely. "Mr. Mordaunt, you will alarm Constance by your promises of ill happenings as much as did Lord Percy during the voyage ——" here he stopped upon seeing her frightened pleading look, lest he should repeat Mistress Primley's tale. Mr. Mordaunt's observing eyes caught the troubled glance also, and did not fail to notice the rosy flush that mounted to her cheek. Who was this Lord Percy? And what was he to her? Perhaps she was not free to be won. That were a pity, for there was a charm about her not at first discovered—an electrical play of soul in the features which continually lighted and varied their expression. Mr. Mordaunt found himself studying her face more than once, and now that there was a possibility of a rival he felt that the preference of such a woman would be a high honor.

"Who is this Lord Percy of whom thee just spoke?" asked Lady Moody.

"A nobleman in high state at Metje Wessell's inn, who arrived in the same ship with Constance. He has some matters to transact with the Director. You will doubtless see him soon, for he told me he desired to assure himself of my cousin's health and safety after the fatigue of the voyage." Constance's eyes were fastened upon her plate while he spoke. "Baltazzar Stuyvesant will accompany him," he continued, "and will doubtless prove his chivalry in your ladyship's service. This is for your comfort, my cousin, lest you fear a dearth of fine gallants in our pleasant country."

Even Lady Moody, always so tranquil, laughed audibly at the thought of the unwieldy Baltazzar, playing the nimble gallant. Sir Henry immediately described him with exaggeration.

"His breeches are no less than four at one wearing, and his jackets, three. His cue is the longest and broadest plaited in New Amsterdam, and his hat has the widest brim. He always reminds me of one of Dame Zwaller's Holland cheeses."

"Ah, my son, thee need not spend thy wits upon one who has done thee so many favors. Constance, thee will not find in Manhattan a better heart than this same Baltazzar owns. Christiana Zwaller knows it, and her daughter Barbara, who is betrothed to him, can tell thee how truly I speak."

"We cannot admit her testimony," laughed Mr. Mordaunt.

"I shall be glad to render mine," added Constance. "I have great desire to see also your generous protector, the Governor." Sir Henry smiled contemptuously.

"You will come to learn that he is more of a tyrant than protector. Governor Keith was a more liberal guardian of our rights than he."

"Has any thing new come to thy knowledge to-day?" anxiously asked Lady Moody.

"No, mother. I had in mind his new proclamation, forbidding the worship of any sect save the Calvinists. You will have no more freedom here, than in the English colonies. Only for savages and beasts, we might still follow the sun with profit."

"'Go further and fare worse,'" suggested Mr. Mordaunt, as they arose from table, and returned to the library.

Constance withdrew early, not to sleep, but to talk long of the sacred past with her aunt. It was a precious interchange of joys and sorrows, such as won her heart, and bound them together in sympathy and love. When at last they said good night, she forgot the smooth neckerchief and threw her arms lovingly around Lady Moody, exclaiming,

"I have indeed found a mother! I am happy!"

III.

Before breakfast the next morning, Constance stood by the shelves in the library, lost in a book. Mr. Mordaunt came sauntering through the hall. Catching a glimpse of her, he stopped in the door-way to admire the effect of her simple blue morning-dress, loosely girdled, her hair fastened without ornament, and the small foot almost hidden by the huge rosette of her slipper. Even the bend of her neck, and the droop of her shoulders, did not escape his critical survey. Eyes thus fastened upon one are always felt. Constance turned without knowing why, and seeing him, wished him a cheerful good-morning, and restored the book to its place.

"Lost in book-lore so early?" said he, glancing over the rows of volumes as if to know their titles.

"Only a quaint poem, I chanced to see." Mr. Mordaunt noted its Latin title.

"Ladies do not often amuse themselves with learning, even in England, Mistress Aylmer."

"Oh, I am not learned. But my mother caused me to be taught as my brother. She thought embroidery and the harpsichord pleasant trifles, but not worthy to serve one at all times."

"Learning helps one to endure hardness," returned Mr. Mordaunt. "You will have need of that and the harpsichord too, in this wilderness home. Can you truly find content away from the gayeties of London?"

"Truly I can, for, having never tasted those gayeties, I shall not miss them. I have always lived at Atherton Hall."

All the time she answered, Mr. Mordaunt was watching the changing expression, the frank, confiding look in her eyes, the play of dimples around her sweet mouth, and then the modest falling of her eyelids under his too studious gaze, which sank more deeply into his heart for after-dreaming, than any coquettish brilliancy he professed to admire. It was more dangerous pastime for him than he knew. Even at breakfast, while talking with Lady Moody of the affairs of the colony, his eyes wandered so often toward Constance, that when he had gone, Sir Henry drily remarked, that he continually mistook her for Lady Moody.

"Is my hair disordered? Is my toilet awry or unseemly, aunt Deborah?" was Constance's question as soon as they were alone.

"I see no fault. Why does thee ask?"

"Mr. Mordaunt scanned me so well," she laughingly answered, "that I believed he thought me unfitly attired."

"Thee must pardon him, for he has not seen one of his own countrywomen of gentle birth, these many months. He was used to much courtly society before he came hither. He seeks to repair a broken fortune in Virginia, and will doubtless return to England, when his wishes are fulfilled. Will thee come now and learn the windings of the house?"

Constance followed Lady Moody in her usual

morning rounds to the great kitchen, where Chloe, black as ebony, presided over kettles swinging upon the crane, in the huge fireplace, or delighted herself at the pastry-board. The tiled floor was spotless in its neatness, the cross-beams above were festooned with strings of apples drying, and bunches of sweet herbs swung from hooks in the wall. Beyond the kitchen, was the dairy, with its cool stone floor, and its rows of full pans crusted with delicious cream. Rose stood there, just bringing up golden butter from the depths of the churn. It was a pleasant sight, suggestive of a plentifulness which Lady Moody generously shared with those who lacked stores of their own. The rooms above displayed piles of linen, woollen fabrics, and coarse material, the sum of the industry of old Cæsar, and Phillis, and young Jinney, who spun and wove in an outer building, a stone's throw from the house. The finest of the wool and flax, were reserved for Lady Moody's wheel. It was woven in the house-loft by Rose, whence came the soft blue fabric that curtained the pretty room under the eaves.

When the morning round was finished, and the two returned to the library, Constance hesitatingly asked,

"Are all these black people slaves, whom I have just seen, aunt Deborah?"

"No, my daughter, they have earned their freedom according to their faithfulness. Tobee, the herdsman, gains his papers the first day of the New Year. Mingo and Peter, the field hands, belong to Christiana

Zwaller, whom I have entreated much to sell to them their freedom. She believes it would cause mischief, and waxes indignant when I press the matter."

"She is not a gentle mistress," said Constance, remembering the shrill, impatient voice.

"She is the best housewife in Manhattan," replied Lady Moody, unwilling to lessen her friend in any one's esteem. To end the subject, she went out upon the piazza and into the garden, where she busied herself in pruning the leafless rose-bushes. The air was soft and hazy like a returned Indian summer. Its pleasantness tempted Constance to walk outside the palisades, and then, seeing Mingo with his oxen and cart trundling along the road that led toward the forest, the idea came to go also, and gather bright leaves in the hollows.

"Stop, Mingo!" cried she, "take me in your cart." He could hardly believe his ears, but seeing her in earnest, he stripped off his jacket and spread it over the bottom of the cart. Constance sprang lightly in, and seated herself with a smiling "Thank you." Mingo gave the word of advance, flourishing his long whip over the ears of the oxen as proudly as if he were postillion to a princess. The old cart was instantly dignified above every other, and Mingo was so elated at his honor, that he kept up an incessant hallooing at the quiet oxen to display his skill and the speed of the unheeding beasts. After much ado, the woods were reached. Constance bounded out and was soon plunging her hands among the fallen leaves, exclaiming now and then at sight of a maple or sumach leaf, gay and fresh yet.

"Woa! ah! whoo!" rang through the woods. The unearthly sound sent her scrambling and out of breath toward Mingo.

"The Indians!" she gasped.

"Woa! ah! whoo!" came again the shout, wound up by a prolonged screech. Mingo was convulsed with laughter, shaking his head all the time and begging pardon over and over when he could speak.

"Dem's Dutch women drivin' cows. You see 'em straight through dis yer strip o' wood. Go in dat path an' you see 'em," said he, pointing to a small, winding path at a short distance.

She followed it, half afraid to venture, yet longing to see from what woman's lips such a sound could come. She soon reached a small clearing where stood a house, with peaked, thatched roof, and walls blocked in blue and yellow. In front were two cows yoked to a plough. A dark-faced woman, in short-gown and striped petticoat, guided it, shouting her yisht! yisht! woa! in a high key each time she reached the end of a furrow. Constance sat upon a fallen tree to look and to listen to the wild sounds. Then she bethought herself of a pencil and paper in her pocket. Using the inside of a smooth piece of bark for a portfolio, she quickly produced a sketchy little picture of the thatched cottage and the gipsey-faced woman, with her cows and plough. She was too absorbed to hear the soft steps behind her or to know that a pair of eyes were looking intently over her shoulder at the picture.

A low ejaculation close to her ear made her spring to her feet with fright. A harmless Indian girl stood before her. Constance's eyes dilated with fear, then grew calm as they rested upon the beautiful, dark face. She scanned the mantle of fine feather work, the skirt bordered with porcupine quills and the deerskin moccasins. The two remained looking at each other, Constance with half-parted lips and brilliant eyes—the Indian girl with folded arms and quiet aspect. At length, the girl pointed from the Dutch woman to the sketch, nodded her head and gave a soft, low laugh.

"Come to Moody Hall," said Constance, "and I will picture you." The wild beauty shook her head. She could not understand. Constance pointed to the path, to herself, and repeated, "Moody." The unmoved face nodded assent. Now she wished to know the name of this forest belle. She gently stroked herself, repeating her own name, then laid her hand timidly upon the stranger waiting for her to speak.

"Omanee," was the reply to the silent question.

"Omanee! Omanee!" said Constance over and over, and Omanee gave another soft, low laugh, at hearing her own name from the lips of the white girl. Then they parted, and it was time, for Mingo was already coming in alarm at the prolonged absence of his venturesome charge. Constance gathered in her broad hat the nuts and leaves she had chosen, and went back bareheaded in the old jogging cart to the very gateway. As she entered the house, Mr. Mordaunt met her.

"I must believe you are the Spirit of the Wind, and that a breeze has whirled you in with the autumn leaves," he said. She was quite unconscious of the bright glow, the animation, the graceful abandon of manner which awakened his admiration, and laughingly replied,

"You would have named it a lazy breeze for a spirit, and truly Mistress Primley would have called it an unseemly coach for a lady, but it was a delightful trundle for all that. Who, think you, I saw in the woods? Omanee. Her face is like a picture at Atherton Hall. Her eyes are full, dark, soft; her hair glossy black; she moves like a queen. You have seen her, then?"

"I have seen her," said he quietly. "She is the daughter of a chief. Her beauty can in no wise be denied, but it has not the unspeakable charm that I have seen in another face—the Archeress of the Island."

"I have never heard of her," said Constance, innocently waiting further explanation.

"Ask Sir Henry. He can tell you better than I," continued Mr. Mordaunt, smiling. Constance turned away wondering, and not a little disappointed that he was not more enthusiastic in regard to Omanee. Upon reaching her room, she threw herself into the deep chair by the window to rest, but remembering that the morning was nearly spent, hastened to renew her toilet. A small mirror in a quaint, beaded frame gave back the poor reflection of herself.

"What a fright! What a tousled head! What

wonder that he believed me a piece of a hurricane!" she exclaimed, surveying her disordered hair frizzled and tossed over her neck.

"And my shoe!" cried she, looking down in dismay at her foot. At that moment Lady Moody came in, surprised to find her ready to cry with shame and vexation.

"What troubles thee, Constance?"

"Look at me, Aunt Deborah. Mr. Mordaunt just told me he thought me the Spirit of the Wind. Why should he not smile and gaze at me? Truly he had need; see my slipper!"

"Where did thee go in those fine shoes?"

"In Mingo's cart, and in the woods to see the Dutch woman," said she, still perplexed as to what Mr. Mordaunt must think of her. Her aunt could not refrain from smiling.

"Thee need not trouble thy head. Thy health is of more account than dress, and Edward Mordaunt is too sensible to think less of thee for the disorder of a morning's ramble. But thee had not better walk in slippers, nor so far without thy cousin."

Her mild voice, and view of the matter, restored Constance's composure. She brought the sketch, chatted of Omanee, laughed over her alarm, and while talking, busied herself in fastening the brightest of the autumn leaves above the little mirror. At last, rearranging her dress, she sat upon a footstool at Lady Moody's feet as placid and as smoothly neat as if the wind had never kissed her cheek or tossed her hair. It was a new pleasure to her aunt, this possession of a daughter, and she will come often to fill this pleasant seat by the window, while conferring, as mother and daughter only can, upon the cares, the pleasures, duties, and sorrows that are in store for both.

Constance did not see Mr. Mordaunt again that day, nor for several days, he having gone to Midwout. She was not sorry, for she still felt ashamed of the ragged *deshabille* in which he had seen her. A few evenings later, some allusion to Omanee reminded her of what she intended to ask Sir Henry.

"Can you tell me," said she at the first opportunity, " who is the Archeress of the Island?"

"Archeress? No," he slowly replied, "I remember none such." He cast an inquiring glance toward his mother, but she was equally at loss. Constance then added,

"She is lovelier than Omanee, Mr. Mordaunt said. He bade me ask you." Sir Henry's face suddenly gleamed with suppressed merriment.

"It is your ladyship!" laughed he outright.

"Is it I?" exclaimed Constance, amazed. "I do not understand." The color was fast creeping to her very brow.

"I told him, before he had seen you, there was not a net-maker could tie a stronger mesh, nor yet an archer on Long Island who could send an arrow surer to the mark. He took my word, and thought to behold an Amazon. He owns the skill of the Archeress, then!" Here he laughed so immoderately again, that his mother could not refrain from laughing also. But seeing Constance's increased confusion, she said,

"Thee need not let his boyish roguery disturb thee. One would hardly think thirty-five years had gone over thy head, my son. When will thee cease to be a boy?"

"Never, I hope, mother!" Lady Moody gently diverted the subject; turning to Constance, she said, "Omanee makes baskets of crab-shells and acorn-cups, more ingeniously fashioned than any other Indian work. It is long since she came to see me."

"Perhaps she will come. I tried to persuade her. She may fancy seeing her own picture, which I promised."

"A bauble or a gay ribbon would draw her sooner," suggested Sir Henry.

"She must weave a basket for me. If I were to make a pattern, think you she could imitate the form?"

"Thee can try." Constance immediately busied herself with cutting, weaving, and twisting paper into unique shapes, while Sir Henry amused himself over a volume lately added to his library.

Mr. Mordaunt returned from Midwout the next noon. Constance was on the piazza, balanced on one of the prongs of a column, and striving to reach one of the few clusters of scarlet leaves that remained on the vines.

"Let me serve you," said he, approaching. She descended quickly with a smile and welcome, and in another moment he had obtained the tendril, and offered it to her.

"Thank you," said she, "I have been watching it

wishfully. I wanted to wreathe it in my hair," and she immediately placed it there.

"Not rightly adjusted," Mr. Mordaunt said. "The larger leaf should hold captive that stray curl; the smaller ones should stoop to your shoulder. Thus, and thus." He turned the leaves this way and that, tangling his fingers among the soft curls, touching by accident the smooth cheek.

"You need not bestow so much labor upon it. It is twice well done, I am sure," remonstrated Constance, turning away to hide her heightened color. It was worth ten journeys from Midwout to this nice critic to perform such sweet service. But at that moment the sound of horses galloping along the road caused both to look toward the open gateway, for the road was hidden by the high palisades. Immediately two horsemen stopped at the gate, and alighted. Mr. Mordaunt went to meet them.

"That is Lord Percy!" said Constance, entering the house quickly, flying along the hall, up the staircase, and to the refuge of her room. There she heard the bustle of arrival, the noise of feet and voices. She threw open her window, sat down by it and looked out upon the unruffled bay in the distance.

"I wish I could hide!" she whispered to herself. "They could not find me in the wardrobe! But Mr. Mordaunt knows I am here. It would trouble dear Aunt Deborah, too." Then she sighed, and still sat looking out upon the quiet scene.

In the meantime, Lord Percy and Baltazzar, the Director's son, who accompanied him, had entered and been welcomed by Lady Moody. She was not agreeably impressed by the stranger; perhaps the firmly set mouth, the restless grey eyes and powerful form, or the extravagance of his manner, and excessive compliments, more courtier-like than true, did not please her. A mass of curls fell upon his shoulders. His doublet was of velvet, the sleeves slashed with buff satin ; his hose were ornamented with buff ribbons, and buff garters buckled with jewels. These were just visible above the wide-topped Spanish boots.

Lady Moody sent for Constance. As soon as she appeared, Lord Percy overwhelmed her with so many compliments, that she was at loss for a reply, and, covered with confusion, was retreating to a seat, when Sir Henry reminded her of the presence of another guest, by presenting his friend Baltazzar. As she raised her eyes, a round, flushed face, with a pair of dancing eyes and a plump mouth sporting the kindest of smiles, all set upon a figure as broad as it was high, was before her, claiming to be the veritable Baltazzar. She thought of the Holland cheese ; her face broke into a voiceless laugh, merrily reflected back in that of her new friend. It was an honest face, that won her good-will at once. His lazy moderation, too, put her entirely at ease.

"How is my good chaperone, Mistress Primley?" she asked.

"Beaming as a sun-flower. But she has great fear of the savages, and my brother takes wicked delight in tormenting her. We had a pleasure voyage to the

Kaatskills, in which she joined, but it was a sorry pleasure to her."

"What are the Kaatskills like?" queried Constance.

"Hills, with their heads in the clouds. But Mr. Mordaunt must tell you. He is a poet. I am only the keeper of my father's bowery, and know better how to describe the fat kine and the best meadows than misty hill-tops that I can never climb. But you should have seen the woods along the shore. Such colors never go into the loom. There is nothing like our autumn foliage, in Holland."

"Is the Hudson as large as the Thames?"

"Yes," replied Baltazzar, laughing and shaking gently. "The Thames is only a brook beside it."

"One needs to remember you live by the Hudson, and not by the Thames," suggested Lord Percy, joining them.

"True; I should not forget that I am boasting to English friends;" saying this, he rolled his jolly self toward Lady Moody. The genial look vanished out of Constance's face as Lord Percy seated himself beside her.

"You look serious when I approach you. Why do you shrink like a sensitive plant when I turn my eyes upon you? . You have not forgotten what I told you during the voyage? *Ma belle*, I promised you I should persevere."

"There is no need, my lord."

"I have been impatient for this meeting," he returned without regarding her words, "and will you mar its happiness by withholding smiles so easy to bestow?" Constance's eyes were fastened upon a cluster of flowers embroidered upon her dress. She was silent.

"You veil your eyes as well as your heart," he continued in a low, tenderly modulated tone, so that none but she could hear. "I am yearning to read them both. I fear that you wilfully hide them." She looked up with a pleased, twinkling glance.

"Your lordship is so good an interpreter that it is needless to make a task of so easy reading." Her heart thumped at her own boldness, but she did not know how to soften the truth. Thus agitated, she caught the half-troubled, half-scornful look of Mr. Mordaunt, who had just noted the earnest devotion of one and the blushes and bright glance of the other. He turned away indignant that one so pure should favor the address of a flippant courtier. Constance saw and felt the reproach. She was vexed and pained. Lord Percy saw her cheeks crimson. His vanity was flattered.

"You are jesting," said he, "but your very jests are arrows that transfix me. Grant me a leaf of the vine twined in your hair, that the wound may be healed. They say some wild leaves have power to heal."

"You can have all you wish from the portico," she replied coldly.

"But you will not refuse the one just ready to fall. It twirls upon the stem."

"Not one; even though all were ready to fall!" she repeated, with an emphasis he had not expected. He concealed his chagrin, and seeing Sir Henry approach, arose.

"Your discussion is very earnest. What is the result?" asked Sir Henry.

"We were differing as to the healing virtue of certain leaves. Your cousin grants them only power to irritate." He spoke carelessly, and changed the subject. In a few moments dinner was announced. Lord Percy was appointed to a seat next Constance. Mr. Mordaunt filled his usual seat opposite.

"I have the happiness to hold you in durance an hour at least," whispered Lord Percy.

"I am afraid it will prove much like holding a thistle," was the reply.

"The wounds even are sweet," he retorted. Thus he took delight in tormenting her till sometimes the tears stood in her eyes. She felt that Lord Percy had the power of acting the accepted lover, whatever might be the undercurrent of words, and was troubled at the averted eyes and haughty looks of Mr. Mordaunt. How long the ceremonies of dinner seemed! She was glad to be released at last.

Sir Henry went with his guests after dinner to inspect the town and surrounding lands. Constance remained alone, and amused herself before her embroidery frame; but her fingers tangled the floss, and her eyes were not quick to accord the colors. It was useless to pursue the delicate work in this mood. She leaned back idly in her chair. Mr. Mordaunt came in to look for papers. He bowed, as if to excuse his intrusion, and, without a word, obtained what he sought and went away, not to return till the next day.

"What is it to him if I have a suitor that does not please him? He is not my guardian. What right has he to watch me daily—to scan my attire, till I am always in fear lest it does not please him? Why need he reprove my conduct when he sees only, and does not hear?" said Constance indignantly to herself. Then she added more softly, "What is it to me if he is offended? Why should I care if he thinks even that I love this hateful man? But I do care!" She looked quietly at nothing, and lost herself in a reverie half troubled, half pleasant.

When the guests returned, Constance took care to place herself between Baltazzar and Lady Moody. She soon found interest in their spirited conversation as to the character of the Indians and the best mode of preventing hostilities. Baltazzar would employ military force. Lady Moody contended for justice, and the gospel of peace. Lord Percy cunningly drew forth the savage characteristics of the natives, and the horrors of their warfare. When the evening was spent, and they arose to separate, he drew near Constance and said in a low tone,

"You see what a home you have chosen. Would that I could entice you back to England. I am in danger of lingering here always to protect you."

"I have the best of protectors already," she returned coldly. "I am content to stay with Aunt Deborah, in any case."

IV.

The guests left the next day, with the intention of returning before the end of the week, to join Sir Henry in a hunt. Iyano, a famous Indian hunter, was to serve as guide. This prospect of a speedy return put Lord Percy in excellent spirits at parting. He had gone away as gayly as an accepted lover, assuring Constance of his intention to persevere.

The adieus had hardly been said when a Fiscal arrived, to inform Lady Moody that the village was in commotion at the news just received of the refusal of Governor Stuyvesant to ratify the election of the town magistrates. These had already served one term, and had been almost unanimously rechosen by their townsmen. This interference in their choice was a violation of their charter which could not quietly be permitted. The reason of it no one knew. One declared it was a whim, another that the Director's last cargo of Rhenish wine was sour. A little Dutchman wagged his head and said it was his High Mightiness's demon, and nobody need try to better the matter.

A town meeting was at last called, when one John Tilton was appointed to bear a remonstrance to the Governor. Sir Henry gravely rose in the assembly, and asked if John Tilton would be willing to remove his hat in the presence of the Director.

"That I will not!" was the sturdy reply.

"Then, my friends, the Fiscal is a fitter messenger, if you would have our case obtain a hearing."

For this reason the Fiscal was chosen and sent. He returned the second day with a firmer answer than before, and also a plump refusal from the Director to give any reason. To submit quietly to this tyranny was impossible. But what was to be done next? It would be a great gain to know the Governor's reasons, and who could discover them better than Lady Moody? At least her judgment and advice might show them a peaceful way out of trouble without sacrificing the freedom of their charter. They appealed to her, and left the matter for her to manage as graciously as she chose. She immediately sent despatches of her own to the touchy Director.

In the meantime, Mr. Mordaunt had returned from Midwout. Although he had been absent but two days, he must have thought it very long, for when he met Constance he held her hand in a warm grasp till she shyly drew it away. The pleased glow in her face when he first came in, charmed away all the resentment he had felt since the coming of Lord Percy. He forgot this, he forgot everything in her presence. Only yesterday he had promised himself to think less of this simple girl. She was not the brilliant beauty upon whom he should bestow the honor of his ancient name; he wondered that he could have been so moved at her possible preference for another. But to-day he found himself jealously watching every glance and expression with a keen interest, to know if his absence had been felt, and if his return gave her pleasure. One moment he was thrilled with her happy look, the next tormented with doubts when she turned from his tender glance, or instinctively drew away from too near approach. While making himself thus happy the days flew uncounted.

The messenger sent by Lady Moody returned, in company with Lord Percy and Baltazzar, the latter bearing the reply of the Governor that he would confer with her at the Hall the next week, Tuesday. There was now hope of a peaceable result. Lady Moody and Baltazzar were in close conference most of the evening, leaving Lord Percy altogether to the entertainment he most desired. Constance busied herself winding silk from a reel, and gave cold attention to the flatteries and adroit words offered her. Yet he would not be repulsed. He admired her the more for her scornful retorts, and her coldness seemed only to incite him to new and more persevering efforts to win her favor. At last, seeing how little he was able to awaken her vanity, he sat thoughtful and silent. Then, in a quiet tone, he asked her if she knew of Castle Cairne and its wild scenery. That was his ancestral home. He was reminded of it by her industry. When he was a mere boy, his mother used to gather the maidens from all the country about and teach them how to embroider tapestry hangings with strange legends. Then he described the castle, the forest behind it, the great sea that stretched away before it, the high black cliffs, the angry roar of the surf at their foot, and the booming of the distant breakers. Constance, little by little, stopped her reel, and presently the ball of silk lay idle in her fingers. Her face was animated, and her eyes turned upon him with interest. Seeing this, he cunningly continued to fill out the sketch, telling her romances of the castle, his wild adventures in the forest, and his daring feats upon the sea. Then of a wreck that happened off the coast while he was once alone at the castle; of the wreckers' refusal to go to the ship in the awful storm; of his own reckless bravery in reaching it; the saving one by one of eight suffering beings, and his own narrow escape from death when returning to the shore. So skilful was the painting of his own action that Constance looked upon him in astonishment, wondering if this was the same Lord Percy who had been speaking to her hitherto. She had listened an hour, forgetful of everything but Castle Cairne, its forest and sea, noting only that at the beginning Mr. Mordaunt left the room with the same haughty disdain as once before. She unconsciously looked toward the door whenever it opened, but he did not return.

The next morning the gentlemen were gone before sunrise, with Tobee for an attendant. Lady Moody's time was much taken up by the village magistrates and their friends, each of whom had advice to offer in regard to the Governor's visit. Constance was amused to notice how invariably each interview ended with leaving the whole matter to the judgment of her aunt. The whole village was talking of the Director's reception as the great event of the quiet year. Only Lady Moody herself was calm and patient, although upon her exertions and tact rested the welfare and peace of the colony.

"Aunt Deborah, you have not once this day knit your brows. How do you carry your cares with so peaceful a face?" asked Constance, tired herself at the end of the day of troubles.

"I am not disturbed within. Why should I frown, therefore? I am weary, but not troubled, since I know whence to get the wisdom needed in this matter. God is able to melt Petrus Stuyvesant's heart toward us."

"And if He should harden it?" questioned Constance, in doubt.

"We should be afflicted, yet continue to possess the peace that passeth all understanding. It is war with God that gives unrest to the soul."

"But, Aunt Deborah, I have seen people at peace with God, yet who fret grievously at their cares."

"If the cares are selfish, as through a desire to gain riches, thee can see the treaty with God is broken, and the unrest comes. But if the cares come through a desire to work with and for the good Lord, there is peace within, and the soul does not chafe and fret under the burden."

"Ah, Aunt Deborah, if I can but grow like you, rather than like Dame Zwaller, how pleasant it will be when I am old!"

"Thee will be in danger of copying many faults," she replied, smiling. "Thee had better take a perfect model. I know of one only—the serene Saviour." Lady Moody leaned her head upon her hand, and her arm upon the chair, as if weary. Looking toward the window, she saw a movement toward the gate.

"Look, Constance; are not those our friends returned? Thee can meet them at the door."

Constance saw them from the window, but she hesitated, lest her welcome should be too pleasing to the conceit of Lord Percy. She went, however. As she opened the door, Rose, the dairy-maid, hastening along the path, tripped and fell upon the stones. Lord Percy laughed coarsely, and called her an awkward wench. Baltazzar instantly stooped, helped her to rise, and good-naturedly asked if she was hurt.

"No, massa, thank you," said Rose, grinning with shame, and hiding herself quickly in the garden path that led around the house. This glimpse of Lord Percy's coarse nature confirmed Constance's strong aversion. Her frozen courtesy when he came in was the more marked when he saw it melt into a generous smile for Baltazzar. Fire was in his eyes, but he hid it under his eyelids, and set his will the more firmly to attain his object. He played his old part, of the accepted lover, all that evening, enjoying the scornful looks of Mr. Mordaunt, and seeking to interpret the troubled glances which Constance returned.

The next morning, when the guests took leave, Lord Percy spoke some words to Mr. Mordaunt, which were received with the frigid politeness of a sworn enemy. In bidding Constance adieu, he grasped her hand too quickly for her to resist, and raised it to his lips with the action of an adorer. Mr. Mordaunt saw it, and disappeared. Later in the morning, he returned from the village and announced his intention to be absent several weeks. He was going up the Hudson. Urgent business was the excuse to Lady Moody. After writing a note to Sir Henry, who was not in, he turned to Constance, sitting with her fingers between the leaves of a book, looking intently at nothing.

"I must bid you adieu," said he, taking her proffered hand. Their eyes met for a moment. Constance's voice trembled when she spoke.

"I am sorry you are going. We shall miss you." Mordaunt wished she had said, "*I* shall miss you." He gazed earnestly at her as if he would say something, yet feared to offend, then turned away to say farewell to Lady Moody who came in.

"Thee will be very welcome here at thy return, as thee well knows, Edward. May God give thee safety and good speed."

Now he was gone. Constance heard his footsteps along the walk, and afterward the clattering of the horse's hoofs as he galloped away. Then it was still. How still and vacant the house seemed! How heavy her heart! She longed to cry, but refused the tears.

"It is only because Lord Percy vexed me so sorely this morning," said she, striving to busy her fingers. with her needle. But the work did not interest her. She sewed it wrong side out, and twisted the seams hopelessly. Throwing it down, she went to the bookshelves and cast her eye along the rows of books. There was "A little Eye-Salve for the Kingdom and Army," "The Dippers Dipped, or the Anabaptists ducked and plunged over head and ears at a disputation at Southwark," "Voyage of Ferdinant Mendoz,". "Sylva Sylvarum," and many others of like titles. She passed these, and fixed at last upon Spencer's "Fairie Queen," which had lately been added to the precious store. She was lost in this till Sir Henry came in and read the note left by Mordaunt.

"How now, cousin mine? You have put all your lovers to flight."

"What have I done?" she asked wonderingly.

"Bewitched them—for which I hold you accountable. Mordaunt supposes Lord Percy is to take you to England at the beginning of the New Year, and so he makes business the excuse whereby to escape the misery of seeing you his lordship's bride."

"Does he say that?" said Constance, blushing deeply, though believing not a word.

"He means that."

"I believe nothing you tell me," she replied, bending low over her book to hide her face.

"Read, you wicked unbeliever! You should not have left him to convey such news to me." Constance read the note thrown in her lap.

"It is all about one Sudbury's law matters. What know I of that?" she said laughingly, yet reading for the sake of a half-conscious pleasure in the writing. "Oh! what is this?" she exclaimed, glancing further at the postscript: "Lord Percy informed me this morning of his expectation to bear with him to England, at the beginning of the New Year, your fair cousin. I will detain my congratulations till a more fitting time." Constance sat speechless, crimsoning to her very temples.

"It is true then?" said Sir Henry, unbelieving in his turn.

"No! no! no!" cried Constance. "Lord Percy is base to say it." Rising quickly, she fled from the room to hide her emotion in her own little chamber. Presently there came a light step, and a gentle tap at the door. Lady Moody entered.

"Thy friends have plagued thee to-day, my daughter. Can thee tell me which disturbs thee most?" said she, seating herself in the deep chair.

Constance burst into tears, and sat down upon the footstool at her feet. She soon felt the soothing influence of Lady Moody's hand in soft, loving strokes upon her head.

Thus encouraged, she confided to her aunt all the annoyance and fear she had felt since her first meeting with Lord Percy, and how carefully he strove to represent her falsely.

"He has stooped even to a base falsehood. How can I meet him again with the respect due to his degree?" said Constance, looking up.

"Thee must not lower thy gentle manners because he holds his honor light. Neither would I have thee otherwise than courteous to him whom Petrus Stuyvesant recommends to our good entertainment. But, Constance, art thou quite sure this nobleman, in his riches and high estate, has no charm for thee?"

"I am sure, Aunt Deborah. Though he were a prince, even the crown-prince of England, I should fly from his love." Lady Moody looked down upon Constance's earnest face with tender, motherly interest.

"Thou hast removed a load from my heart, dear child," said she. "I feared greatly lest he had already won thy affection. I will not say aught against him, lest I do him wrong; but he is not one I should choose for thee. Thy confidence has made me very happy."

V.

Tuesday was a holiday in the village, in honor of the Governor's visit. The Prince's flag floated from the staff in front of the Town House. Children huddled together near the town-gate to see the Governor pass, and the magistrates went out to meet and escort him to Lady Moody's. The cavalcade delighted the eyes of the lookers-on when it came at last. There was the body-guard of four halberdiers; the magistrates, in Puritan grey; Nicasius de Sille, the Lord Councillor, in velvet and gold lace; Lord Percy, distinguishable by his English hat and plume and riding-cloak; and conspicuous among them all, "His High Mightiness, the Lord Director," as he was fond of hearing himself called. His vest was scarlet, and his breeches yellow. A brave sword dangled at his side; and even his wooden leg, strapped with silver bands, had a brave look. With due awe and ceremony, the magistrates conducted him to the Hall, and left him with profound obeisance; for which attention he regarded himself with great complacency.

The stately drawing-room was open, and cheerful in the warm light of a crackling fire in the wide chimney-place. The confusion of arrival was over before Constance came in. She advanced with no slight heart-beating to meet this doughty Governor, whom she so much dreaded, yet wished to see. She was not quite sure, after all that Sir Henry had told her, whether he would suffer her head to remain fast upon her shoulders or not. If he happened to think the curls, or the simple roll at the back of her head, a reproach to the ribbon-bedecked braids of the Amsterdam belles, how did she know but he would shave the whole off at one sweep of his valorous sword? Doubless the awe with which she approached him, pleased him; for he immediately greeted her with a kiss on either cheek. She was not used to this Dutch mode of salutation, and dared not raise her eyes to behold this Gorgon, who was as likely to deal a blow as a kiss. But a question unexpectedly kind made her look suddenly and full into his rubicund face. She did not soon forget it. A wide, bald forehead; arched brows, now raised almost to a point; small, penetrating eyes, and a prominent curved nose, were features too marked not to make a distinct impression at this first glance. He regarded the timid girl before him, as if wondering to find her there, and finished his inquiries with the exclamation,

"By my troth, you would make a fine Christ-child next Christmas. I will tell Dame Zwaller myself."

De Sille, the councillor, explained to Constance the honorable office proposed for her, which was only in gauzy disguise to distribute gifts from a Christmas tree. He delighted her with accounts of many German customs of the Holidays. The announcement of dinner broke the pleasant chat, but it was resumed again at table by the goodness of Lady Moody, who placed the fatherly De Sille next to Constance, keeping Lord Percy attentive to herself and the Director.

The discussion of the rights of patentees, and some sharp strokes from Sir Henry as to usurping such rights, would have waxed too warm for civility, had not the sumptuous dinner and the succeeding meerschaums soothed all irritability.

Constance withdrew at the earliest possible moment, going for quiet's sake to the deserted library. She was but just there, when the door opened softly and Omanee glided in without a word of salute. She brought, as a gift, a curiously wrought basket of basswood fibres, interwoven with fine, brilliant feathers, and elegantly shaped.

"Oh, how beautiful this is!" exclaimed Constance. "I am glad you have come." Her mute visitor stood unmoved, her arms folded in her mantle. Constance talked and gestured to no purpose. Then she remembered her promise, found pencil and paper and began rapidly to sketch the forest beauty. She succeeded in transferring a similarity, if not a likeness of the beautiful face and stately form, the picturesque robe and wampum-girdle, the plumaged mantle, and the necklace of white shells pierced and strung upon a scarlet cord. The sight of it, completed, won a smile from Omanee.

"Good! good!" she said. Then she wished to possess the magic pencil. Constance allowed her to guide it over the paper. Finding that in her own hand it produced nothing but random lines, she threw it down, and passing her fingers slowly over Constance's head and eyes, indicated that the power was there. She touched her hair and smoothly fair features,

3

the shoulders just visible beneath a fine laced handkerchief, and the round white arms within the open sleeve, with the mingled fear and admiration that a little child might feel when venturing its hand upon the marble image of its own beauty. Her eyes at last fell covetously upon a small gold pin that fastened the gossamer kerchief. Constance perceived it, and, immediately unloosing it, gave it the place of the long sharp thorn which fastened Omanee's robe. At this moment Lady Moody entered with Lord Percy. Smiling a welcome to the Indian girl, she passed to Constance.

"I desire thee to divert our guest while he remains. Our business will have no interest for him. The councillor will soon depart with him for New Utrecht." Saying this, she returned again to the drawing-room. Nothing could have been more pleasing to Lord Percy than this *téte-a-téte*. But his eyes had been instantly attracted to Omanee. He stood silently gazing at her while Lady Moody remained, with such bold admiration that she sullenly turned her back.

"What a splendid creature!" he exclaimed at last.

"Your lordship will offend her. She can read your countenance, if she does not know your words," said Constance.

Omanee cast a glance at the gayly costumed gallant, and turned toward the door. He intercepted her. She looked at him contemptuously, and then at her new friend, who arose to expostulate.

"You forget that I have never seen a Pocahontas. This mantle, these ornaments, are novelties in costume.

This wonderful border! What is it?" he queried, laying his hand upon the trimming of quills. Omanee struck it from his touch, and, too quick for him to interfere again, glided out of the room.

"I warned you of offence. Though uncivilized, she is as conscious of offered rudeness as one of your own country," was Constance's earnest rebuke.

"Your plain speech never leaves me long ignorant of my offences," he returned, seating himself near her. "With you to check my wild impulses, what might I not become? I am sorry to have so often forfeited your good opinion by my thoughtless rudeness, but you would not judge me too hardly if you knew how isolated from softening influences I have lived. My mother died in my boyhood—my father a few years later. An only sister entered a convent. I have since gone like a thistle-seed, blown hither and thither by chance. I return to Castle Cairne at long intervals, but for the most part roam restlessly in search of a happiness that I never find. The first sight of your face recalled that of my pure sister, lost to me now. It filled me too with a sense of what I am alone, and what I might be in a home brightened by such gracious presence as yours." He paused as if overcome by early recollections, and was lost in sad thought. Constance's sympathy was aroused. She remembered her own losses. She reproached herself for her harsh judgment, and wondered that she had not before discovered so tender a heart under his frivolous exterior. Lord Percy saw that her eyes were intently fixed upon him.

"You know the desolateness of a home from which all have gone," he continued, "but ah! you do not know the weariness of a heart that can claim the love of none. You have a mother in Lady Moody—a brother in Sir Henry. But to whom can I turn in suffering? Who gladdens at the sound of my voice? Not one. Even you, to whom my whole soul has turned—even you have deigned me only cold words and reproaches, when I have yearned for the sweet gentleness you hold for others."

"I am sorry," said Constance, overcome by the extreme sadness of his tone and manner. "Indeed, I am sorry ever to have pained you. I did not know ——"

"You will deal gently with my offences, then. You would forgive them all, for the sake of the love I bear you, if you could but know the half of it," he continued, drawing nearer. "Can you not make the rest of my sad life a joy? Can you not save me from evil?"

"*I* save you from evil!" she exclaimed, astonished. "I could not do so great a thing as that."

"Yes, with your precious love, your innocence, your truth: it would lift me heavenward. Will you not love me? Speak, Constance!"

She was bewildered. Sympathy and pity had awakened feelings she could not understand. Ought she to make this miserable man happy? The shadow of another rose before her. Her heart beat so fast and heavy that the delicate kerchief rose at every throb. She was silent. But when he stole his arm around her, she turned away her head and attempted to leave him.

"I do not, I cannot love you, my lord. Do not speak of it."

He would not release her, and bending till his lips almost touched her cheek, whispered,

"You shall live in my beautiful home—old Castle Cairne—and Lady Moody shall come with you. Oh! Constance, make glad the life of an unhappy man. It is in your power. Say Yes!"

"No! no! my lord, I cannot," she pleaded, shuddering at the thought of the weird, grim castle and this man its master. "Pray let me go." She struggled to be released, but he held her fast.

"Hear me, Constance. May I hope yet to win your love?"

"Impossible! It is not right that I should promise hope. Pray let me go."

"Constance Aylmer, you must—shall be my wife! You shall! I swear it by this!" he exclaimed, holding her firmly and imprinting kisses on brow, cheek, and lip.

At this she became entirely calm. She raised her head loftily, her delicate nostrils dilated, her lips curled with pride. Her timid blushes were gone. She was pale as a statue. She suffered her hands to remain imprisoned in his, without an effort to withdraw them. And her eyes! With what a flash of indignation they met his! They stood thus an instant, he quite taken by surprise.

"You have taken advantage," said she, "of a

sympathy which you have now as thoroughly extinguished, as you before had kindled. When you have the honor to release me, I am ready to go."

Her majesty and dignity were not to be resisted. Lord Percy relinquished her hands instantly. She turned, and with a deliberate, stately step left the room. He gazed after her, astonished. He was angry now at himself.

"What a fool! madman! to spoil that which was so well begun!" He stood flushed and scowling. He ground his teeth. "I will have her yet!" He paced the room, stopping now and then, his head bent, his face working intensely, his eyes blazing. "She is not to be tampered with. She is no child. She is lofty! Royal! But I will have her yet. Yes, I will have her!" He could have growled like a raged tiger, so great was the tempest within him. Voices in the hall cautioned him to restraint. He pressed his hands over his eyes to collect and master himself. Presently the door opened, and Councillor de Sille announced his readiness to proceed to New Utrecht. He was too preoccupied to notice the passion that agitated the face of Lord Percy.

VI.

Lady Moody was still in earnest converse with the Governor. She had spoken in so plain terms against his proceedings, that he was offended at her boldness, and replied in high passion. She expected nothing less. A year had scarcely passed since the same magistrates she defended were foremost in a petition from several townships, for redress against various acts of tyranny. In case of refusal, they had threatened to apply to the superior council of the Netherlands. The Governor's only reply was, to "disperse, and not assemble again upon such business." Lady Moody well knew that this offence was not forgotten, and she had not scrupled to charge his present action to its account. She waited calmly therefore till the little tempest subsided. Then she replied,

"Thee need not be angry with me, friend, because I do not oil my tongue with pleasant lies. I speak truly when I say thou art too hard upon the most peaceable citizens in all thy dominions. The men whom thee would appoint are strangers of thine own nation, and would produce only discord in our English town. Complaints would clatter in thine ears like hail. Thy revenge would turn upon thee and rend thy peace. I pray thee, as a Christian Ruler, deal justly."

There was no cringing in word or manner, and no

taunt in her calmness. She spoke with an earnest candor that commanded his respect, and so persuasive and gentle withal were the tones of her voice, that it soothed and controlled him. He serenely replied,

"You ply me wrongly. As a Christian Ruler, I am bound not to recognize the election of Baxter and Hubbard, and to install in their places those who will enforce the decree that the Reformed worship alone shall be tolerated. I am bound by oath to the States General to see it executed."

"Friend Petrus, thee need not wrongly construe thine oath, nor keep back that part of thy instructions which only forbids our worship in public. We have no meeting-house in Gravesend. We worship in our houses, and thee cannot disturb us there by any right." At this, the Director's face grew red and threatening. Lady Moody continued firmly,

"Our patent secures us liberty of conscience. Its violation would tarnish thine honor. William Kirft, who gave it, left us unmolested. I look to thee to be no less generous than thy predecessor, and to grant even the half of that freedom which thee claims for thine own persuasion."

Had any other than the good Lady Moody spoken thus, the boldness would have cost her liberty.. The Director furiously struck his fist upon the polished table exclaiming,

"Baxter and Hubbard shall not ride over me with their straight coats. I'll not ratify the scoundrels! So hear me, Saint Nicholas!" Another thwack on the table-top helped the assertion. Silence followed.

Then said Lady Moody, as mildly as if the Director had not shown anger,

"Thee has no need to call upon the saints. Yea or nay for thine answer will suffice." She extended her hand across the table. "Now, friend, lay thine hand upon mine and say, for peace sake, who thee will have for our ruling magistrates. I only insist upon Englishmen. I ask this for thy peace as well as ours." He could not intimidate her. Her self-control shamed him. Her confidence in extending her hand overcame him. He hesitated a moment, smiled, took it, and said kindly,

"God knows I will, for peace sake, and for your sake. Choose the magistrates yourself."

"If the people accept my choice, will thee abide by it?"

"By my honor, I will. Write quickly."

Lady Moody wrote two names upon a slip of paper, and gave it to him. He read, and nodded assent.

"Here, Sir Henry, bear the message yourself. Tell them to accept my Lady's choice, or I'll send them a couple of schepens who will straighten them, I'll warrant." Sir Henry delivered as much of this message as he saw fit to the citizens, who impatiently waited at the Town House to know the Governor's temper in the matter. Applause and doubt greeted the decision. Was it wise to yield in any degree to the dictation of the Director? Would it not prove disastrous to their freedom in the end? And was it not beyond all precedent for a woman to nominate the town officers? Was it not illegal? The discussion was spirited and prolonged. The farther it advanced, the more threatening it grew. Sir Henry, fearing at last that some worthy gossip might carry these proceedings to the Director's ear, threatened them with the rule of the schepens and the loss of the charter. This quieted the dispute, and the choice of Lady Moody was accepted, and a vote of thanks returned to her and the Governor.

The Councillor and Lord Percy returned late in the evening. Constance escaped to her own room on their arrival. Making herself comfortable in a warm wrapper, and cosily grouping the deep chair, the footstool, the tripod stand and tall wax-light, she took for a companion a favorite book of Mordaunt's which he had recommended for her entertainment. Pencil-notes and marked passages added to the interest of every page. She was admitted into the sanctum of his thoughts, without feeling his watchful eyes. The very handwriting had a charm of its own. So she read and dreamed, and dreamed and read, caring nothing for the good-night voices, thinking nothing of the hush that settled upon the household. Leaning back in the cushioned chair, busy with her own sweet thoughts, she fell fast asleep. The candle slowly burned away. At last it flickered and flared, sunk almost into darkness, flamed up again without waking her, and then went out in a puff of pungent smoke, that curled about her head, and roused her with a sense of suffocation. She thought she had slept but a moment, till she remembered how tall the candle was when she closed her eyes. She was frightened to find herself in the dark at midnight. The door was open too. If that were only shut!

"Happily this is not old Castle Cairne," she said to herself, smiling, "else I might well fear the sight of ancient knights and ghostly ladies." She began hastily to unloose her dress. Suddenly she stopped and listened. That was a footstep! Nor a ghost's either! Stealthily, quickly it passed along the hall. Constance stood rigid as stone. It went down the stairs. Should she fly now to her aunt's chamber? She could not stir. It was as if nightmare possessed her. The library door creaked. She thought her heart beat as loudly as the clock and would betray her, but she neither dared to go nor stay, and so stood terrified. Waiting a long time and hearing no sound, she began to believe the whole a fancy. Trying to soothe her own fears, yet standing like a statue, she heard the footsteps again upon the stairs. This time she sprang toward the door, closed it with a force that rang through the house, leaned against it with all her strength, and held the latch till her fingers were numb. The noise alone would have frightened ghosts back to their resting-places, much more a cowardly prowler. She did not think of this. She thought only of that tall, powerful man who held her yesterday in his grasp. An army of Black Knights were not half so terrible. What wonder, then, that she guarded the door till the coming of morning was announced by the crowing of the cock; then believing all was well, threw herself upon the bed and slept.

The guests had risen, breakfasted, and gone. Still

Constance did not appear. Thinking she might be ill, Lady Moody went to her room and found her just awakened, and lying there in her wrapper of yesterday.

"Has thy good sense left thee, Constance?" she asked, amazed.

"I was foolish, Aunt Deborah, but oh! so frightened!" She told how she had watched, and why.

"I heard no stir, save the noise of thy door. I thought little of that. But why did thee charge it to Edgardo Percy? Perhaps Friend Stuyvesant was ill, or the Councillor may have sought warmth in the library."

"The Governor could not tread like that with his wooden-leg, neither has the fatherly Councillor such stealth in his heart. How then could he put it in his foot?" Constance shook her head.

"Thou art paying a sorry compliment to thy countryman. If it was he, doubtless he was careful not to disturb us. Thee mistook his kindness for stealth. I recollect Rose told me the coals were opened on the hearth. Thy reading turned thy head last night." Lady Moody took up the book that lay upon the floor just where it had fallen from Constance's sleepy fingers.

"Let me take it, Aunt Deborah," she said, unwilling that other eyes than her own should read the underlined passages. Lady Moody noticed the blush stealing over her face, and laid the book down unopened.

"Hasten and dress thyself, my daughter. Thee must not disappoint Mary Tilton, who looks for thy coming this morning."

VII.

The monotony of the following weeks was only broken by two visits from Lord Percy. Constance escaped the first by a fortunate absence. At the second, she was not to be found, which Lord Percy grimly suspected to be a wilful disappearance. Soon after a messenger came from Dame Zwaller, claiming the promised visit. She urged Constance's return with the escort the next morning, in order to arrive in time for Elsie Roosevelt's birthday.

New Amsterdam did not look, under the snow of winter, as at her first arrival in the bright autumn days, and she observed it now more leisurely and more composedly from the ferryman's boat, than from the ship that brought her to a new country. The mud walls of the Fort were topped and rounded with the white snow, and the stone bastions bravely defined its limits. Upon the outermost bastion toward the river stood a windmill and a tall flagstaff, where signals were hoisted upon the arrival of ships in the bay, or where the Prince's flag floated on gala days. The new church, with its square tower, its weather-cock and bells, and double peaked roof, rose prominently above the ramparts. The Governor's house, of Holland brick, stood next the church. Its red-tiled roof was visible above the walls of the Fort, though now it was sheeted with white, as were all the houses. The reed-thatched roofs could only be distinguished by the chimneys of plastered boards; the tiled roofs, by the better ones of brick or cobble-stones. The walls of the houses, painted in blocks of yellow, blue, or red, gleamed gayly from under the shelving roofs. The gable ends invariably stood toward the street.

Near the landing were stone warehouses. Paul Schipper's shop was here, as all the children very well knew. A chubby, dumpy group, in close caps, stood now looking at the wonderful show in the window, of little animals moulded in clay, wooden lyres, cakes shaped into shoes and hearts, oil-skin tobacco bags, brightly painted dutch pipes with fat people figured on the bowls, and a host of other toys which the sign over the door affirmed to have come from Holland. Farther up the street stood the imposing Stadt Huys, and beyond was Metje Wessel's inn. This gave more signs of life than all the toy-shops together, for here tobacco and beer were dispensed to the Herrs who met to talk over the last proclamation, or the latest arrival from the Old World.

When Constance arrived at the Zwallers' home, she found them in busy preparation for Elsie's festival. The wheels and the reels were stowed in their corners, Dame Zwaller had already donned her best tabby gown, and hung a new pocket at her side, filled with worsted balls, ready to begin a gay kassaveika for Christmas. Like all the aristocratic dames, she provided herself with a china cup and saucer and teaspoon, and went early, in order to enjoy a whole afternoon of gossip. Constance and Barbara followed at their leisure. Elsie met them at the door, and assisted to remove their wrappers, eager to see the face of one who was likely to become her rival. She surveyed Constance with a critical glance from head to foot, when unobserved. The rich garnet silk would have become a princess. There was no fault in it. The pearl brooch was simple and becoming. Her hair was without ornament. Elsie fixed her eyes upon the fresh, sweet face. There was an air of grace and purity about her too high for vanity; that could never stoop to rivalry. Elsie felt this without understanding it, and regarded her only with admiration and love. Her own nature was of another order. Vivacious, coquettish to the last degree, craving conquests as a soldier craves glory, she was in a perpetual state of brilliant excitement. Her eyes sparkled, her white teeth shone, her cheeks glowed; her motions were quick, her voice running always into laughter, her words into merry badinage. Her sympathies were cold. She laughed at the sorrows of her lovers. She was intensely selfish. Yet she was charming in the eyes of more than one of the gallants of Manhattan, and no one could deny that she was pretty to-day. Her long glossy braids, blacker for the interplaiting of scarlet ribbons, hung far below her waist. The red stomacher, laced with gold chains (the gift of her last admirer, Nicholas Stuyvesant), closely fitted her round full form; and a short blue petticoat fully displayed the prettiest foot and ankle in New Amsterdam.

That this was her eighteenth birthday, was signified by the number hung in the centre of the evergreen wreaths that decorated the walls of the rooms. A lyre of moss over the fire-place was also duly inspected by the arriving guests. Among those who seated themselves in an inevitable row, after saluting friends, Constance noticed a wiry, restless little woman, whose round black eyes shot hither and thither, as if intent upon knowing every person and every article of dress, as if to secure the pith of every remark and every incident. Constance's unfortunate attention did not escape her. Flattered by it, she instantly occupied the nearest chair, and resumed her knitting. The needles clicked so fast that one would never have believed they raised a solitary loop of yarn, had not the rapid growth of the dangling stocking proved it beyond dispute. Her tongue clicked in good time with the needles. She did not hesitate to address Constance.

"Nicholas Stuyvesant must have helped to make the lyre. I saw him bring a covered basket yesterday. He came into the street by the landgate, and must have been to the woods for moss. I ran for my hood to see if he came here, and truly he did come. Elsie wont refuse him—the Director's son. Will she?"

"I know nothing of it," replied Constance, amused at the earnestness with which the little woman talked of her neighbor's affairs.

"There comes Nicholas himself," whispered Lisbet. Constance turned with some interest to see him, for she had often heard his name. She was disappointed to see him almost boyish, slight, pale, blue-eyed, and wearing his hair in curls in the English style. His dress was half English. He entered with a careless, languid swing which indicated his creed, "Leave care for to-morrow."

"Nicholas is a good fellow, but he is a lazy stripling," said Lisbet. "He gave Elsie her gold chains this morning. There is no end to his generosity. But it is easy enough to give away other people's earnings. If he would bend his own back to the burden like his brother, doubtless his guilders would not slide so deftly out of his fingers. He borrows till his debts tease him, and then, to lift him out of trouble, his good brother pays it all. More's the pity for him, that Baltazzar has so soft a heart!" Constance was shocked at this revelation of family affairs, but regardless of her troubled look, Lisbet rattled on.

"There is Baltazzar now, he's his father's staff. The Director would sooner part with his other leg than with that son. Barbara will bring him a fine dowry, wont she? I know, for I have been in Dame Zwaller's loft. She has more quilts and linen and stuffs from her own looms than you will find in another house this side of Holland. And nobody knows how much gold is stowed in the iron chest." Lisbet was forced to stop at the approach of Baltazzar, who came to speak to Constance. After a few words, he went away. In the meantime, a new arrival started Lisbet's tongue anew.

"That is Carl Van Loot, the richest man in Manhattan. You see his clothes are rusty, and his face pinched with hunger and cold. He was a suitor of Elsie's. She told him she would marry him if he would build her a house all of Holland brick, and fill it with gold-laced chairs and silk hangings, and that he must furnish a purse of guilders to roll to beggars on their wedding-day. She sends all the alms-seekers she meets to his door, and punishes him with every petition for money she hears of. He groans at his folly in making love to such a giddy-head." Constance laughed in spite of herself at all these—the miser, the coquette, and the gossipper. Yet she shrank from this rude unveiling of characters, and would gladly have escaped from Lisbet had it been possible without drawing upon herself the eyes of all. The next moment, however, she was glad to retain her neighbor. Lord Percy came in. The buzz that had filled the room ceased at the announcement of his august presence. The mass of curls upon his broad shoulders, his velvet coat gold-laced, the scarlet stockings topped with Flanders lace, the high-heeled shoes of Spanish leather, attracted the gaze of every one for a moment, and then the buzz of chit-chat was resumed. Lisbet turned to Constance with a wise nod.

"Lord Percy will wish this seat. I will find another."

"Stay!" said Constance in so commanding a voice that the little gossiper remained in her seat, frightened into a short silence.

Lord Percy, like any earnest lover, discovered Constance at his first entrance. He saw Lisbet's movement and detention, and understood it. But he was occupied now with Elsie, and, soon after, Herr Roosevelt appointed him to lead Elsie to the great room where the feast was spread, and hither followed all the company.

This feast was not a French sleight of hand. It was a banquet of solids, every one of which had been watched from the seed, the egg, the tree, by the hostess herself, and finally concocted in tempting forms by her skilful hands. Even the silver was mainly of her earning. The savory smoke of the preparing feast had for some time foretold what was in store. Geese stuffed with chestnuts or prunes, turkey garnished with necklaces of sausage, oly-koeks, noodles swimming in sauce, pungent saurkraut and a host of lesser dishes left no spaces on the long table. Conspicuous in the centre was a mammoth bowl of punch encircled by eighteen wax-lights, reminders of the happy occasion. At one end of the table sat Dame Roosevelt, behind a large swinging silver kettle. Her shining face told as plainly as words that she had personally superintended all the brewing and stewing to the latest moment. The guests were seated, the silent grace followed, and then, above all the clatter of serving, rose the voice of Dame Roosevelt as she filled each thimble cup with tea.

"Stir or bite, neighbor Zwaller? stir or bite, Lisbet? Herr Van Loot, will you stir or bite?"

Each suited his own whim as to nibbling the lump of sugar beside his plate while sipping the fragrant tea, or whether he should permit Dame Roosevelt to sweeten the celestial draught. Herr Van Loot chose the latter, and reserved the lump beside his plate for his rare and solitary cup in his dreary cabin. Lisbet nibbled and chattered right and left, pronouncing every thing perfect, though Herr Zwaller could not see that she took time to touch or taste.

"This pretty Mistress Aylmer is to be your Christ-child, I hear," whispered she to the burgomaster.

"Ah ha!" exclaimed he, from the midst of an oly-koeks.

"The Lord Director himself chose her," continued Lisbet, enjoying his puzzled look. He laid down his oley keok and turned his moon face full upon her.

"Well, how do you know it?" was the sharp question.

"Baltazzar told it to Barbara this afternoon," she answered, a little alarmed. The burgomaster's head slowly revolved to the other side where his wife sat intent upon discovering any slovenly flaws in the entertainment.

"Christiana, do you hear this? His High Mightiness has made an appointment for your Christmas rejoicings."

"I chose Constance long ago without the aid of the Lord Director, or Lisbet either. Let him see to his state affairs, and Lisbet to the run of her own tongue."

Next Herr Roosevelt sat Lord Percy, all devotion to Elsie, except his eyes, which continually wandered across to Constance. She carefully avoided meeting his gaze, and politely listened to all that Nicholas Stuyvesant had to say. But poor Nicholas was absent and distracted. He felt ill at ease in Constance's grave company. While he thought her beautiful, he was afraid of her. She had none of the attraction for him that the saucy, flirting Elsie exercised, and he was annoyed and angry to see that Elsie seemed to forget him altogether, and spent all her lively glances upon her new admirer. He felt indignant at Lord Percy too. Had he not spent many an hour with him in friendly chat at the inn? Had he not confided to him his intentions concerning Elsie? Had he not devoted himself to him in every way? Gambled, drank, assumed his manner, imitated his dress? Been, in short, his humble pupil? This was his friendship then. He did not scruple to win Elsie under the very eyes of his devoted servant. But Nicholas had to endure it, and take his first valuable lesson in self-control.

Lisbet was not blind to all this. Whatever she could not discover by leaning forward or backward, she knew by intuition. The knowledge obtained, she felt an irresistible desire to tell it. She could not speak without gossiping. Her head had never contained anything but her neighbors' affairs, and to be silent concerning them would be simply to become forever dumb. When she opened her mouth therefore, it was with no malice, but the natural overflow of her thoughts. Dame Zwaller's reproof, a little while ago, only caused her to choose a more amiable auditor. With the best possible intentions, she began to entertain Mistress Primley, who sat next below her quietly enjoying the feast.

"Do you see Lord Percy, yonder? Elsie is setting her cap for him. She need not take the trouble, for he is to marry that pretty Mistress Aylmer very soon, I hear." Mistress Primley looked aghast at this bit of news.

"Is it true, Lisbet?"

"Yes, I know all about it. He has crossed the ferry twice a week to see her. And the gifts he has bestowed! The pearl brooch that fastens her kerchief must be one of them. There never was one like it in Amsterdam. You can see for yourself how his very eyes would eat her up." Yes, Mistress Primley saw it all. Her feast was ended. Lisbet might as well have poured gall in her tea.

"I feared me it would end thus," said she, agitated. "My lady may live in a fine castle, but her dear heart will pine. Ah me! no good will come of her seeing that owl."

"What of the owl?" queried Lisbet. She was soon in possession of the whole history of the voyage and arrival. Her gossipy soul was delighted.

Now Elsie's health was drank in many flagons of beer, many pipes were produced, long-winded legends were recited, and the banquet was ended. The tables disappeared. Cato with his fiddle came in, and the great room resounded with music and the tread and shuffle of dancing feet. Constance was only a spectator. Lord Percy had opened the dance with Elsie. As soon as he could withdraw, he came to her side and addressed her in his lowest tones.

"How can I atone for my rudeness at our last

meeting? I crave your pardon. Can you not grant it?"

Constance had no courage to reply as she wished. Her face was downcast and perplexed.

"Shall I construe your silence in my favor?" he whispered, bending respectfully.

"No!" was the sudden reply. "I can grant your request only on one condition, my lord."

"What may that be?" he asked, pleased and eager.

"That you leave me altogether." She trembled, and dare not encounter his look. He, perceiving her timidity, said boldly,

"I cannot accept forgiveness upon terms that would fill me with misery. Neither can I leave you now till you grant the pardon I so humbly crave. To prove it, I will kneel to you as to my sovereign, sweet Constance, in the presence of all these witnesses."

He made a movement as if to drop upon one knee before her. She arose quickly to prevent it.

"Do you pardon me, then?"

"I do if you will but leave me now," said she, vexed tears filling her eyes. Lord Percy smiled, bowed gracefully and went away triumphant. When Constance ventured to look up, she saw Lisbet's curious eyes fixed upon her. That worthy gossip was unable to wait till to-morrow to tell what she imagined she had seen and heard, and, turning quickly about, whispered to Mistress Primley,

"I heard Lord Percy, with my own ears, say that he loved her, and with my own eyes saw her blushes. There is truly to be a wedding after all that. I wonder how soon it will be?" Intent upon this question, she went over to Barbara, who was resting after the fatigue of the dance. Poor Mistress Primley went for her cloak and hood, sighing and murmuring over the fate of her *protégée*. The rest of the matrons were rolling themselves in their mufflers, in order to reach home at the decent hour of nine. A little later, the last vigorous couple who had outwaltzed every other, finished with a flourish, and Cato gave a long-drawn scrape across the fiddle-strings, then a short sharp squeak which announced the end of the festivities.

Nicholas Stuyvesant had proudly avoided Elsie the whole evening. He had danced incessantly with the daughter of a rich burgomaster, and, at a moment when he knew Elsie must hear, asked the happiness of escorting the heiress to her father's stoop. But Elsie did not care. His services had been valuable the previous day, and she possessed a gold chain for her bodice. She enjoyed immensely her new flirtation with the English nobleman. His flattery elated her. What was it to her, then, if Nicholas went away pained and with a vague feeling that he was loving a woman without a heart?

VIII.

The next day, Barbara and Constance sat in the midst of gay bits of ribbon and silk, paper cuttings, little bunches of bright bird plumage, and acorn cups, which they were busily making into fancy articles for the expected Christmas tree. Perle and Engle Zwaller, to whom Santa Claus was to transfer them, were at this hour imprisoned in the school-house under the shadow of the Fort, and were wholly innocent of the delightful hurly-burly of brilliant things at home, the moment their feet pattered over the foot-path to school. Barbara was hurrying the work, in order to remove all traces of it before their return. Both she and Constance were so absorbed as not to notice the double stamping of feet upon the stoop, or hear another voice than Herr Zwaller's. Dame Zwaller left her spinning-wheel, and made haste to lay a pair of slippers near the door, lest Mynheer should track the newly sanded floor with his heavy wooden shoes. Constance did not look up even, when the two entered. A voice caught her ear that made her start. She turned quickly to meet the smiling face of Mr. Mordaunt. She was surprised, agitated, confused at his sudden coming, and in rising overturned her work-basket, so that its contents went rolling over the floor in every direction. She was ashamed of her confusion, and he standing there so composed with his always watchful, critical eyes upon her! He was pleased at her embarrassment, pleased to find her there in the midst of childish work. It was better than seeing her at Moody Hall busy with a bridal *trousseau*. If she was to become Lady Percy, there was a respite at all events. But what did the happy glow in her face at sight of himself mean? Thinking thus in the intervals of greeting, a painful suspense of fear and hope oppressed him. He looked again at Constance. Her face was quiet and cold now, her manner reserved. He did not imagine how heavily her heart beat beneath it all. His own sank like lead, as he judged that friendship alone had moved her. And yet it was such a rare glow that had lighted her countenance.

Mr. Mordaunt talked with Herr Zwaller of the events of his journey, turning now and then to Constance, to explain items of interest to her. Afterward the Herr went away, and only Dame Zwaller remained, with her ever noisy wheel accompanying the chit-chat, but instead of interrupting, it seemed only to make conversation flow the more readily. The hours flew swiftly to both Mordaunt and Constance. He gave himself up to the happiness of her society for this once more. Perhaps it was the last time. He was obliged to sit near her, that the buzz of the wheel might not drown his voice; he offered suggestions about the little silk bags she was making; he picked up her scissors when she dropped them; he found her missing thimble rolling away, and playfully took her hand and replaced it himself, telling her he wished she would drop it again. The hours were bewitched.

In the meantime, Barbara had gone to the Fort to get Nicholas to come and act Knecht Rupert that evening. He was too much out of humor, but offered to go to the bowery and bring Baltazzar, who never refused any kind office. Then she hastened to secure Elsie's presence, that the evening need not pass without a frolic. Elsie's mother was ill.

"Never mind," said Elsie; "Mistress Primley shall come and stay with her. I shall be glad to get away. A house is hateful and dull with sick people in it."

"But," said Barbara, feeling guilty for tempting her, "your mother may need you. She will not be pleased." Barbara thought of the mother's labors to make her daughter's birthday happy. "I will put off Knecht Rupert till another evening," she added, "rather than take you from her."

"Fie!" laughed Elsie. "Mistress Primley will serve her better. She complains that I make her broth too salt, that I never place her pillows right, and —so, so. I can't please her. Besides, it is rueful to sit all the evening by a faint taper and keep silence. You may be sure I shall come to see your Knecht Rupert."

The all-dutiful Barbara went home with an uneasy sense of having done something very wrong herself. She would still have put off the frolic, but for Baltazzar, who would not fail to come all the way from the bowery. And he did come.

As soon as supper was served and carried away, there was much whispering and laughter, and going in and out of an adjoining room. Elsie was closeted there also; but Nicholas remained quiet and thoughtful, amusing himself occasionally with teasing the children, who, half frightened and half pleased, waited the advent of the wonderful Rupert. There was an unexpected addition to the guests. Lisbet, who had seen the arrival of a stranger that day across the street, and watched Barbara going to and fro, could not resist catching up her wheel after tea and running into neighbor Zwaller's to see what all the commotion was about. Once arrived, she was a fixture at the fireside. She did not fail to survey Mr. Mordaunt from the top of his brown locks to the tip of his pointed boot, and decided him every inch a gentleman.

"Who is he?" she whispered to Constance at the first opportunity. "He looks the nobleman far better than Lord Percy. Who may he be?"

"A friend of Aunt Deborah. He is a Virginian, I believe," replied Constance, endeavoring to look indifferent, and changing the subject. But Lisbet was not satisfied. She was soon conversing with Mordaunt himself, as if she had known him all her life. She felt no awe or reserve. If he had been the Prince just from Holland, she would have entertained him all the same with the latest news in New Amsterdam. Mr. Mordaunt knew of her, and it occurred to him immediately that she might be able to tell him what he most wished to know. The first moment that Constance was called away, and while Perle and Engle were noisily romping with Nicholas, he adroitly alluded to Lord Percy. This was enough to lead Lisbet off in full description of all she knew and all that she did not know, but had repeated so often that she now honestly told it for truth. Every word went like a dagger through his heart. He was newly disappointed. He could not understand Constance. The unconscious betrayals of love in the happy afternoon just gone, had thrilled him with hope. But she was capable of giving her hand to one for the sake of a title, while her heart was possibly another's. The tumult within kept him silent, while Lisbet rattled on about indifferent matters, till interrupted by the jingling of bells and the announcement that Rupert had come.

One that looked like a giant, wrapped in furs, stalked in. He wore a tall fur cap, with three fox tails hanging behind; a heavy robe, edged with bells that tinkled at every step; great boots, lengthened out like Esquimaux snow-shoes; and two large quivers strapped on his back, one filled with cakes, the other with birch-rods. Perle flew to her mother, scrambled upon her lap and hid her face in her bosom. Engle stood bravely up, with his hands clasped tightly behind his back, and his eyes wide open. Not a foot would he stir before Rupert, even though he had gone over him like a car of Juggernaut. So Rupert stopped, looked smilingly down upon him, and spoke in a voice that seemed to come from a cave in a mountain. Engle was awed and amazed that Knecht Rupert knew all his conduct at school, and that he had thrown paper balls to the top of the wall that very day. He thought Rupert had been down the school-house chimney, and saw them sticking on the wall. But his monitor reprimanded him kindly, and, to his great relief, took down the load of cakes instead of the rods, and showered them over him and Perle. Both Perle and Engle were ready to throw up their arms in delight that no rods were left for them, for now they were sure of having the Christmas tree. When Rupert turned to go, Engle followed him at a safe distance, bent upon seeing him perform the feat of flying up the chimney; but when he was able to open the door that closed behind Rupert, nobody was there. So he ran quickly to the chimney, and shouted with all his might,

"You all up?"

"All up!" said a muffled voice that Engle was sure came from the chimney-top, and he went back with intense satisfaction to distribute his cakes among the company. A space was now cleared for blindman's-buff. Just as the game was about to begin, a loud knock startled them.

"Knecht Rupert has come back," exclaimed Engle. No, it was Lord Percy. The burgomaster ushered him in, and hastened to obtain a chair from the upturned furniture, apologizing for the confusion. He begged not to spoil their entertainment. He had come only for a few moments to make his adieus, having to leave early next morning on urgent business. He was going to the New England colonies, and expected to be absent some weeks.

"Lisbet was right, then. This is the reason of the delay of the marriage," thought Mr. Mordaunt, who showed himself stiffly reserved in the new presence. After a few words with the Zwallers, Lord Percy approached Constance, who had remained at the upper end of the room with the blinder still in her hand.

"Once more, Constance Aylmer, may I return to claim you as mine?"

"Never!" she replied, in a low, calm voice.

"You are obstinate. You will repent it yet. I never abandon an undertaking till it is accomplished. I leave my heart with you, and shall demand its equivalent."

"Which you will never receive!" The stern decision of her words and look would have checked any other than him. He was the more reckless for her coldness, and seizing her hand as once before, kissed it passionately, turned quickly away, bowed his adieus to the assembled company and went out. What a marvellous change this sudden raid worked in those who remained. Constance stood still, pale and frightened. Elsie's vanity was wounded at the slight recognition of herself, after all his adulation only the evening before. A great load was lifted from Nicholas' heart at the departure of Lord Percy, for more reasons than concerned Elsie. As for Mr. Mordaunt, his very soul was on fire. He had the evidence now of his own eyes that Constance was affianced to Lord Percy, and the words had been pronounced too distinctly for him not to hear,—"return to claim you as mine." He could not stay near her longer. He could not bear to look upon her face. Pleading illness, he turned to bid

Dame Zwaller good evening. Barbara endeavored in vain to detain him.

"You may go in peace, Mr. Mordaunt, if you will promise to return to us Christmas eve," said she, intercepting him as he was about to depart.

"Impossible! I cannot," he replied, casting a look at Constance, who was earnestly waiting his answer. Barbara withdrew from the doorway, a little chagrined at his manner, and allowed him to pass out. He went to Metje Wessel's inn, making himself as wretched as was possible. The party he left were scarcely in better humor.

"I hope Knecht Rupert will carry him a bag of ashes to-night, for spoiling our sport," said Elsie, pouting her red lips and turning away in a pet from Nicholas. He needed but very slight repulse now, and went quietly to talk with Constance. This did not suit Elsie.

"I am going home. I have pressing business that requires my attention too," said she, mocking the tone of the two gallants who had so unceremoniously taken themselves away. "Come, Lisbet, are you not going? You must begin early to-morrow, or you will not be able to recount all that has happened. Good night, Barbara." She put on her hood and cloak, and was out of the gate before Nicholas was half ready, and, if she had not condescended to wait there, he would have disdained to follow her.

The good-natured Barbara could not understand the queer humor of her guests. She wondered and chatted about it till she talked herself to sleep that night, not knowing that while Constance answered her cheerfully, her cheeks and pillow were wet with tears. She was as unhappy as Mordaunt. It takes so little to make lovers miserable!

The following days were as busy as those that had gone before; there was so little that could be bought for gifts, so much that must be patiently made into comely shape or use. Dame Zwaller was as occupied with preparations for Christmas, as any modern housewife for Thanksgiving, and Barbara's services were often needed. Naturally indolent, she much preferred to sit by the fire and mould clay sheep and shepherds, than to spend all the morning frying noodles or making pigeon pies. There was often a struggle in her mind between self-indulgence and filial duty, though one would hardly suspect it, so readily did she always answer her mother's call.

"But," said she, on one of these busy days, "when you come to my house, good mother, you will see the milk in stone bowls that will never want to shine; the floors shall be dyed as yellow as the sun, and I will put iron dogs in the fire-places, that will need no fine polish every day, and so my Minxey will have time to fry and stew and bake, and leave me to please myself."

"So, so! We shall see," laughed her mother. And the preparations went on, and might have gone on indefinitely, if Christmas had been postponed. But the last day came, and the last touches were the most important. The parlor underwent a thorough renovation, although Dame Zwaller unfailingly swept, dusted, and aired it every week, and shut it up again, allowing the children to inspect it only on tip-toe from the door-sill. The floor was now scoured white, waxed, and polished till it shone. The green russet-leathered chairs were carefully dusted, and the silver-lace uncovered. The flowered tabby curtains were looped back in precise folds, and an extra polish given to the black oak table. Engle and Perle danced about delighted, but after seeing a tall fir-tree carried into the forbidden room, they were permitted to behold nothing more, for the key was turned and the tree left for the gifts of the Christ-child. After listening in vain for the fluttering of wings, they went away with little Jansen Müller and his sister Margaritta, to make a fort of snow like the grand one in which the mighty Governor lived.

Before dark, Nicholas and Baltazzar came in, then Elsie Roosevelt, and later, Mr. Mordaunt arrived from Gravesend, surprising and pleasing all at his change of purpose. Early in the evening the locked room was thrown open. A huge log in the wide fire-place, fronted with pine knots, threw a brilliant light over the room. In the farthest corner was a cone-shaped tree, shining with wax-lights, and hung with gifts of every color, shape, and use. The tree was firmly planted in a large box filled with earth, and covered with moss to represent a field. A stag with gilded horns, storks, dogs, sheep, and two shepherds with long crooks stood watching their flocks in the field. Above them was suspended an angel, to represent the announcement of the birth of Christ.

Behind this gay tree, and partly concealed among evergreen boughs, was the dispenser of the gifts, called the Christ-child, to whom Knecht Rupert had given a faithful report. Thin drapery was lightly thrown over the figure, of which only one fair arm and the half-averted face was seen. A pair of transparent wings spread upward. The voice called Herr Zwaller. An oil-skin bag, gayly colored by Perle's own hand, a silk purse, silver shoe-buckles, and a porcelain tobacco pipe upon which was finely painted one of the favorite sports in the Fatherland, were the love offerings to him.

"O, honored Herr, thy children strive thus to assure thee of their tender love," said the voice.

"And for thee, good mother, their industry has brought this from the Fatherland."

Dame Zwaller received a tea-pot of solid silver. Surprise and happy emotions overcame her for a moment. She understood now why Engle and Perle had stored away their little earnings, and why Barbara had denied herself all new ribbons and the silk bodice she should have had for Elsie's festival. She was moved to take all her children in her arms at once and weep happy tears, had she not feared to astonish them by such an unwonted show of affection. Now it was too late. Barbara was called.

"Receive thy tokens of love. May thy truth and thine unfailing duty be as bright a glory in thy future home as in this!"

Modest Barbara had not expected so much praise, and was glad to retreat with the shower of beautiful

things that fell to her share. Among them was a
gold bodkin and chain for her bodice, and a pair of
stockings with tall clocks of alternate red and blue,
like Elsie's. Then Baltazzar was summoned to receive
a soft eel-skin for his cue, a costly china pipe,
and a chain of Barbara's hair, woven by herself.
Then the little ones held up their arms for the treasures
that seemed to them endless. It was as if an
angel had shaken a tree of Paradise, and let fall about
them golden fruit and all manner of precious things.
They were too elated at the sight to hear any of the
gracious words of the Christ-child, and ran away to
place the gifts in showy array. Engle began at once
to try his bow and arrow, making a target of anybody's
head, till his father gave him a gilded apple
and sent him elsewhere to practise his skill upon it.

Elsie Roosevelt, who came only as a spectator, was
wholly astonished at receiving a golden butterfly, so
fine, so delicate, of so exquisite workmanship, that it
announced itself foreign and costly. It conveyed a
doubtful compliment, but she did not heed this in her
desire to know the giver. Could he be Nicholas?
His countenance betrayed nothing. Could Lord
Percy have bestowed it?

"Lisbet alone can tell me," said she, turning to
Mr. Mordaunt. "I have only to give her the faintest
hint, and she will pursue it to the death, like a hound.
I need allow her but one day, either."

"Can she furnish you with sound evidence?" he
asked, with a smile of doubt.

"Sound or not, it is all one to her," added Elsie.

" You slander an absent friend," said Nicholas.

" Truth is not slander," retorted Elsie, turning away from him and devoting all her smiles and bright glances to Mr. Mordaunt. At that moment, Constance came in, divested of wings and gauze, and was led by Herr Zwaller to the tree to receive her share of the tokens. A little box was placed in her hand. She opened it. Two rings lay at the bottom. One bore the letter P emblazoned in diamonds; the other was a coiled serpent of fine gold, its ugly head reared, and fangs protruding as if to strike. Its eyes were two rubies. Constance stood looking in the box, so silent and so abstracted that the curiosity of the lookers-on was excited.

" What is it so wonderful?" cried Elsie, peeping over her shoulder. " Oh what a magnificent sparkle! Alas! my butterfly is nothing!" As Constance raised her eyes, she met the inquiring gaze of Mr. Mordaunt.

" He will recognize the letter," she thought, " and will find new cause to distrust me. But he may misjudge me if he chooses." She gave him the box proudly, expecting to see his face assume the cold, haughty look she had seen there before, with less reason to provoke it. Instead, he carefully examined the two rings, admired them and returned them to her, smiling, and fixing his eyes upon hers in a manner so full of confidence and love that she was abashed. Then she remembered he had been to Gravesend, and Sir Henry must have told him of Lord Percy's false representation.

"The serpent-coil reminds me of the story of the poisoned ring," said Mr. Mordaunt. "I should be loath to wear it." Constance looked at it again. She fancied she saw a choice offered her of which the rings were emblematical. Either was hateful. She quietly closed the box and replaced it among the branches of the tree.

"Herr Zwaller, I cannot accept this gift. If you know the donor, you will return it as gently as you are able."

"Not keep the rings! Not wear those diamonds!" exclaimed Elsie, clasping her hands in her amazement. "How can you resist ornamenting your hand like a princess?"

"Or like Omanee, Aunt Deborah would say," returned Constance, smiling.

"Are you so much a Puritan? I did not think it." Then, aside to Mr. Mordaunt, she whispered, "What a pity!" Constance was quite willing that her rejection of the gift should be put upon this ground. It would prevent surmises about the giver. There was no occasion to answer Elsie, for the Herr had unfastened from the tree and presented to her a bow and quiver filled with silver-tipped arrows, plumed with the feathers of the blue-bird. This gave rise to proposals to practise archery early in the spring, and compete for a prize. Then burgomaster Roosevelt came in, and, after admiring the presents, was persuaded to stay and join in the games that followed. Even dame Zwaller herself, always so staid and anxious, consented to forget her dignity and her cares on this "Happy Evening," and play at blind-man's buff. The burly Herr had all he could do to keep himself out of the way, and at last was compelled to sit down and hold up his fat hands as a shield against the rush that sometimes threatened to overturn him. He rolled from one side to the other with laughter at the poor wight who chanced to stumble, and trip the rest in full flight at his heels.

Constance had escaped till Mr. Mordaunt was blindfolded. Now she tucked her long skirt under her bodice here and there, looped her sleeves, and gathered her hair into hasty braids, like Barbara's. She was captured in the first skirmish, and so skilfully that Elsie protested Mr. Mordaunt could see, unfairly. Yet he was slow in identifying his prisoner. Holding her, he daintily touched her features and smoothed her silken hair, with so satisfied a smile that Nicholas Stuyvesant was certain he knew whom he held. Constance knew it to be a caress and struggled to get free.

"*Is* it Mistress Aylmer?" he asked, releasing her and raising the blindfolder.

Just then the tall clock slowly tolled nine strokes. This was the signal to disperse, and as Herr Roosevelt was ready to go, Elsie decided to go also. After some chatting about the church going and the dinners of the next day, the guests all departed. Dame Zwaller immediately put out the wax-lights, while the Herr covered the glowing brands in ashes. Barbara and Constance put the silver tea-pot and the most costly of the presents into safe hiding-places till the next day, when they were to be locked in the strong chest. After all these things were done, they went to rest, wondering if they should wake in time to hear the Christmas bells, and doubting if Engle and Perle would open their eyes soon enough to sing carols at their mother's door. Constance and Barbara chatted and laughed long over the events of the evening. When at last they fell asleep in each other's arms, it was for both a deep, dreamless slumber.

Constance found her eyes wide open when the clock chimed one. Some other sound than the bell-stroke had awakened her. The room was dark and still. She listened. Nothing broke the silence, and believing her own fancies alone had disturbed her, composed herself to sleep. Hark! what was that? A light stroke upon the floor of the room below. She was not mistaken now. She leaned upon her arm, listened, then softly parted the curtains and slipped down from the lofty bed. Wrapping a shawl about her, and thrusting her feet in slippers, she went noiselessly down the stairs. She hesitated as her hand was upon the latch, but the sound of suppressed voices urged her to open the door. She uttered a cry of horror. A tall man wearing a mask stood before the dresser, holding a light above him as if in search of some object. The mask was lifted. The upheld light fell clearly upon the features—the strongly marked features of Lord Percy! But it was as if a gleam of lightning had revealed the face, so quickly was the mask dropped and the light extinguished.

"Fly, Disco!" cried he, in a hoarse voice. At the

alarm, a person standing without, fled. The other turned to follow, but sprang back toward Constance. She heard the approach as she was retreating. With a piercing scream, she bounded up the stairway and into Dame Zwaller's chamber, bursting off, at one push, the wooden button that fastened the door.

"Quick! Quick! Herr Zwaller! Some one is in the house!" she exclaimed, in a terrified voice. Mynheer was already upon his feet and bundling into his endless suits as fast as he could in the dark. Constance stood with her back against the door. Poor Barbara was outside, pushing with all her strength. Constance resisted in an agony of fear, till she recognized the voice of her friend. Then she gave place so suddenly, that both were nearly thrown to the floor.

"What has happened?" cried frightened Barbara.

"What is it, my children?" reiterated Dame Zwaller, who stood wrapped in a blanket, shivering with cold and alarm. The clumsy Herr was trying in vain to strike a light with a flint. Tchick! Tchick! but no spark appeared. He was too hasty. Great drops stood upon his forehead, and the heart throbs of the rest were almost audible. Tchick! Tchick! At last a light. This revealed Engle and Perle clinging to their mother's blanket, and too frightened to utter a word. The whole troop now cautiously set out for the room below—the Herr foremost, holding the light above his head. Finding no one there, they all ventured in. The door stood wide open, the snow drifting in from the stoop. The Herr closed it, and raked open the ashes for the sake of light and warmth.

"Oh!" screamed Dame Zwaller, catching sight of the strong-box, wide open. "Our gold is gone! All gone! Yes," leaning over it, "every guilder is gone! My heir-loom, the goblet; even the gold beads* for Barbara's bridal, which she has so hardly earned; all are gone!"

"The ear-rings too," said Barbara, in tears. Constance looked on confounded. Mynheer was greatly excited. He searched for a weapon of defence, with intention to follow the burglars.

"You can do nothing alone; arouse the neighbors," interposed his better half, frightened lest some greater calamity should befall her. He regarded her caution; he hurried to the Fort to give the alarm to the sentinels, rapping at his neighbors' doors and shouting as he went along. But, alas! it took them all so long to awake, so long to get on their five and twenty garments, so long to strike their lights, that the nimble miscreants had ample time to laugh at the pursuit, and betake themselves to a place of safety.

Two soldiers from the Fort, in passing Carl Van Loot's cabin, heard a lusty cry for help. Rushing in, they found him stretched upon his back, bound hand and foot.

"What does this mean? Who did it?"

---

* The number of beads worn by a Dutch bride indicated her industry; each one representing a certain amount of cloth woven, or flax spun.

"Two fellows in masks. How should I know the villains? Look there!" he shouted, mad with rage. His bed lay in a confused heap, and the floor where it had stood was torn up, exposing an empty hole— Carl's treasure had disappeared. He was no longer the richest burgher in New Amsterdam. He was too angry to receive sympathy, and indeed little was likely to be offered, since he might as well be poor as rich, for all the use he made of his gold. He joined the party gathered in the street to aid in the pursuit, but one would have thought him an accomplice of the burglars, intent upon betraying the direction of search, so loudly did he boom his rage through his long nose. The stir and confusion awakened the whole city. Some seized their guns, thinking of an Indian attack; others, not so brave, barricaded their doors and windows, and waited till daylight before venturing out to learn the cause of the tumult.

IX.

Dame Zwaller stalked about in her blanket, to discover the whole extent of their loss. Constance and Barbara thought of the Christmas gifts, and went to the parlor; opening a little door above the fireplace, the precious tea-pot and the dear love-tokens flashed pleasantly in the light of their tapers, as if to say,

"We are all here!"

"Ah!" said Constance, shivering, "he sought that upon the dresser. I remember how carefully he surveyed it when you showed it to Baltazzar."

"What is that you say? Do you know the robber?" said Dame Zwaller, looking at her in wonder.

"It was Lord Percy! May God forgive me if I wrongly accuse him, but I saw his face."

"Constance, how dare you say it?" sternly replied Dame Zwaller. "He went to Salem more than a week ago. He could hardly have arrived there, much less return in that time."

"That is true; yet I saw Lord Percy last night."

"I see'd him dis yer night!" whined a thin, timid voice. Minxey's woolly head appeared in the doorway, followed by old Mable, who held up her hands, and repeated over and over, as if she did not know how to express her dismay and sorrow,

"Oh, missus! oh, missus!"

"Did you see him, Minxey? How? Tell us," they all exclaimed. Minxey lapped her hands under her arms, like wings, to keep them warm while she told her story.

"I thought mornin' was broke sure 'nuf, an' ran out to make a fire. He said, 'Go to bed, you brack squirl;' so I ran back, and while I was tellin' mammy, de house was full of screams."

"Did you see the man's face, Minxey?" asked her mistress.

"I 'specs I see'd his back. He talked English like de great Lor' dat wears laces and colors."

Dame Zwaller reprimanded her sternly for daring to speak of Lord Percy, and sent her back to bed. When they were alone again, and sat by the fire, Dame Zwaller said, almost in a whisper,

"I dare not think Lord Percy is only a robber—perhaps the leader of the horde that has so long been the terror of the Long Islanders. How can you believe it, Constance? He is a nobleman, and a gallant gentleman."

"He acted the gay gallant well," replied Constance. "But his manner did not always befit a gentleman, and sometimes frightened me. I feel that he is an impostor, and betrayed his true calling last night." She shuddered as she remembered his wooing.

"What will the Lord Director say to that!" suddenly exclaimed Dame Zwaller. "It might ruin us; he will never admit that he has been imposed upon, and will punish us for the scandal. No more of this;

it will not be safe." Barbara looked sad at this suggestion. What mischief might it not work for her and Baltazzar! tears rolled over her cheeks at the thought. Constance looked at her, crouched upon a low stool, close in the chimney-corner, and saw the tears shining like diamonds in the firelight.

"Ah, dear Barbara, I am sorry I have spoken of it. Let us forget it. No one shall know it, unless such proof comes to light as will convince the Director himself."

The next morning, Cornelius Dirksen brought an important letter on his return from Breuklyn. Such a missive rarely fell into his hands for transportation, and he examined it with no little curiosity. It was addressed to Constance Aylmer. The immense seal bore the Moody coat of arms. He concluded it to be of importance, for he was bidden by the messenger who delivered it to make his best speed. He accordingly carried it himself to the door of the Zwaller's. A group of neighbors were there talking over last night's fright and loss, and found a new topic for gossip and wonder in this rare arrival. Constance broke the seal with a trembling hand and read the letter, while the rest waited, full of impatient curiosity.

"Aunt Deborah is dangerously ill, and wishes me to go to her quickly," said she, much agitated. "I must set out immediately."

"You cannot go to-day," said Barbara. "The ferryman goes but once in a day, and he has already been there."

"He will be well paid for another trip."

"Who is to go with you?" questioned Dame Zwaller. "I dare not let you go alone."

"My cousin writes that a servant will be in waiting with horses at Breuklyn. I do not fear the journey."

"It will be very late before you reach the Hall," remonstrated her friends.

"And what can a young thing like her do if Lady Moody should die! It would be a lonesome happening for the dear child," said Mistress Primley, fussing about in great distress.

"Oh, Mistress Primley!" exclaimed Constance, her eyes filling with tears, "do not name so great a misfortune. But if Aunt Deborah should be long ill, you will come, will you not?

"Most truly I will. I knew this morning I should soon walk upon strange ground, for my foot pricked sorely." And Mistress Primley, full of all manner of forebodings and condolings, followed Constance up stairs and down till she was ready to say her adieus. Barbara said nothing, but did much. She had gone to the inn for Mr. Mordaunt at the first thought of the journey. He arranged for a trip with the ferryman, and came to the Zwallers' to tell Constance he should be glad to go with her to Gravesend. Her face as well as her lips thanked him for the timely courtesy. Amid the regrets of all she took leave, and was soon gliding away from the landing.

The shores looked dreary in their winter dress. The whirling arms of the two windmills, and the striking of the bell of St. Nicholas, were all that gave life to the receding town. A single sloop lay at anchor in the bay, and a few boats were moored near the shore or lay keels upward on the beach. The Long Island shore rose thickly wooded. A few patches of brown earth could be seen on the low white hills that had been cleared, showing that the sun was not powerless even in these short days. While Constance was glancing at the long shore line before her, a canoe shot out from a sheltered cove and moved swiftly over the water.

"It comes like an arrow out of its hiding-place," said she, watching it.

"The fellow will soon reach the other shore with those strokes," said Mr. Mordaunt. "See! the boat fairly leaps. Who is it, Dirksen?"

"An Indian water-dog," growled the ferryman. Now the rower turned in a smooth curve and was passing across the track of their own boat.

"That is Hihoudi, the brother of Omanee. You —." Whatever else the ferryman would have said was cut short by something falling at their feet, evidently thrown by the passing Indian, yet so quickly that no one perceived the movement. Mr. Mordaunt picked up a piece of smooth bark having figures rudely stained upon it. Cornelius Dirksen saw it and turned away, muttering,

"I always heard Injuns were devils. I believe it now. No honest man could have tossed that without my seeing him. It is one of his cursed charms."

"It has a meaning," remarked Mordaunt. "Indians often carry tidings thus. See him yonder, rowing as swiftly as if his errand were not done!" Constance looked. He was skimming over the water like a bird. She examined the bark again with interest.

"That is intended for an uplifted hand. But what is this red figure? And what does the figure of a canoe mean?"

"The hand must mean danger, and the canoe haste," suggested Mordaunt.

"Ah, that is it. It warns me to go quickly to Aunt Deborah. She must be very, very ill," said Constance, vainly longing to transport herself instantly to the bedside of her aunt. Mordaunt sat quietly questioning with himself why Hihoudi had need of stratagem. It was evident that he wished to avoid observation from the shore. But what occasion was there for mystery in the tidings of Lady Moody's illness? The red symbol too, what did it mean? It had an ugly look. Mordaunt expressed nothing however of his surmises, and waited patiently till they reached the landing.

"That copper-skinned imp did not sink us with his charm. I hope it bodes no ill to your journey," said the ferryman, shaking himself as he leaped out on the shore, and whistling his satisfaction.

"Shall I leave it in the boat, Dirksen?"

"Not there!" cried he, frowning. "Throw it to the fishes, if it please you, though it may breed a storm." But Mordaunt stowed it in his capacious coat-pocket, greatly to the Dutchman's amazement, and followed Constance up the hill. They found, as had been promised, a servant and two horses waiting.

5

"How long have you served at the Hall?" asked Constance, surprised at seeing a stranger in charge of her favorite Lightfoot.

"A fortnight yesterday, my lady, since I went to the Hall. Sir Henry bade me fetch you in haste, and sent your own horse for your riding. It is a high-mettled creature, my lady."

"How is Lady Moody? Is she very ill?"

"Rose told me she is like to die." Constance was much agitated.

"Let us make haste. But stop! we must have another horse," she said, turning to Mr. Mordaunt, who stood watching the man Rupert. The latter did not seem pleased with the scrutiny, and busied himself in a restless way, adjusting the saddle while answering his questioner.

"Sir Henry said nothing about any gentleman I was to fetch. I have brought only two horses," said he, doggedly.

"Go ask Hans Jasmin, in the new house you see. Tell him we desire to go to Lady Moody, and he will not refuse," commanded Constance, impatient to begin the journey.

"He has no horse fit to ride. I heard him say a while since, he is going to Gravesend to-morrow with his wagon. The gentleman could ride with him."

"Precisely what you can do yourself," returned Mordaunt, sternly. Rupert stammered angrily,

"What! lose my place, Sir? I must obey orders, Sir. I was bid to come for the lady, Sir, and bring her safe to the door." He spoke in a more respectful tone as he finished, for he was somewhat cowed by the cool suspicion and threatening looks with which Mordaunt eyed him. Constance interposed a bright thought.

"A pillion!" she exclaimed, smiling. "Fleetfoot is strong, and can bear us both. Go now, Rupert, quickly to the same Hans and ask the favor. Go instantly!" she repeated, seeing him reluctant.

"I dislike him," said she, when he had gone. "I will tell my cousin as much. Why could not Peter or Mingo have served me as well? They are slow. Doubtless that was the reason." Mordaunt answered nothing. He looked as if about to speak; but not wishing to alarm her, held his peace. She, with a confiding smile, said frankly,

"I am glad you are to go with me. I shall feel quite safe."

"Thank you," he replied, only too happy to protect her from all harm.

The pillion was obtained, and both soon mounted and set out, much to the chagrin of Rupert, who averred that gentlefolks never rode in that plebeian fashion, and followed them in sullen humor. The whole party were silent while they picked their way along the rough and muddy road. They travelled thus for an hour, when the road struck into a forest, which closely bordered the way a long distance. Mordaunt seemed impatient to get through the dreary route, and urged Fleetfoot to a quick pace. Rupert grumbled, and at last spoke aloud.

"Sir Henry will take it amiss that I have ridden the horses fast over these bad roads."

"I am responsible. Be silent, fellow, and fall back," commanded Mordaunt, harshly. He obeyed, and kept at a respectful distance. A little later, he gave a long, sharp whistle. A similar shrill sound came from the depths of the valley they were just entering.

"Was that an echo?" asked Constance, "or a reply to Rupert?"

"A reply. There are persons waiting for us in the valley with evil intent. Now sit firmly, and do not be frightened. Hold your arm fast about me, and be prepared for Fleetfoot's spring or sudden curveting when we reach them. Have courage, my precious Constance." Those last words caught her ear even in the terror of the moment. They assured her how devotedly he would protect her in any event. Hitherto not a suspicion had entered her mind as to the nature of the danger for which Mordaunt had been on a keen look-out all along the way. Now she saw two persons emerge from the woods, and walk along the road-side toward them. One was tall, broad-shouldered, powerful. Constance fastened her eyes upon him with a feeling of horror stealing over her. A dreadful thought occurred to her. Threats flashed upon her memory. The two rings hung before her eyes. She clung to Mordaunt with both arms. They approached within a few yards of the men.

"Now, my beloved, courage!" whispered Mordaunt; and instantly, with whip and spur and tightly drawn rein, he caused Fleetfoot to leap in the very faces of the armed men, who were crying,

"Stop! stop!" One was thrown to the ground. The other, in whom Mordaunt instantly recognized Lord Percy, reeled, but recovered himself, and, cursing with rage, fired after Fleetfoot, who had dashed past and was speeding away like the wind.

"Follow them, Rupert! Fire upon them! Knock the horse under!" shouted he in a hoarse voice. He disappeared among the trees, and soon came crushing through the underbrush, mounted on a heavy horse. Rupert was already clattering fast after the fugitives. He fired. A sharp whiz went by them.

"What was that?" Constance exclaimed.

"A bullet. I will return the villain's compliment." Still urging Fleetfoot forward, he turned and aiming a small pistol, sent a ball through Rupert's hat. It served to check his speed, for he had not counted upon so well-directed a retort.

"Fire again! Fire again!" cried Constance. "Lord Percy is coming!"

"I cannot. I have neither ball nor powder. Fleetfoot must outspeed them." He turned again to see their chances. Neither of the pursuers were fitly mounted. They had not expected the necessity.

"Their clumsy horses will soon fail. We shall be out of reach of bullets in another minute;" and renewing the whip and spur, they plunged on till the forest was passed and the road lay between open fields. Mordaunt lessened their speed but slightly, as some miles yet lay between them and Gravesend. He hoped also to give the alarm before Lord Percy could escape from the neighborhood. Neither he nor Rupert were now visible.

"You are exhausted, Constance," said Mordaunt. "Let me place you in front of the saddle, and you can lean upon me."

"No, I am strong, very strong."

"Only because you are intensely excited. It is best for you to change position."

"Not yet! Oh, ride on! They may pursue us by some cross-path." On they went for one or two miles. Then Mordaunt insisted upon a change. Dismounting, he moved the saddle and lifted Constance in front, and in a few moments resumed the flight, he clasping one arm about her and causing her to rest her head upon his shoulder. It was a doubly precious weight to him now. It was rest to her, and gave her a profound sense of safety. Both were silent. It grew dark slowly, and then the stars came out clear and twinkling. By and by objects grew familiar. A small Dutch village came and went; the bridge that everybody feared would cause a mishap, yet which nobody mended, rattled under the horse's hoofs; the great white oak spread its arm over them for a moment, and then receded like a shadow. A little farther, and the welcome sight of the palisades and thatched roofs of Gravesend, was before them. Constance was grateful that home was so near, for she felt her strength failing.

"Be brave a little longer," said Mordaunt tenderly. And now Fleetfoot bounded to the gateway. Dismounting, Mordaunt lifted Constance in his arms and carried her to the door.

"Pray set me down. I am not faint, I am only very tired," she urged.

"No; I shall carry you."

By this time the door was flung wide open, and Sir Henry stood holding a light and peering out at the comers. Lady Moody approached behind him, attracted, as he had been, by the quick clatter of hoofs, the sudden check at the gateway, and the sound of voices.

"There is Aunt Deborah! She is not sick! How glad I am!"

"Just as I surmised," added Mordaunt.

"You, Mordaunt? And you, Constance? What has befallen you? What does this mean? Is Constance hurt?"

"No, dear friends; only tired, and he is determined to carry me." Her voice was hoarse and unnatural, so that Lady Moody's anxiety was not appeased by her cheerful reply. Mordaunt placed her gently in an easy-chair in the Library.

"She has just escaped Lord Percy's clutches," said he. "He and his minions waylaid us on the road through the woods. Thanks to Fleetfoot, she is safe."

"Do you say Lord Percy attacked you? Are you in your senses? Where did you get Fleetfoot?" questioned Sir Henry, profoundly surprised at the whole affair.

"Your new servant waited with him at the ferry.

Did you not send him? Did you not write me that Aunt Deborah was very ill, and bid me haste?" asked Constance.

"Zounds! I know nothing about it. You speak riddles."

"Come, friend, we will explain afterward. First let Fleetfoot be cared for. I have pressed him hard, and he carried us both nobly. Let us rouse the villagers, and hunt these outlaws." The two went out together to get fresh horses for the pursuit, and messengers were sent to form a party to accompany them at the earliest possible moment.

Lady Moody had given Constance restoratives, and ordered tea to be served immediately in the Library. She urged her to rest quietly till tea was brought in.

"I cannot rest, dear aunt. It was such a cruel ruse to tell me you were dying. I should have come alone, and have fallen into the hands of that desperate man, but for Mr. Mordaunt."

"Thank God, my daughter, for sending him to thee! But I doubt if thou art in thy right senses to speak thus of Lord Percy."

"He robbed Herr Zwaller of all his gold last night. Even poor Barbara's beads are gone."

"Constance!" exclaimed Lady Moody. "How can this be true?"

"I saw his face unmasked. For Dame Zwaller's sake, I should not have told even you, but to-day's crime will convince the Director."

Sir Henry and Mr. Mordaunt came in to partake

hastily of some refreshments, while waiting for the villagers.

"Mingo tells me," said the former to his mother, "that some one came for Fleetfoot yesterday."

"Margaret Haller sent for him to visit a friend. I knew he would bear her gently, and the ride would be a wholesome medicine for her," explained Lady Moody.

"A clever knave manufactured that message. It must have been Rupert himself," said Mordaunt. "Now I bethink myself, here is a message that an Indian tossed into the ferry-boat. Can you read hieroglyphics?" He drew forth the piece of bark, and gave it to Sir Henry.

"Pity you should walk into the lion's mouth with this warning in your hand!" said he, drily. "The red figure means a lover, the uplifted hand, intended harm. The white spot represents one day, or this day. The other symbol represents a boat; meaning possibly, that the lover was to bear Constance away in a boat."

"Henry, does thee remember hearing yesterday of a sloop near Coney Island? May not that be the retreat of these men?" Mordaunt and Sir Henry looked meaningly at each other. Their thought was simultaneous—to direct the pursuit thither.

"We have no time to lose. Let us be off," said Sir Henry, drawing on a fustian doublet. "Our townsmen will be forthcoming while we mount."

"Tell me first, my cousin, how your seal could have been thus imitated," urged Constance, giving him the letter of yesterday.

"The seal itself stamped that!" he exclaimed. "I have searched in vain for it. Have we a dishonest servant?" His face flushed, as he looked inquiringly at his mother.

"There is not one that I should permit thee to charge with theft," remonstrated Lady Moody, firmly.

"Aunt Deborah, nothing is beneath Lord Percy's stooping. Remember my alarm when he was here with the Director. Was it not he who walked with stealthy steps through the halls at midnight? Did he not come hither and relight the fire?"

"It is true, my daughter. It was no fancy of thine."

"What a scoundrel! To insult thus our hospitality! A viper!" cried Sir Henry, stamping with rage. He turned upon his heel, went out, and flung himself upon a horse, not waiting for Mordaunt to overtake him, that he might hasten the slow-coming villagers. At last they all set out together towards Coney Island.

X.

The party returned the next morning, unsuccessful. They had learned however, from a fisherman, that about midnight two boats had put off for the sloop, with five men and an Indian girl. They had forced him to carry a light to the shore and aid them in loading one of the boats with boxes, which weighed amazingly heavy for their small size. His description of the men left no doubt that Lord Percy was of the number, and the mantle worn by the girl could have belonged to no other than Omanee. Sir Henry could not contain his rage at having so narrowly missed them.

"There is no end to that pirate's deviltry!" he cried. "But the bold fellow shall be caught yet. Let us go to New Amsterdam, charter whatever craft we can find, and hunt out the dogs. They will take shelter in some cove, haply. We can find cavaliers enough for the adventure. What say you, Mordaunt?"

"I am at your service," was the reply. "But hold, I have been in the saddle many hours, besides patrolling the streets of New Amsterdam a good portion of last night. I will back to the Hall for rest, and join you by night at Metje Wessell's inn. You will not be in readiness for sailing till to-morrow."

This being agreed upon, Mordaunt returned to the Hall. The news he brought pained Lady Moody even more than all that had already occurred. She knew that Iyano had negotiated for Omanee to grace his own lodge, and she felt an affection for the artless and half-tamed girl.

"Oh, missus," exclaimed Mingo, overhearing the facts as he stood warming himself before the broad blaze on the kitchen hearth, "oh, missus, I snuffed dat ar. Dat gemman in de fine close a prowlin' in de woods like a roarin' lion—'twan't for no good. I'se sure she'd run away wid dat ar."

"Why did thee not tell me, Mingo?" asked Lady Moody, reproachfully.

"You see, missus, I make it de great principle neber to meddle in de course ob true love."

"Thee should have told me," she repeated, sadly.

"Next time I will, sure, missus," said he, ready to tear the wool from his head for his woful mistake. He was glad to do his part toward repairing the mischief, by preparing the horses for Mr. Mordaunt's journey to Breuklyn after dinner, whither he was to accompany him.

Constance arose very late, and spent the little that remained of the morning in busy idleness. She was winding gay-colored silk from a small wheel, when Mr. Mordaunt came in with a pleasant good-morning, and many inquiries for her health, after the fatigue and fear of yesterday. He told her of his adventures last night, of the renewed pursuit proposed by Sir Henry, and his intention to join in it.

"But I cannot go," said he, "till you forgive my

foolish misunderstandings, and the unkind resentments that have been so ungallantly manifest."

"You recall what I should have forgotten," returned Constance, bending over her work.

"Then I caused you no pain," said he, coldly, at the same time closely watching her face. He saw the rose-color deepen in her cheeks, and her fingers tangling the silken thread into hopeless knots.

"Is it not painful to be always misunderstood?" she asked, timidly lifting her eyes.

"Yes, if by one you love," he replied, with a look full of tender inquiry. She bent her head quickly over the tangled knot. Mordaunt came near and took the thread from her fingers.

"Leave it," said he. "Listen to me now. Till within a few days, I thought you were to become the wife of Lord Percy. I believed his title attracted you. Can you forgive me that I could impute to you so base a motive? Believe me, jealousy alone distorted all your conduct. And where jealousy is, love is. My great love for you is my only apology. Are you indifferent to this?" He stood there intensely agitated, waiting her answer. She had no voice to speak. Her heart beat violently. She could not make her lips say what her thoughts were asserting.

"You are offended," said Mr. Mordaunt. "I have presumed too much."

"Oh, no!" said Constance, extending her hand and venturing one look, so glowing, yet so timid that Mordaunt's heart bounded within him at the possible realization of his hopes. He sat down beside her, and drew her toward him. She hid her face upon his breast.

"Not a word for me yet, to complete my happiness?" said he. She attempted to speak, and burst into tears. Mordaunt could not understand this. He smoothed her hair with gentle strokes—the silken hair he had so longed to touch; he tenderly kissed the forehead he had often looked upon as so fair and sacred. It soothed her. Composing herself, she looked up at last with a smile full of contentment, and said softly,

"I am too happy. That is all."

Mordaunt thought her never so bewitchingly lovely as at this moment. Her eyelashes, still glistening with tears, modestly shadowed her cheek, and dimples chased about her sweet mouth with the agitation of her new happiness.

"I am not worthy of you, Constance," said he sadly, with a sudden sense of the sacred trust that he had called forth—the soul-absorbing first love of a pure, high-minded girl. He spoke truly. He was not worthy. Selfish, exacting, jealous, he should never have found a place in her heart. But the veil of love was thrown over it all, and transformed him in her eyes. Through it she worshipped an ideal, and dreamed her ideal was Mordaunt.

An hour passed sweetly. Few such hours come in a lifetime. Many, many days were to pass before they would come again to Constance. Mordaunt made his final preparations to go in a dreamy kind of confusion; he dined hastily, not knowing if he ate mortal bread or not, and went away with a farewell kiss to Constance, saying with supreme happiness to Lady Moody,

" She has given me the right!" Aunt Deborah was not ignorant. She had graciously consented to his seeking that right, four days ago.

In the evening of the day of his departure, Lady Moody and Constance sat talking by the fireside—Constance upon a footstool at the feet of her aunt. As her eyes followed the lines of her revered face, she thought how fresh, smooth, and fair it was. There were sunny wrinkles like rays diverging from the corners of her eyes, and furrows in her cheeks where smiles loved to run to and fro. Her hair was perfectly parted, and smoothed back in plain bands under a close-fitting lace cap. Its filmy border lent delicacy to her still fine complexion. Altogether there was an exalted, refined, pure look, wholly different from the melancholy resignation of Dame Roosevelt's pale face, or the placid good-nature of Mistress Primley's round visage. But to-night the shadow of a subdued trouble was upon her countenance. She was deeply anxious for Omanee.

"I have not instructed her as I ought. I have no excuse," said she, sadly.

Constance looked up, wondering how she could find reason for self-reproach—she who was so patient, so tenderly thoughtful of others—who lived not for herself. It was upon her lips to say this to her aunt, when a low exclamation behind them caused both to start with alarm.

"Ah! Iyano," said Lady Moody, as she turned and arose, "thee is so still of foot, I did not hear thee enter. Does thee bring better news of Omanee?" His lip and nostril curled with scorn and pride.

"Iyano knows nothing. Sunny-eye chose the pale-face. She may go."

As Constance glanced at the piercing eye, the fine face, and athletic figure of the Indian, she believed it impossible that Omanee could have preferred Lord Percy.

"It could not have been her choice to go," she said, shaking her head slowly, while her eyes were fixed sorrowfully on Iyano. "Can you not go in the ship, and save her? bring her back?"

"The brave will not have the bird if he must clip the wings," he replied, sadly.

"Thee must think kindly of her, friend, till thee knows her story."

"The serpent will hold the bird," was the fierce reply. "Iyano will not seek it. The good mother no seek it." He stood silent a moment, then, with hatred firing his eyes, he continued,

"The mother of the Inglis has power over her people. She talks to the Great Spirit, and He hears. He will destroy them, if she says it. The mother can tell her Maniton to kill the serpent that has stung Iyano."

He gazed at Lady Moody so fiercely, that for a moment she was at a loss. She pressed her hand over her eyes, then motioning Iyano to sit down, she took from a table a large copy of the Scriptures, bound in thick vellum, and fastened with an iron clasp. Iyano looked at it with superstitious awe; he believed she was about to exercise some wonderful power by means of it. The fire of gratified vengeance lighted his face.

"Friend," said Lady Moody, "I am not a prophetess, as thee seems to think; neither can I entreat the death of him who has injured thee. Thee must wait God's time. Here is his message—listen, Iyano: 'Vengeance is mine, I will repay, saith the Lord. Therefore, if thine enemy hunger, feed him; if he thirst, give him drink; for in so doing, thou shalt heap coals of fire on his head.'"

This was read slowly and distinctly. Iyano did not fail to catch the meaning; he looked disappointed.

"Iyano does not hear!" was his laconic answer.

"Friend, thee can hear better when thee is not angry. Thee desired me to ask the Lord concerning thine enemy, and I have read what he says. Edgardo Percy cannot go unpunished; God will snare him in his own net."

Iyano's face was less sullen. With another fierce glance, he asked,

"Did the Great Spirit speak again to the mother? Will He slay the Inglis?"

Lady Moody arose and placed the open volume on his knee.

"Read it for thyself, friend."

He glanced full of awe down the sacred page,

much puzzled at the mysterious characters inscribed upon it.

"It does not speak to Iyano," said he.

"Neither does it speak to my ears," returned Lady Moody. "It talks to my eyes. Now, if thee will have it talk to thine eyes, thee can come every day, and I will teach thee. It will tell thee what to do when thee has sorrow. It will tell thee what manner of man thou art, and how to live forever."

Iyano had learned to place implicit trust in all that Lady Moody said, and now the suggestion that this book would always tell him what to do, and tell him how to escape death, as he understood it, awakened strange hopes of attaining even more than a conjuror's power. He sat pondering a few moments, and then, as if it was too much for his credulity, pushed the book from him, rose suddenly, drew his wolf-skin about him, and stalked out of the room, much as a white man, indignant at an insult, might have done.

"Is he angry?" questioned Constance, who had watched him with the anxious fear that he might tomahawk either, or both, for vengeance.

"Nay; thee will get used to his rude ways. He will come back another time. If I am away, thee must not fail to tell him more of the Sacred Word; his interest is awakened."

"I am afraid of him," said Constance. "Perhaps Omanee was afraid, but she might well have feared Lord Percy far more."

"His gay ribbons pleased her. He was gallantly dressed, as thee knows, and the wits of the poor Indian girl were no harder to turn than many a civilized damsel who should be wiser."

XI.

When Mr. Mordaunt reached New Amsterdam, he found it alive with excitement and preparation for the expedition. The large schooner, "White Duck," was being made ready to sail the next day, and although it was not a strong craft, Sir Henry hoped that somehow the spirit of the adventurers would make up all that was lacking in it. At all events, he was strong-headed, and determined to go even against wind and tide. Burgomaster Zwaller and Herr Roosevelt were enlisted, and four soldiers from the Fort, a schepen, and a few other citizens were to make up the party. Carl Van Loot refused to go; he was willing enough that others should regain his lost fortune, if they could, but he had not courage to risk either the dangers of the coast, or an encounter with the pirate ship. Nicholas Stuyvesant held back, strangely enough; he was pale and silent since the first news of the robbery, so that there was not a little raillery at his expense. He promised that either he or Baltazzar should go in the schooner, and went out in the afternoon to the bowery, to consult with his brother. Baltazzar was struck with his haggard looks.

"What is in the wind now, Nicholas?" said he, leaving his work, and entering the farm-house with him. They sat down in a retired office, rough with rubbish, and disorderly with papers and account-books. Nicholas closed the door.

"The townsfolk are manning a schooner to pursue Lord Percy. He has been traced to Coney Island. I cannot go. You must go in my stead, Baltazzar."

"Nick, you are not a coward, but there is something in this affair that gives you the look of a poltroon. Now out with it; you know you can trust me."

"Well, Bal, that man and I have been close companions since he came. We have been friends. I can't hunt him down now like a wild beast." Nicholas sat uneasily, and trembled. His brother eyed him anxiously, and after a little silence, he said, in a tone of doubt,

"That is not all, Nick."

Nicholas remained silent, his eyes cast down, and his face irresolute. At last he gave way.

"You are right; I have not told you the worst," said he, with impetuous feeling; "it is through me you have all been robbed. I have betrayed my friends into his hands; but, God knows, I did it ignorantly. I have been flattered, fooled, cajoled, intoxicated. I have been the tool of Lord Percy. All the money I borrowed of you is in his hands; I have gambled it away. It was only by the merest chance that he did not obtain the city treasure, and even rob my father. It is I who told him every thing he would know, like a prating fool. Bah! I trusted him like a woman. I am deceived, betrayed, and thrown to the devil!"

"Why then are you not ready to throw yourself

into battle with the villain?" cried Baltazzar, wiping the perspiration from his brow.

"No, the remembrance of my folly sickens me. I am too filled with shame. I wish to hide myself, lest I betray to others what I have told you. I would fly to Holland, if I could."

"Pity you cannot! You might find something there better than mischief for your idle hands to do," said Baltazzar, with bitterness. He was wearied with helping the wayward youth out of the miseries that continually befell him, and of shielding him from the anger of his father. "You have involved me more seriously than ever," he continued. "I told you I should require the money loaned you, in three months, for the payment of stock already shipped from Holland. Herr Zwaller's loss will interfere too with my marriage, for his dame is too proud to give Barbara away without a handsome dowry. You have abused a too indulgent brother."

Nicholas sat like a statue. He knew all that Baltazzar said was true. Could he count upon his goodness any longer? He wanted one more sacrifice from him. He wished him to leave Barbara, and risk this venturesome expedition in the old schooner, and encounter the fugitive desperadoes, all for the sake of shielding him. Still he sat silent, and crushed by his brother's rebuke. Baltazzar saw it, pitied him, and yearned to draw him from the cloud that rested upon him. They talked long and sorrowfully of all the evil influences that had surrounded him the past few months.

"Perhaps this scrape may bring you to your senses," said Baltazzar, when they had recalled every thing. "It may make a man of you, Nick. Yes, I will go in your place, and you can stay here and manage the bowery till I return. When I come back, I will talk over that windmill business with the Governor, and see if you cannot run it. Better do that than dress like a thieving courtier, and go to cockfights and races!" Baltazzar started to his feet. "When does the schooner sail?" said he.

"To-morrow morning."

"No time to lose, then."

"Bal," cried Nicholas, rising quickly and placing his hands on his brother's shoulders, "count me no longer a scapegrace and spendthrift. I cannot make Herr Zwaller's losses good, but I will return your loan if I have to work like a dog. I pledge my honor."

"Well, well, never mind the money, so only you turn yourself into a solid man," said Baltazzar, turning away to hide the moisture in his eyes. They went out together to make arrangements for his absence, and soon afterward Baltazzar was on his way to the town.

Early the next morning, the schooner sailed away amidst the hearty cheers of the lookers-on along the shore, if the tender-hearted women be excepted. They waved gay colored handkerchiefs one moment, and the next, had them buried close under their hoods to hide their tears, for they knew very well, notwithstanding the brave cheers, that the husbands and brothers might never return. Mistress Primley strove to console

Barbara, by telling her she was just as sorry as if her own lover was going away, never to come back. Dame Zwaller was silent, and climbed up the snowy road back to the house, when they had gone. She worked all that day and the next, and the next, with greater energy than ever, and kept up such a din with scouring, sweeping, and spinning, that she nor anybody else could get time to talk of the absent ones. Lisbet came in with her wheel to chat. She sat all by herself for some time, and then went in search of the dame, whom she found in the loft stuffing a featherbed. Minxey, who had turned somersaults behind her mistress' back, stood in the midst, the white down waving tremulously on her woolly head, and stiffer feathers standing upright upon it. She showed a fair row of teeth when Lisbet opened the door and shut it quickly again, exclaiming as loudly as Dame Zwaller, at the intrusion. Lisbet retreated, picked the downy bunches from her hair and eyelashes, took up her wheel, and tripped away down to Dame Roosevelt's.

When Elsie spied her coming along the road, she left her household occupations for her mother to finish, as usual, and hastened to welcome Lisbet. She threw open the door, and, with many mock courtesies, protested her delight at seeing her "dear budget of news." When the little tumult was over, and both were fairly seated at their spinning, Elsie looked up with a roguish twinkle and asked,

"Why not begin?"

"Begin what?" innocently asked Lisbet.

"The news, of course. You are longing to tell me, and I am like the weather-vane on Hansen's gable yonder, wriggling every way to catch a steady breeze of gossip. So begin." Lisbet colored slightly, and looked offended.

"I do not gossip; I came to listen to you. Though you may be ever so ill-natured, you raise one's spirits. I stopped at Mistress Primley's, but she was nodding over an old tabby cat purring in her lap. Then I went to Dame Zwaller's, but, dear me! she was floundering among feathers; and Barbara and old Mabel made such a thumping, weaving counterpanes, when every body knows they already have more than enough, that I could no better hear my own footsteps than if I had been a ghost."

"Is not Barbara trying to earn a new set of beads? Ah me! If I do not get married till I can count my beads, I must stay always Elsie Roosevelt. When is Barbara to be wedded?"

"Who knows, now that the treasure is gone? Dame Zwaller is too proud to give her away without her weight in gold. Mistress Aylmer's wedding will come first."

"How do you know?"

"Mistress Primley says she is betrothed to the English cavalier who was here Christmas eve," quietly answered Lisbet, closely eyeing Elsie's face.

"I do not believe it!" exclaimed Elsie, with warmth. "It is not two weeks since you declared her the expected bride of Lord Percy. I wonder if she is to have Nicholas too?" She jerked the wheel as she spoke, and her thread snapped. She attempted to join it.

"Fie!" she exclaimed, angrily, "I never can spin smoothly. There!" and she caught up the rolls of flax, and sent them flying overhead and across the room. Leaving them where they alighted, she seated herself upon the floor before the fire and sat looking into it, while Lisbet laughed and continued her gossip. They wondered together where the schooner might be, and what success the gallant adventurers had met. Dame Roosevelt came in with the long blue stockings she was always knitting, patiently gathered up the scattered flax, and added her surmises to the rest. Lisbet staid till after tea. When ready to go, she noticed how suddenly the wind had risen. Hurrying on her mufflers, and catching up her wheel, she hastened away, calling back from the door,

"How cold it is! How the wind blows!" and sped home, half carried by the force of the gale.

The wind moaned and wailed all that night, shaking doors and windows as if with a strong hand; whirling into the wide chimneys, or whistling lamentable cries around the steep gables. Sleet was driven in long ghostly columns up the streets, coating the roofs and steps with ice, and sheathing the trees in glassy armor that rattled dolefully in the wind. People stayed by their own hearths the next day, and gathered close around the fire to escape the chilling currents of air pouring through every crevice. The gloomy day was more dismal yet, for the sad forebodings of the fate of the absent friends. Nothing else was talked of.

The Gravesend people shared in the anxiety. Lady Moody alone seemed cheerful and hopeful.

"They have gone upon an errand of justice and mercy, and I believe the Lord will return them safely," said she.

"Every one frets but you, Aunt Deborah. My heart sinks with fear; for does not God sometimes permit misfortune to fall even upon those who are doing good?"

"In any event, the will of God is supremely the best," was the reply. "Thee will never find a kinder, wiser, or stronger arm to rely upon than that of the Almighty. Leave thy friends in his care, and thee will roll off that load that weighs upon thy heart."

"I try, but the fear remains."

"Because thee does not truly believe. My precious child, when thee has given thyself and all thou hast to the Lord Jesus, thee will understand me. Now, thine own poor human strength is thy support. It will fail thee in time of need. Remember what I say."

Fear was lessened, and hope began to rise in the hearts of all when the next morning opened clear and mild. It was impossible to resist the cheery influence of the sun, yet the day seemed long to those who looked yearningly out upon the bay to descry the sails that nowhere appeared. Constance thought every passing horseman a messenger, and every footfall the coming of tidings; and at last, wearied with the springing heart-beats and the sinking back into disappointment, applied herself industriously to work away the dragging hours. Toward evening a messenger came, but not such as she looked for. It was Iyano, who came in unannounced, while she and her aunt were busily but silently at work.

"Does thee bring tidings of the 'White Duck'?" asked Lady Moody, quickly.

"Iyano knows nothing. The Great Spirit sent Omanee to her people."

"Has she come?" cried Constance. Lady Moody, pushing back her chair, said,

"Tell us. How was she returned to thee?"

"The winds and the waters fought the ship, and beat and tore it. Iyano saw it fly to the rocks, and he was glad. He watched while the day slept, and listened to the talk of the waves. They said, 'Omanee is coming.' When the day awoke, they said, 'We give her to Iyano.'"

He was silent and downcast. Constance had listened with breathless anxiety, hoping one moment, fearing the next. When he paused, she gazed at him, waiting for him to speak again; then advancing timidly, laid her hand upon his arm and almost whispered,

"Is Omanee dead?"

"Omanee sleeps with her people. Enough." There was no sign of grief in his face, except that it lacked the fire and energy she had noted before, and there was a nerveless lassitude in his figure that told of suffering. Constance saw it. She burst into tears. Lady Moody sighed deeply, and said,

"God knows best, friend. It may bring a precious blessing to thee."

Iyano drew something from his wampum belt.

"The white man's gift cannot go with Omanee," said he, scornfully. It swung upon his finger, and then he flung it upon the table. It was a necklace of gold beads.

"Barbara's beads!" cried Constance. "How happy she will be! But poor Omanee! were these upon her neck?" Iyano assented, and turned to go. Lady Moody detained him.

"I have somewhat to tell thee. Will thee listen?" He folded his arms in respectful silence, while she told him of the eternity to which Omanee had gone, and of the Saviour. She read from the Scriptures, and explained simply the passages she wished most to impress on his mind. She promised to tell him more, as often as he would come. He deigned no reply, and went away with an indifference that would have discouraged any but his patient friend.

XII.

"Dame Zwaller, have you heard the news?" cried little Lisbet, rushing into the kitchen without ceremony. Dame Zwaller rested the churn-dasher a moment, but, upon second thought, did not believe Lisbet's stories, and splashed it quickly again into the thick, yellow cream.

"The ship is coming," rattled on the gossiper, "and they must have Lord Percy in irons, and all the treasure safe. Run, Barbara, for your hood, and we will go with all the town to the landing." The busy dame did not believe the story, and it was only by dint of pulling her by the gown, that Lisbet urged her to the gate, where she could see with her own eyes the unusual stir down the street by the water-gate. Then Lisbet and Barbara hurried away, and the housewife returned to her churning.

"The ship will sail none the faster if I stand watching it, and the butter will spoil if I leave it," said she, plying the dasher with energy. In due time she ladled up great golden lumps, drained and patted them into a solid roll, and then sent Minxey for her quilted cap and cloak. A little later, she was on her way to join her neighbors at the landing. There was the ship, just arrived; ragged, battered, dismantled. The crew had given no answering cheers to the lusty welcome from the shore, but, as they landed, haggard and worn, thanked God they were safe at home once more. No prisoners. No gold. Both were beyond reach now. The pirates were doubtless in a stronger prison than Holland could have given them, for the same storm from which this lorn crew had escaped, cast the sloop upon the rocks. The returned found loving greetings. Even Barbara forgot that she stood on the landing when she saw Baltazzar, held out her arms to welcome him, and returned his joyous kiss.

"Give thanks, my heart, that you see me alive and whole. Mordaunt has not fared so well. His leg is broken. I go to fetch a litter for him."

Lisbet stood by and heard this. Away she ran to Elsie Roosevelt.

"Elsie!" cried she, panting, "that handsome Englishman has broken his leg quite off, and will have to hobble like the Director the rest of his days. What a pity such a fine gentleman should be spoiled! How pale you look! What is the matter, Elsie?"

"Nothing; I'm not pale," was the sharp reply, and she reddened with anger at the keen glance that had read her through and through. Happily her father espied her at the moment. Without waiting to allow a daughterly welcome, he shouted,

"Run, Elsie, and make a room ready for Mr. Mordaunt. Be quick, now!"

Elsie obeyed this command with novel readiness. She frightened her mother with the sudden order, and went to work so vigorously herself that the good mother paused in her hasty plans to wonder. The parlor was opened, a bed was put up in the roomiest corner; a generous fire displaced the holly branches on the hearth; an ample square chair, stuffed to portliness, stood near the bed. These arrangements were scarcely finished when Mr. Mordaunt was brought in. Elsie was shocked at his altered countenance. Its pallor suggested death, and she went away and wept.

"There, Mordaunt, you could not be in better hands, save in my blessed mother's," said Sir Henry Moody, when his friend was safely deposited in the pleasant quarters. "Dame Roosevelt is a famous nurse. Keep quiet, and your bones will mend with good speed. I'll warrant the setting." This service he had performed himself, at the time of the accident; and now, with the surgeon's authority, he cleared the room of all lookers-on, and left him to Dame Roosevelt's care, promising to return for messages before leaving for Gravesend.

The people at the landing went to their homes, or to Metje Wessell's inn, to talk over the expedition. The Zwallers had hardly reached their homestead, when a messenger arrived from Gravesend with a package for the good dame. She opened the carefully sealed wrapper, then a box, and lo! within lay coiled the lost gold beads.

"Oh!" shouted every voice, one after another, "Barbara's beads! Barbara's beads have come back again!"

The mother held them up tremblingly before the Herr, too overjoyed to utter a word, while he stared as if he could not believe his senses. Then he threw back his head and laughed till his face grew as red as the tassel on Engle's cap.

"Think of their getting home before us, after all. I believe nobody but a witch on a broomstick carried them off. Eh!" said he, turning to Barbara, who stood with her hands clasped tightly, and her face shining with joy, "eh, Barbara, we'll have the wedding."

"No wedding without a dowry," interrupted Dame Zwaller, dropping the beads into the palm of her hand. "It will be many a year before so much gold is locked in the strong box again. My looms and wheels will be worn out before the good day comes when we are rich again."

"Bless me!" cried the Herr, "haven't we a fine house and plenty to eat and drink, miles of wood to keep us warm, and counterpanes and feather-beds and bodices and petticoats, and linsey-woolsey enough to cover a whole troop of grandchildren! And here am I, home again, alive and whole, and here is brave young Engle and my round little Perle—who cares for the lost guilders? Ho!" shouted he, catching up Perle and tossing her till her flaxen curls touched the wall overhead. He sung snatches of jubilant student-songs till out of breath, and then went to the chimney-corner, filled his pipe, and sat down to soothe his excitement in its sleepy fumes. Dame Zwaller smiled, in spite of her sorrowful regrets. Chancing to look again in the box from which she had drawn forth the necklace, she saw a note lying at the bottom. Barbara read it. It contained the unhappy story of Omanee and Iyano. Barbara sighed as she dropped the note in the box, and asked her mother to keep it with the beads. The Herr anathematized Lord Percy between his teeth, and puffed more vigorously.

"The most wonderful thing of all," said Dame Zwaller, "is, that an Indian should have brought back gold."

"Lady Moody has taught him," said mynheer, significantly nodding his head. "Doubtless we might find Iyanos in our woods, if we dealt as fairly with them."

"There may be wrong at somebody's door, but not at mine. I have had no dealings with them," frowned the thrifty housewife, who truly never gave a thought to the heathen beyond her door, or such as chanced within it, except to be watchful of their pilfering fingers. It never occurred to her that there might be another way of wronging them than to drive hard bargains. So she closed the box tightly, tied it securely, and put it away for safe-keeping till the day when it would be needed for the bridal. Mynheer watched her with a pleased look for the happiness thus restored to Barbara. Presently a mischievous twinkle shone in his eyes. He called loudly for Minxey.

"Run, Snow-ball! Bid vrow Lisbet to come this way as fast as her two feet can carry her." He chuckled as Minxey darted out of the door before her mistress could forbid, and when Lisbet arrived, all out of breath with the sudden summons, he rubbed his hands in a delighted way, drew a chair to the hearth, and bade her be seated. Dame Zwaller stalked out of the room, vexed at the gossiper's arrival.

"Have you heard what has happened to us?" queried he, looking drolly at her. "Lord Percy has sent Barbara a wedding present! Chut! chut! let me tell it," said he, noticing Barbara's parting lips. But instead of telling any more, he sat quite still and smoked his pipe. After a little silence, he added,

"It is all of gold, solid gold!"

"He can afford it, after robbing you of all your guilders," said Lisbet, impatiently.

"But it is worth more than all the guilders," returned the Herr, smiling graciously at Barbara, whose lips opened again to speak. "Chut! chut! keep silence, child."

"Where is it?" asked Lisbet.

"You shall see it at the wedding."

"When may that be?" she queried, in surprise.

"When Domine Megapolensis says the ceremony."

"I do not believe a word you are telling me," said Lisbet, rising to go, yet seeing in Barbara's face that her father's story was not all a fable.

"Very well, go," retorted the Herr, "you will find it true one day." And he would not tell her another word, but sat smiling and purring in the chimney corner as contentedly as if a fortune had fallen to him. Lisbet might have lingered longer, had not Dame Zwaller come in frowning, and sharper than ever at the exasperating sight of the Herr's happy face, when he knew very well how long and hard they must labor to recover from their loss. Lisbet was afraid of Dame Zwaller's sharp words, and went away sorely puzzled at what she had just heard.

XIII.

Edward Mordaunt recovered slowly. Nearly four weeks had passed, and he was only able to sit in the stuffed chair, his limb supported upon an ingenious fixture contrived by Nicholas Stuyvesant. Poor Nicholas secretly accused himself for all the misfortunes that had befallen his friends, and made all the amends possible. He had watched Mordaunt through the feverish nights of his earliest illness, had been thoughtful of many comforts and beguilements for the long hours, and had not only taken care that his notes and messages to Gravesend were faithfully transmitted, but more than once went himself, to gratify the whim of the invalid.

And where was Constance all this time? The short, but violent illness of Sir Henry after the voyage, followed by a painful and longer sickness of Lady Moody, had required her continued presence at the Hall. But her thoughts winged at all times to Herr Roosevelt's little parlor, and lingered with the invalid there. She sent him tempting jellies and confections, the newest book from England, and the sweetest of notes. But all this did not satisfy him. He hungered to see her, to hear her voice, and, not least, he wished to scold her, to show her that he was irritated because she had not chosen to neglect all for him. So he was cross to Nicholas, he was ungrateful to Dame Roosevelt. Elsie alone could bring him cheerfulness, with her saucy ways and coquettish graces. At first he was amused, and then interested in studying her character and testing her heart. Vexed at Constance's continued absence, he revenged himself by securing all that was possible of Elsie's time and thoughts. When Dame Roosevelt came with her knitting, he begged that Elsie might come also. Then he kept her as long as possible, telling her of his travels in distant lands, and spun out long stories which had to be finished while the good mother went to superintend the dinner. This, with the dainty compliments he cunningly wove into his sayings, was fast casting a spell over her. It was easy and delightful to perform every possible service for this handsome cavalier, and just as pleasing to withhold them when it suited Elsie to try the sincerity of his admiration. She called him selfish, cross; and sometimes went away a whole afternoon, or sat in the next room and sung cheerily at her wheel, that he might know she cared not a whit for his comfort. When she came back, she made him own that he was ill-natured, ungenerous, and guilty of a whole catalogue of sins, and was exceedingly sorry, till he was forced to laugh at his ludicrous helplessness. She catechised him; she made love in mockery; she held court, in which she declared herself both judge and jury and he the culprit, always found guilty. She was wilful, wayward, gay; pouted and laughed in the same minute; sung for him, petted him, scolded him, all in a manner which charmed him, and beguiled the hours and days. Dame Roosevelt was bewildered with her audacious way of entertaining a gentleman of his degree, and often called out, "Elsie! Elsie!" in a reproachful voice.

"Leave her alone," Mordaunt would say, with a smile that said plainly to Elsie, "she pleases me." Then she would flash back a smile that said, "Thank you; you understand me."

Mordaunt could not but discover the interest fast awaking in his behalf. It was not difficult to read her face, or to interpret her various moods. He enjoyed the discovery that he could torment her, in return for her vagaries; half seriously, half in play, he flirted with the gay coquette, who he assured himself was not one to pine and sigh and die of a broken heart. He did not care to arrest the tender interest now.

At last Lady Moody recovered so far, that Constance could contentedly leave her for two or three days. Nicholas Stuyvesant, still eager to serve Mordaunt, came for her and attended her safely to Dame Zwaller's. She was presently on the way to Herr Roosevelt's with a beating heart. She had not seen Mordaunt since that day of sweet plighting. It seemed like a dream, and she was half afraid she had only dreamed it. How she longed to see him again, to be under the spell of his eyes, to feel the magnetism of his presence, to hear him speak to her tenderly and reassure her of his love! How much she intended to tell him! Every day she had stored away some precious thought of him, had seen or read something which he must see, till she had accumulated a heartful that must be told sitting beside him, with her hand trustfully in his. She had gone over this first visit in imagination many, many times, and now that its realization was near, her heart fluttered so that she could scarcely command her voice, to return the greetings that met her when she entered. There sat the Herr by the fireside, there stood Dame Roosevelt with the never-failing blue stocking, there was Elsie, bathing Mordaunt's brow with her pretty hands, and there sat the ever-present Lisbet, chirruping her chick-a-de-dee of gossip. Constance was abashed. She walked straight to Mr. Mordaunt, thinking a hundred thoughts of disappointment in the instant, hoping he would not kiss her before all these people, yet longing to throw her arms about his neck and rest her head upon his shoulder. He looked so pale as he sat there, that she wanted to tell him how pained she was at his suffering, and what joy it was to see him again. But instead of all this, at the end of those few steps, she only reached out her hand, permitted it to rest in his a moment, called him Mr. Mordaunt, gave him one dizzy look more frightened than loving, told him simply she was sorry for his long illness, and then accepted the seat which Dame Roosevelt brought near for her. The Herr questioned her about her friends. While she answered, Mordaunt looked at her intently. He had not seen her for a long time. He had grown accustomed to the piquant liveliness and frankness of Elsie. Constance looked reserved and self-possessed, and even cold, but for the color on her cheek, which he plainly saw deepening painfully while he gazed at her. There was an ineffable sweetness in her face and manner that charmed him anew, and made him forget for the time to find fault with her absence. Could it be possible that he had folded her in his arms, that he had kissed that lovely mouth, and beyond all, that she had acknowledged that she loved him? Yet she sat there so distant, her eyelids quivered and dropped so persistently when his own eyes were questioning her soul, and she was so much more ready to speak to any other in the room than himself, that he was puzzled, and wondered if it was possible she regretted that precious confession. Perhaps she did regret it. He grew thoughtful and silent. Lisbet's chattering annoyed him. Elsie's nervous movements and usual attentions disturbed him. He wished all these kind people would be considerate enough to go away and allow him to talk freely with Constance. But they knew nothing of the relation in which she stood to him, and regarding her simply as their distinguished guest, were unceasing in their efforts to make her visit as agreeable as possible. Mordaunt looked wearied. The sun was declining. Seeing the afternoon gone, Constance arose to go. She approached Mordaunt, and in a low voice asked,

"Will it be long before you come back to Gravesend?"

"The surgeon says I must not move in two weeks yet."

"It is very long," she replied slowly and sadly.

"You miss me, then?"

"As you perhaps miss me." A smile played quickly upon her lips, and her eyes rested upon his a single moment. Mordaunt took her hand in both his, and kissed it reverently.

"Good-night," said she, withdrawing it gently, but not displeased.

"You will come again to-morrow?"

"Yes."

"Come in the morning and spend all the day with us," suggested Dame Roosevelt. "Mr. Mordaunt likes company. And I suppose you are glad to hear from your friends," she added, turning to him.

"Very glad," he returned, smiling. "I am refreshed by what she has told me."

Constance assented to Dame Roosevelt's kind proposal, and went away with Lisbet, who, after striving in vain to hear the few words that passed, wrapped herself up and patted along the street at Constance's side.

"Mr. Mordaunt is long in mending," she chatted, "but he has no need to fret about it, so long as he has pretty Elsie to wait upon him. She manages him just as she pleases. Yet of all the gallants she has jilted, she never found her match till now. I cannot quite see which will get jilted this time!"

"I am glad she has been so helpful," said Constance simply. Her gentle heart did not feel one twinge of jealousy. Earnest, trustful herself, it did not occur to her to doubt Mordaunt one moment. Lisbet looked up at the reply, and then ran on praising and berating Elsie all in one breath.

"Lisbet, do you see the sky in the west?" interrupted Constance. "Was there ever such burnished gold? And do you see how softly it melts away into the blue?"

"It is as yellow as my spring daffies," said Lisbet. "That signifies a fair day to-morrow. That will be fine for Dame Zwaller, who goes to Baltazzar's bowery to see what is to be done there for Barbara. You know we shall soon have a wedding, and a gay one it will be." Constance saw that no sense of beauty could enter into her soul through such a pair of round, whisking eyes, and was glad when she reached the gate, and could escape from the whirr of empty gossip. She lingered on the doorstep, with her hand on the huge latch and her face turned toward the shining west, thinking what must be the brightness and glory of heaven, if even that could not represent it. She went in with a smile on her lips. In the chimney corner sat Mistress Primley, waiting patiently to see her. She arose quickly, courtesied low, and expressed her gladness at meeting again.

"So much has happened since I saw you," said she. "Poor child, I always knew that screech-owl did not sit on the chimney for nothing. If the Herr had only minded the warning, he would never have lost his guilders. And you, my precious heart, should never have gone on that journey, after such a dream."

"But I had made it twice before that sorrowful adventure, dear mamma Primley," laughed Constance, sitting on the stool at her feet.

"It was tempting Providence," said she, shaking her head slowly.

"Would you have me stay always at home for a foolish dream?"

"It would be safer for such as you, in this wild country," replied Mistress Primley, smoothing her hair lovingly, and thinking her whilom *protégée* grown more beautiful than ever. This was true, for the precious shining of peace and joy and love was in her face, and there is no beauty like it.

"I am not afraid, with such brave cavaliers as are here," returned Constance. "One feels stronger too, having gone safely through danger. It is good to test the nerves and use them to alarm, just as high-mettled horses are trained to the sound of drums and cannon. I believe I could listen to an Indian's war-whoop with less terror now, than before I heard that shout of 'Stand!' from the highwaymen springing out of the woods."

"Oh! my precious child!" cried Mistress Primley, clasping her hands. "What will be the end of all this? It does not befit you to go about unguarded, with such a head on your shoulders. You are too heedless of danger."

"Would you have me journey in state, like the Director, with four halberdiers at my service, or like a princess with a train of plumed knights, ready to challenge every shadow we met?" asked Constance with a merry, ringing laugh. "But you may be sure, mamma Primley," she added, seriously, "I will never go alone, as many do. Mary Tilton rides often many miles by herself, and more than one good wife thinks it not ill to carry a bag of grist to the mill, with none to defend her."

"All wrong. I wish you were safe back in England. But tell me, child, of your escape from that wild Percy, that I knew was never a shoot of a noble race." Urging Constance, she learned part of the story, the tragic fate of Omauce, and the return of the gold necklace. This led to Barbara's affairs, which Dame Zwaller was ready to discuss fully. After Mistress Primley went away, the evening was filled with plans for the bridal, the house-furnishing and the all-important wardrobe. Constance made some pretty suggestions, and busied her fingers in fashioning a tuft of rosettes for the slippers. It was a pleasant, happy group about the fireside that evening, and none felt happier than Constance. Had she not seen Mordaunt, and was she not to see him and listen to him all to-morrow? In all the day she could find some moments to speak the stored-up thoughts that had waited so long to be told. What wonder if she fell asleep that night smiling to herself, slept profoundly, and awoke in the morning with a dreamy consciousness that something happy was in store! The waking to a new day was joyous to her soul, untouched yet by pain.

She went early to the Roosevelt's, for she knew Mordaunt would be waiting, and the day would be only too short at the longest. Arriving, she found Mynheer Roosevelt consulting with him as to a knotty law matter. But it was pleasant to listen to his voice, to see his face, to catch his frequent glance when she looked up from the dainty bit of work brought from Barbara's basket. Later, the Lord Director came in, and jocosely assured him it was no small distinction to stump about the world on a silver-chased leg, and was sorry at the prospect of losing his company in such good fortune. Suddenly perceiving the presence of Constance, he exclaimed,

"Bless me! Here is my Christ-child! When did you arrive, Mistress Aylmer? By St. Nicholas! Mordaunt, I should think you would be afraid she would unfold her wings and soar upward. How is the Lady-mother, my child? Does she manage those straight-coats as well as ever? Herr Roosevelt, if there is anybody in the world who can exorcise the devil out of me, it is Lady Moody. That is high praise. She anoints with the oil of peace all who pass her threshold."

"I wish she might come to the Stadt Huys!" said the Herr, quietly folding the papers which he had been overlooking.

"Yes, yes," retorted the Director, "such a testy set of fellows never sat together in council. They need to be dipped in the oil of peace. Why, sir," said he, turning fiercely to Mordaunt, "they wont listen to having the street paved. And yesterday I came near locking them all up till they should agree to light the street with lanterns hung out on poles from the window of every seventh house. 'Foolhardy,' said they, 'to make a beacon of our city, and let the savages know where to find us!' Faugh!" said he, in infinite disgust. "As if wild-cats cannot see as well in darkness as in light. We should never have had that pretty pack of thieves prowling through the city, but for the lack of lanterns. Faugh! A blind set of bull-dogs I have to manage at the Stadt Huys. And I must be about it," said he, taking his hat, bidding a gruff good-morning, and walking off with the air of a duke among his retainers. Mordaunt smiled.

"He carries himself so like an old admiral, that one forgets his misfortune," said he.

"He forgets it himself," added Constance. She was not sorry at losing sight of His High Mightiness, who always inspired her with fear, especially when followed by his four halberdiers with their four grim axes. "If I were poor Barbara, I should be afraid he would order my head off in one of his passions."

"She must not dare to oppose his whims," said Herr Roosevelt, his own temper ruffled at the last words of the Director. "Yes," continued he, as if talking to himself, "he may forget his misfortune, but he never forgets that he is master." And he continued to grumble in a low voice till he also took his departure for the Stadt Huys. When he had gone, Mordaunt motioned Constance to come with her work and sit beside him.

"I wish you to tell me why you remained away so long," said he, abruptly. "Could not Rose have cared for your aunt as well?" Constance looked up surprised.

"I explained it in my note. Aunt Deborah is as my mother. I would not leave her till assured that she was recovering."

"I would have forsaken father or mother to have gone to you, at least for a single day," replied Mordaunt.

"I should have told you, you are an undutiful son, and sent you back," was the spirited reply.

"Do you owe nothing to me, then?"

"Yes; more than I can tell you now," said she with tremulous lips. "Yet so long as I am under my mother's roof, I owe my first loving duty to her. She had no physician. Would I trust her to servants?"

"Where was Sir Henry?"

"He is not a tender daughter." A silence followed these words. Constance continued to sew, bending her head low to hide her emotion. Mordaunt resumed in a low voice:

"I supposed the love of woman for her affianced husband surpassed every other earthly love."

"It does! oh! it does! If I had consulted my own heart only, I should have flown to you at once. Yet I am sure I did right to remain."

"You are a bit wilful, Constance."

"What do you wish? That I should say I did wrong to wait?"

"Yes. If you bear the same love to me that I hold for you, it would not be difficult for you to see how cruel was the long waiting, and therefore wrong." Constance felt as if her heart was ground under a millstone.

"I do love you with all my soul," she replied, "yet I cannot think as you do. Would you have me speak an untruth?"

"What a Huguenot you would make, Constance. You put duty and truth above your love for me."

"Oh, Edward Mordaunt," said she, dropping her work with a gesture, as if she would have thrown her arms around him, "do not trifle with both my heart and my conscience. It is exquisite pain to be doubted thus."

"It is because I adore you, my beloved," replied Mordaunt, drawing her toward him and kissing her burning cheek. "I hunger for the whole of your love. I would not divide it with any on earth"—or in heaven, he would have added if he dared. Dame Roosevelt opened the door at that moment, and, seeing the fire low upon the hearth, came in to replenish it. Constance went to the window to get more light upon her delicate stitching and to hide her agitated face. Elsie soon joined them, and was satisfied to see her friend so reserved and occupied by the window, and Mordaunt with his head thrown back against the chair, and his eyes closed as if he meditated a nap. She was hurt yesterday at noting how admiringly his eyes rested upon his beautiful guest, and thought then, and even yet, that she would not remain in his way to afford the contrast of her own prettiness with the nameless charm that won every heart to Constance. She had remained in her room this morning, heroically enduring the cold till worried by her mother into proper hospitality. Though now crouching by the fire, she intended to escape at the first opportunity.

After dinner had been served, Nicholas Stuyvesant came in and infused new life into the family group. He was fast recovering his natural buoyancy, and with it, something of his old spendthrift ways, which could hardly conform to a plodding devotion to business. He fully intended to perform all his promises to his brother; but he must have jovial hours now and then outside of that odious mill. What signified a few hours and a few stivers at the inn, or at a friend's fireside! The mill would turn out enough to pay Baltazzar, somehow! So he shook his curls—for he would wear curls instead of the orthodox cue—and tried to recover the good graces of Elsie. But she was strangely sedate to-day, and so he toyed with Constance's work-basket, and chatted gayly with her. She laughed at his foolish sallies, in spite of her sadness. Mordaunt watched them in silence, and saw that she spoke freely to him and looked full into his eyes while speaking.

"Why should she shrink at my touch, and why should her eyelids droop till the lashes sweep her cheek if she catches my ardent gaze? She does not lay her hand fearlessly upon mine, nor caressingly bathe my head, like Elsie. Does she fear me more than she loves me? Could she not care more tenderly for Nicholas than for me?"

Brooding thus, a keen dislike began to creep in his heart toward Nicholas, whose patient, friendly devotion was passing for nothing. He had spoiled the morning for himself, and the short afternoon was quickly speeding away, with Nicholas still there, and other friends coming and going, till there were no more moments for the happy converse that Constance had so long promised herself. It was time to go. She laid aside her work with a heavy heart, and, in the dusky twilight, stood beside Mordaunt.

"I return to Gravesend in the morning," said she.

"Stay another day, Constance. I have scarcely spoken to you yet."

"I should love to stay, for I have said nothing of all I desired to tell you. But I promised to return, and Aunt Deborah would be alarmed at my delay."

"Fie! do not allow her wishes to come always between us," said he, impatiently.

"But I cannot hold my promise lightly."

"You are a Puritan, like your father."

"Aside from this," pursued Constance, with quiet dignity, "I would not willingly test further the hospitality of your good friends. My cousin purposes to bring me next week, and Barbara's wedding will call me here the week following. I hope you will then be able to return to Gravesend."

"You will not stay, then?"

"I cannot."

"Farewell, obdurate Constance," said he, coldly.

"Good-night," she responded in a tender, sad voice.

Slowly walking home, Constance questioned herself. Abstracted and heavy-hearted by the Zwaller fireside, she questioned herself. In the quaint bed where Barbara lay nestled close beside her, she lay wakeful and thoughtful, while all the house slept: Had that day brought the looked-for happiness?

Why did it leave such a weight upon her heart? Did not Mordaunt love her? Yes, she was sure he did. Did she not love him most tenderly? Oh yes, she was very sure of that. Must every other affection be put away for this? All sense of grateful dependence upon others be swallowed up in this one love? Was it selfish for Mordaunt to demand it? "I would not divide it with any on earth," were the words that came back to her now. Was it noble, generous, to refuse even dear Aunt Deborah a share of her loving duty? Her thoughts frightened her. It grieved, wounded her to suspect that Mordaunt was not the perfect being she imagined. She would not have it so, and began to reproach herself for not humoring his fretful mood. He was ill, and weak and weary. She wished she had soothed and caressed him, as others might have done — even promised to stay. Why was she timid and cold and obstinate? Accusing herself thus, and feeling that she was a wicked mortal, unworthy of Mordaunt, she fell asleep at last, consoling herself that to-morrow should repair it all; for she would stay. But when to-morrow came, she reflected that it would seem unmaidenly to linger at the Roosevelt's another day; and she felt that her presence was not welcome to Elsie. Then Aunt Deborah, not wholly recovered, would suffer nervous fears on her account. Nicholas, too, had arranged to go with her that day, and horses were engaged and waiting the other side of the ferry. For this once, Mordaunt must allow her to have some regard for the comfort and happiness of others. She prepared to go with quiet gentleness, and, by the time the morning sun was shining on the chimney-tops, was walking toward the ferry, looking back with a sinking heart toward the little window of Mordaunt's parlor.

XIV.

Dame Zwaller prided herself upon the preparations for her daughter's marriage. Always overwhelmed with cares, she was never so burdened as now. Mynheer wondered why the house needed to be renovated from top to bottom, as if the guests were to inspect it, and could not see what the cellar and dairy had to do with the event further than to furnish good cheer. Old Mabel was weary and sore with scrubbing and waxing. Then such preparations for the wedding supper were never heard of before in New Amsterdam. Lisbet was called in to assist, since she had the art of puffing biscuits and cakes into airier heights than anybody else. What a field of exploration this opportunity offered to her innocent eyes! Perhaps foreseeing this, Dame Zwaller had prepared her house for the ordeal, knowing well that what she saw, all the town saw. In due time she had inventoried the bride's wardrobe, and, in her love for the good Barbara, desired to impress everybody with the queenliness of her outfit. Thus it came about that all the prudent mothers were astonished and censorious over the extravagant number and costliness of articles which, in truth, existed only in Lisbet's imagination.

"Six satin petticoats!" said Lisbet. One, of white silk, was in Barbara's possession.

"Flanders lace by the yard!" she exclaimed to the

wrapt listeners. A single yard had come in a note from Constance Aylmer, that day.

"A set of jewels fit for a princess!" This also, upon inspection, dwindled to a very pretty topaz brooch that came in the same package.

Then, how they all ran to peer from the doors at the passing carts filled with furnishings, Lisbet said, for the house at the bowery! And what eagerness to see Dame Zwaller set out now in the high-backed sleigh for the bowery also, as if she had not been there many times before!

This bowery was a rich one, with a new house of brick, yellow and black. The upper story projected over the lower sufficiently to afford shelter to the Director and his companions, when he would choose to sit there in the summer afternoons. And he might sit there often, for the bowery was his and not Baltazzar's, and he intended to retire to it altogether some day, when he tired of his office, or his office of him. A wide smooth road had been made the previous summer from the city, and this road was already the race-course, the pleasure-drive, and the favorite walk of the young Hollanders. Barbara was not likely to lack for amusement or friendly visits in her new home.

The wedding evening came at last, and with it all the great people of New Amsterdam, to the house of Burgomaster Zwaller. The Governor was there in his most genial mood. Herr Roosevelt came in a new pair of buff breeches, and his quiet wife honored the occasion in new taffeta. Elsie appeared in a velvet bodice laced with a silver chain, and her pretty feet were never so well displayed as now, in her scarlet shoes and the envied Christmas stockings of red and white. She was full of vivacity, and ready for a flirt and a frolic.

The arrival of Domine Megapolensis, his wife Macktelt, and their boyish Heldigond, produced a sensation, for all at once realized that a wedding was in hand. Then the courtly Sir Henry Moody entered with Constance, and was directly offered a chair near the Governor. Constance, always with an air of graceful ease, looked more English than ever in her trailing robe of blue silk, its trimmings of delicate lace, the cordon of pearls in her hair, and the soft laced handkerchief, covering, but not hiding her fair shoulders. Mr. Mordaunt, from his arm-chair in the corner, scrutinized her well, and wondered at her unconsciousness of the admiration with which many eyes followed her. When she came near, he gallantly arose and offered his seat. She refused with a bright smile at seeing him there, with his limb loosed from its wooden prison, though dependant upon a crutch. Nicholas Stuyvesant, always ready to serve either of them, brought his own chair and placed it for her.

Dame Zwaller hastened hither and thither, now looking in to see if the luxurious supper was in certain perfection, now greeting her guests and assisting them to unwrap, watching the fires and the lights, retouching the dress of the waiting bride, and, in fine, performing the duties of host and hostess, servant and friend, while mynheer, her spouse, sat quietly enjoying himself with his townsmen, not once thinking there could be any thing else for him to do. The world moved easily to him, and he was mystified to know how his busy dame managed to make a mountain of care out of such a joyful occasion as this.

Now she was telling the Domine that all was in readiness, then she reminded the father that he was to give away the bride, and then made way for the two whose happy hour had come. All eyes were upon the trembling Barbara. Her bodice laced with the gold chain of Christmas memories, the white silk petticoat blue-bordered, and the white shoes with blue rosettes were duly inspected by all feminine eyes. The full string of golden beads encircled her neck, testifying her industry, and proving her ability to manage a house of her own. Only Mistress Primley was a little frightened at the sight of the beads, and thought it ominous that they had already hung about the neck of a dead maiden.

Barbara looked ruddy and bashful, and Baltazzar the embodiment of happiness. They were doubtless glad when the long ceremony and the long discourse upon their duties were finished, and when relief came in the shape of happy wishes from the friends crowding about them. Then followed the fine supper, the drinking of health to the newly married, the ringing of glasses, the tumult of voices, and afterward music and dancing.

Lisbet was there, buzzing like a beetle, and gay as a rainbow with ribbons. She was almost as tireless as Elsie in the dance. Her frequent partner was a

7*

tall, slender bachelor, whose height contrasted oddly with her small stature. He had fine, thoughtful eyes, fair hair, and moved quietly through the intricate measures, listening to Lisbet's prattle.

"Who is waltzing with Lisbet?" asked Constance of the Director, near whom she was standing, while looking at the waltzers.

"Hans Van Elslant, the poet and schoolmaster," was the reply.

"Have I not seen him bearing the State cushions before Your Highness, on the Sabbath?"

"The same," said the Director, nodding and smiling.

"And is it not he who reads the Commandments and Articles of Faith for the Domine, or a Psalm, while the people assemble?"

"Yes, sweet Mistress Aylmer."

"I thought him the curate."

"We have no curates; that smacks of the English Church!"

"The schoolmaster has a variety of occupations, then," added Constance quickly, lest he should go into a passion over the curates.

"Enough to keep him out of mischief, truly: he rings the bell, provides the sacrament, gives the funeral invitations, catechizes the children, and ought to whip them, but I suspect gives them bonbons and flowers instead. Hans!" he called aloud, seeing he had finished whirling with Lisbet, and stood wiping his brow. Hans obeyed the summons.

"Hans, this is Mistress Aylmer, of Moody Hall;

she wishes to know something of our Holland schoolmaster."

Hans bowed respectfully, and waited for the questions he expected, while Constance stood embarrassed at the abrupt summons. Seeing the Director occupied, however, with a communication from Councillor De Sille, she recovered herself, and was soon interested in a quiet chat about the Old and the New Amsterdam. His heart evidently yearned for the Old.

"One must descend to the life of a peasant, here. Starve, too, for books. Those I brought with me look like bones gnawed by a hungry dog. I miss the atmosphere of learned people. I am sick sometimes for sympathy."

"But you should not live upon the thoughts of others, now," said Constance, timidly. "A new country ought to suggest new thoughts. You are a poet; there is much to inspire you here."

"A rugged country, a rugged people, and a rugged life. It is too real for poetry," he answered, thoughtfully.

"I do not know, for I have no gift," said Constance, "yet I think its very roughness would lend vigor and manliness to your thoughts."

A gleam of pleasure lit Hans' face, and he looked at Constance without seeing her, far beyond her, as if he caught a glimpse of what he might achieve. It lifted his mourning soul as it had not been lifted since he left the Father-land. Recalling himself, he said,

"May I ask you if it is not repulsive to mingle

with rude people, after having been bred in courtly society?"

"I find so much to love in them, that I forget all else," said Constance, sweetly.

"But the ignorance, the emptiness of soul!" said Hans, with an impatient gesture. "Yet I forget," he added; "my home is everywhere: the children's homes shelter me. Sometimes they are difficult to endure. The good dame at whose cottage I am now quartered scolded me soundly this morning, for filling her children's heads with nonsense. 'As if the world turned over every day, and I not know it,' said she. 'A fine story! would'nt my duck-pond have been emptied long ago, if the world turned a somersault every day?'"

"You are a persecuted Galileo!" laughed Constance. "But it is pleasant to be Galileo, after all."

"Thank you, Mistress Aylmer, you have done me good," returned Hans, bowing, and retiring at the approach of the Councillor.

The music ceased, and the older portion of the company began to break up. The young people prepared to escort the bride to her new home, and were laughingly selecting partners while Constance stood talking with Mordaunt. Sir Henry had secured Elsie's promise, Hans Van Elslant was already leading Lisbet to his sleigh, and the rest were making ready for the merry ride, so that it only remained for Nicholas Stuyvesant to beg Constance to accompany him.

"Do not go," said Mordaunt, irritated at the politeness of this gay young Hollander.

"Barbara would be disappointed," she replied, hesitating.

"She will not miss you among so many," urged Mordaunt.

"But she told me this evening she desired to show me her new home, which I have not yet seen. What can I do for you if I remain?" He regarded her with a wounded expression, and replied in the peculiar tone usual to him in such moods,

"I merely supposed you would prefer to remain."

By this time Dame Zwaller, who was still superintending all things, came to express her wonder that Constance was not getting ready.

"I think I will not go, if you please," said she gently.

"But Barbara counts upon you. Her will is law, this wedding-day; you cannot refuse. Come, I will wrap you warmly in my scarlet cloak."

There was no refusing her peremptory tone. Constance drew back a moment, and laying her hand upon Mordaunt's in a pleading way, whispered,

"I shall not be long gone. Wait till I return, for I have something to say to you." Then she submitted to the motherly kindness of her friend, and was presently muffled and seated beside Nicholas. The gay procession now sped away amid the jingling of bells and snapping of whips, making a lively uproar that shocked the ears of all who had not been bidden to the wedding.

A bountiful repast was in waiting at the bowery, quite superfluous, though hospitable. The happiness and long life of bride and groom were drank, and, after many congratulations upon the cheeriness of the new abode, the escort returned over the smooth road, and scattered tired and sleepy to their homes. Nicholas intended to take Mordaunt back to the Roosevelt's in his sleigh, but he had chosen to walk there on his crutch without waiting for Constance. She did not see him again, as Sir Henry was obliged to return to Gravesend early in the morning.

Two weeks more went by before Mordaunt prepared to return to Gravesend. He announced his intention one evening to the Herr, and both to him and Dame Roosevelt acknowledged very feelingly their untiring kindness during his long illness. They really regretted his purpose to leave them. Many hours that would have passed in dull silence had been made delightful by his efforts to amuse; and besides, he had often rendered important service to the Herr in state matters. Certainly Herr Roosevelt would miss his clear-headed interpretations of the law, and his skilful manipulations when an antagonist was to be overcome at the Stadt Huys.

A shadow fell upon Elsie's face when she heard him say he was going. How could she spare that handsome face from her every day vision? How dull it would be without his entertaining chat! How hard to lose the sweet sayings and the gallant services of this cavalier! Every other one was so stupid and awkward. Even Nicholas was insupportable when near him. Her heart uprose against his going. She had been slowly reeling off a fine flaxen thread from the full spindle, but now, pushing away her work, she sprang up, saying impatiently,

"I hope you will break your other leg in starting!"

"Elsie!" exclaimed her father, with stern reproval in his tone.

"Elsie! Elsie!" repeated the mother faintly, as if frightened.

"I mean well enough," explained Elsie. "I only wish somehow to keep him there in his chair."

"What! always?" said Mordaunt, laughing.

"Yes, always," replied Elsie; "that is, as long as you are good-natured, and entertain me with tales and gallant words."

"Oh ho! then any fine-spoken cavalier with broken bones will do. There is the Lord Director—he can tell of his adventures by the hour."

"No; he is crosser even than yourself."

"Well, there is Nicholas."

"Oh, no. I broke his heart once, and he was lively as a spring robin the next time I saw him. He gets mended too quick."

"Then Antony Jansen, who danced so vigorously at Barbara's wedding."

"Wrong again," laughed Elsie. "He is too much a giant. Did you know his grandfather carried ten bushels of wheat up stairs at one going?—one bag on each arm, one on each shoulder, and one between his teeth. Now, if I happened to tease Antony Jansen as I tease you sometimes, I should expect him every minute to catch me up and shake me just as old pussy picks up her kittens."

"Nonsense, Elsie," said her father, smiling in spite of himself; "go back to your reel, and stop your chattering." Always doing as she pleased, Elsie did not stir from her position before the fire, with her hands clasped behind her.

"I cannot work to-night," she said. "I wish Hans Van Elslant would fix all the reels and wheels on the chimney-tops. He said to me once, there is no need that women should spin and weave all the days of their life. He says the wind should be made to do all the work. I believe as he does; that if the wind grinds the corn for the men, it can spin flax for us. I shall ask him some day to put my wheel in the place of the weather-vane."

"What would the world come to, if the women had no spinning or weaving to keep them busy?" said Herr Roosevelt, scornfully. "We should not be able to live for the scandal. What would you do, my fine lady, if you neither knit nor spun?"

Elsie looked puzzled a moment, but she did not intend to give up her view of the matter. She replied, quizzically,

"Oh, I would smoke and sit by the fire, and put on a big wig and go to the Stadt Huys and make laws —good laws, not such as forbid games at Pinkster and forbid Maypoles."

"Aye, woman fashion, you confound the Director's proclamations with the laws," interrupted Mordaunt.

"And what would you have us do?" asked her father.

"Watch the wheels, and see that the wind does not blow them away."

"Then who is to make our linsey-woolsey, dimity and linen, our butter, cheese, oly-koeks and noodles? Ah, bah! we should be starved, poverty stricken."

"But we should have all the more time to fashion these dainties," returned Elsie.

"I thought you were going to the Stadt Huys to make laws!" said her father, drily.

"Truly; I forgot," and she tossed back her pretty head and laughed with the rest at her discomfiture.

Mr. Mordaunt really set out for Gravesend that week, and received a cordial welcome at Moody Hall. Constance rejoiced at his return, for now there would be no misunderstandings which she could not quickly remove; unconstrained by the presence of strangers, she could bestow all the little attentions that her loving heart suggested. Mordaunt was satisfied now. He claimed all her time, with no rivals to trouble him. But, tormented by no real jealousy, he feigned it sometimes in order to test her affection, or to delight himself with the telltale expression of her face while he told his doubts, or the old, and always sweet, story of his love. It was plain that her life was daily more and more absorbed in his.

They were busy with the future. Plans were made for the betrothment at an early day. After consulting with Lady Moody, it was decided that the Zwallers and the Stuyvesants should be present as witnesses and guests. The wedding was to be deferred till after Mordaunt's intended journey to Virginia. Meantime, they occupied themselves with plans for a stone house, which was to be built to receive them as soon as they were ready to go to his Virginia home. Time went softly with downy wing, unnoted, except as it brought nearer the day of betrothment.

Early in the appointed week, a messenger came from Governor Stuyvesant, asking Mordaunt's immediate service in a case which threatened difficulty with England. It admitted of no delay. His High Mightiness wished him to attend upon him at once. The matter was submitted to a family council, and all admitted that it was for his interest to obey the summons.

"It is quite right," said Constance, the day of his departure, "though Mistress Primley would name it an ill omen to postpone our plighting a second time."

"I may not be long detained," replied Mordaunt, half pleased at her downcast look, though pained himself at this new separation.

"Will you make me a promise?" she asked, with a beating heart.

"Tell me first your demand."

"It concerns my happiness."

"I grant it then," said he, smiling upon her in his fascinating way.

"Whatever reason you may have for doubting my love for you while absent, will you tell me plainly, and listen to my explanation before condemning me?"

"Suspend sentence till you have a hearing," added Mordaunt, drawing her more closely. "Granted and sealed," said he, tenderly bestowing a kiss.

Constance was happier for this promise. The possibility of its being broken did not occur to her.

When he had gone, the house seemed wofully vacant. Aunt Deborah and Sir Henry were but shadows in the space he had filled. She perceived now how much he was to her, how entirely he occupied her thoughts to the exclusion of others. Lady Moody saw that she listlessly returned to her old occupations.

"I do not regret the delay in thy formal plighting," she said. "It is well to have time to discover mutual failings, that disappointment may not creep into the heart after marriage."

"And if one does discover?" suggested Constance timidly.

"Thee can better bear and forbear than if suddenly made aware of faults. Thou and Edward are now walking in the moonlight of love. Love idealizes its object, just as the natural moonlight softens and beautifies the face on which it falls. When the full day of married life shines upon thee, it will grieve thee to behold how marred is the visage deemed perfect, unless thy knowledge shall prepare thee."

Constance thought of the many troubled hours that had come already, and comforted herself that they had come now rather than later. She longed to confide this to her aunt, but——no! Love hushed the words. She would have no one suspect that Mordaunt lacked aught that was noble. She would resent the suspicion. She would hide it from her own eyes. He was gone now. She would think only of his manly figure, his handsome features, his dreamy, fascinating smile, and all his precious words.

XV.

It was late in March when Mr. Mordaunt went to New Amsterdam. All of April passed, and he was still detained. During this time he had journeyed into New England, and had suffered some hardships in his travels. But he assured Constance his return was now not far, and added to his letter the request that she would not receive Nicholas Stuyvesant's visits, for he had heard of his going often to Moody Hall. To this she replied that he did not come to see her, but to confer with Sir Henry about Lightfoot, which he desired to purchase for the race-course. If he paid any court to her, she knew that it was for the sake of winning her consent to the sale. "I cannot part with Lightfoot," she wrote, "because I love the creature that bore us so well out of danger, and would not see him suffer the cruelties of the races. Perhaps Nicholas thinks he can overcome my scruples by his importunities, which only serve to increase my love for the graceful brute he would take from me. It was only yesterday that Aunt Deborah chided me for putting my arms round Lightfoot's neck and feeding him with some of Chloe's good bread." To this Mordaunt crisply replied, that "so many journeys to Gravesend were hardly needed for the barter of a horse." Constance sighed, and strove to avoid even the sight of Nicholas.

The sunny days of early May had come, and there was much to be done without and within the house to restore freshness after the long winter. Constance was up with the early sun, and not a bird in the woods beyond the green meadow sung a more joyful song than was carolled from her lips while performing her share of duties. The gardener had commenced his pleasant task, Pete and Mingo were ploughing the fields, Tobee was once more watching his flocks and cows, and when night came called them lazily as of old, leading them to their night enclosure with the monotonous cry of "Home! Home!" Within, Rose was rejoicing over the deepening yellow of her dairy treasures, and Chloe was grumbling that the winter store was failing, that neither field nor garden yielded anything to her purpose, and made great ado that she was expected to concoct fine dinners from an empty larder, yet never failed to serve a feast when occasion required.

On one of these bright days of happy waiting for Mordaunt, Constance was sowing flower-seeds in the borders of the garden walk. A wide-rimmed hat shielded her face from the sun. Sir Henry was standing by the gateway just outside the palisades, looking at his new chaise lately brought from England, and which he and Nicholas Stuyvesant had been trying. Seeing Constance in the garden, he called her.

"Come and take an airing in the new chaise with Nicholas. Tell me if it is not as good as a coach, and better than a pillion."

"How shall I be able to tell you, when I have

never ridden in a coach? The sight of those whirring wheels at my side will make me dizzy."

"No, you will forget the wheels."

"But I am ill-dressed to ride in so fine state."

"Well enough," said Sir Henry.

"Perhaps it would please Aunt Deborah to try it."

"No, she thinks it a whirligig, and not becoming to her staidness," persisted Sir Henry, who, seeing his cousin's reluctance, was all the more determined she should go. It was of no use to oppose his whims. Constance yielded, placed a stone upon the seed-papers and took her seat in the chaise beside Nicholas, with some misgivings. Away they rolled, leaving Sir Henry looking after them in admiration of the vehicle, and drawing after them, for a long way, a troop of boys who stared at it with open-mouthed wonder.

The road was grass-grown; even the cart-tracks were not sufficiently worn to throw dust, so that the wheels rolled almost noiselessly along the way, rattling over a chance stone or rumbling quickly across the rude planks that bridged an occasional stream. It was a perfect day for a drive. The air was velvety to the cheek, and balmy with the new verdure and the May-blossoms. The young, glossy leaves upon the trees stretched themselves in the sun, after their long sleep in the downy buds. One could almost see them shake themselves out and grow. Violets peeped out from the green grass beneath, wake-robins spread out their purple and white petals in gaping wonder at the beautiful world around them, and the spring beauties, delicate enough to wreath a fairy's head, innocently lifted their faces from the mossy knolls, content with their humble place.

Wherever these flowers flecked the ground with their blue, white, and purple, Constance begged to alight and gather, till her broad hat was crowned, and her hands and her lap were fully laden.

"They are wasted," said she, seeing them begin to wilt. "Homesick little things, I am sorry I took you out of the cool grass. Do not gather any more, Nicholas, they please me best where they grow. These have lost their beauty. I do not like to hold them. They are like dead hopes."

Without loitering for more, they sped on, too exhilarated by the fresh breeze and joy in the redundant life everywhere visible, to notice how far they had driven, till a sudden turn brought them in sight of the great white oak. The road was straight for half a mile beyond. A horseman was riding towards them. Travellers were not frequent, and it was easy to imagine him to be Mordaunt. They decided not to turn back yet, but to drive slowly and meet him.

"I am sure it is he, I know his plumes," said Constance. Her face lighted with pleasure. Then she remembered her dusty dress and her tossed hair, and how observing and scrupulous he was. A quick thought of the pretty dimity in which she intended to have met him, vexed her. Then it flashed upon her that Nicholas was beside her, and she would have given worlds if she was only back in the garden sowing seeds. What would Mordaunt think? She was frightened now. Mistress Primley with all her croakings crowded into her thoughts. The dead flowers and dead hopes came to mind, and she shook the withered blossoms all out of her lap.

By this time the rider approached, and was surveying the chaise and its occupants as he came near. Constance leaned forward to speak. Mordaunt looked incredulous, then astonished, then angry; so angry that the veins of his temples were swollen. Striking his spurs into his horse, it leaped forward and dashed along the road in a bounding gallop. Constance dropped back in her seat, and was silent. Nicholas knew she was pained at the angry slight, and tried to palliate it.

"He could not have known us. The rim of your hat almost hides your face. Then too, this grand new chaise! How could he recognize it, when he has never seen it? He did not know us." Turning about, he flourished his whip and followed fast after Mordaunt, who presently disappeared in the windings of the road.

The chaise rolled softly and swiftly over the grassy road, between the same clearings and forest as when they went; but the wayside flowers were not noted, nor did the woods ring with Constance's laughter. The two were as if they had grown old since passing before. Nicholas began to perceive the truth—that Mordaunt was jealous of him. He could understand now the conduct which he had attributed to the peevishness of illness. Why had he been so stupid? Constance avoided him often, and this was the reason! He sat dumb beside her, his eyes opening clearly to his own folly.

8

"Why have I involved myself in this new trouble? Am I to be a perpetual thorn to my friends?" he thought. "Am I bait on the devil's rod, held out to draw all whom I love and esteem into difficulty and misery? and shall I dangle thus always? Those races have got me this sweetness. Oh, that I were back in the mill! Once out of this affair with Mordaunt (and who knows how the mad fellow will end it), I will back to my flour-bags. Bother Lightfoot! I will pay Baltazzar. Good soul! he is tired of grumbling."

The chaise was now rolling along by the palisades; in a moment it stopped at the entrance. Nicholas looked about as if not quite sure as to the kind of reception awaiting him. No one was there, however, but Mingo, who led the horse away as if there had been no other arrival. Constance went quickly to the Library. No one was there. Finding her aunt, she asked, surprised,

"Is not Mr. Mordaunt arrived?"

"Nay. Did thee look for him this morning?"

"He passed us in our drive, and I thought to find him here." Constance told it all, and then asked,

"Was I wrong to go with Nicholas?"

"I see no fault in thee. Neither will Edward, when he knows how it happened." Constance shook her head sadly.

"Has he been thus displeased before?"

"Never so deeply. Aunt Deborah, I ought not to have gone."

"If Edward is jealous-minded, thee must not shut

thine eyes to it. It will mar all thy happiness and his. Be a true woman and tell him his fault wisely, and help him mend. Is not thy courage sufficient?"

"I spoke plainly once, and ever so gently; yet he was angry."

"My child, it is better to pluck the thistles now if they do sting thee, else they will overgrow and destroy all the love-blossoms. Edward's affection will be a torment rather than a joy in thy future, if he persists in this wise."

"Aunt Deborah, *you* tell him all this when he comes, will you not?"

"He would take it more kindly from thee."

Constance sat plucking the flowers to pieces, leaf by leaf, from the wreathed hat lying in her lap.

"Edward may yet come. Thee had better change thy garden dress," said her aunt, smiling gently at the decorated hat. Thus reminded, she hastened away to freshen her toilet.

All that day she watched for Mr. Mordaunt, utterly unable to occupy herself as usual. She went to the door at every sound, only to be disappointed. Every footstep made her heart beat quickly, for she thought he meant to surprise her. Once or twice, when she believed no one saw her, she walked outside the palisades to look along the road for him. Night came without him. "He will come to-morrow," she said cheerfully to herself, yet the next day, and the next, brought the same hope and the same disappointment. A week later, Timon, the Roundhead weaver, came from a trip to New Amsterdam;

in answer to Sir Henry's inquiries, he said that Mr. Mordaunt was at Herr Roosevelt's. Sir Henry was in a rage at the conduct of his friend. He pronounced it unworthy of a true cavalier, unmanly, ungenerous, and would have continued to denounce him, had not Constance astonished him by rising up in his defence.

"It is not easy to serve the fair sex. One never knows on which side of a question to find them," said he.

A few days afterward, he asked Constance to go with him to New Amsterdam. They would go in the chaise as far as Breuklyn. The pleasant weather and the cradle-like chaise were not to be resisted. Perhaps, too, the possibility of meeting Mordaunt was not the least of the reasons why she gladly consented. They accordingly set out in the morning of a cheery day, and reached Breuklyn in time for Cornelius Dirksen's noon trip across the ferry.

When Constance arrived at the Zwaller's, she found Dame Zwaller seated in the doorway, stitching a jacket of linen fustian. A heart-shaped pincushion pierced with needles and pins, a pair of scissors, an oilskin bag of thread, and a bunch of keys, all dangled from her apron-strings, significant of thrift. Mistress Primley sat within, stitching also industriously. She looked up on hearing a voice, and then threw up her hands, as she always did at sight of Constance.

"I knew you were coming, for my scissors stuck fast in the floor, and the pins pointed to Gravesend when they fell," she exclaimed.

"Your scissors and pins are wiser than mine, then, for though they often fall, nobody comes," laughed Constance.

"You should have told me what they said," added Dame Zwaller, "and I would have laid by a bit of that fine cod for her comfort." Saying this, she bustled about, setting a repast fit for a princess, though Constance protested she desired nothing better than her white bread and sweet milk. Meantime, Mistress Primley was reciting some harmless gossip, prattling about Lisbet and Hans Van Elslant, how they strolled on the Battery at sunset, or walked to the bowery on pleasant Saturdays, and how Hans had sported big yellow daffies in his button-hole at church, as if everybody did not know they came from Lisbet's garden.

"A fine couple they will make, with his head always among the stars and hers always in her neighbor's affairs. One would think such a man of learning would be loath to marry a chatter-box," she said, forgetting her work and folding her fat hands pensively. But she resumed it again, as Dame Zwaller came back to tell Constance that Barbara was with her to-day, and had gone up to see the Domine's wife. She would send Minxey to call her home as soon as she had finished standing the dishes in the dresser.

So small a detention as this simple placing of dishes was to make a vast difference in Constance Aylmer's life. If Dame Zwaller could only have seen the little measure of time left in which to save all Constance's dreams of earthly happiness, she would have sent

Minxey on the wings of the wind. But there they sat, quietly chatting in the doorway, while Minxey idled at her task and the minutes were oozing away like life-drops! It is no chance that holds them thus in durance. It is the will of an Almighty Father that joins the insignificant links of circumstance that bind Constance to-day. A bitter cup is preparing, but through it her soul will rise into a nobler life.

Minxey goes at last, but it is no matter if she goes now.

Barbara comes in breathless haste, throws her arms around her friend and kisses her, but her face is smileless and troubled.

"Come with me to Elsie Roosevelt's, will you?" she whispered, "now—quickly!"

Constance assented, puzzled very much by her agitation and evident wish not to be overheard.

"What is it that troubles you, Barbara?" she asked, trying to keep pace with her quick steps along the street.

"I know nothing—I fear only. Domine Megapolensis went there a half hour ago, and I am afraid— no, I will not tell you my foolish fears. We will see."

Could anything have happened to Mordaunt? Was he very ill again? Perhaps dying; and was it her fault?

A few moments' walk brought them to Herr Roosevelt's house. The door stood wide open, but no one was visible. It was very quiet there. As the two came nearer, a voice in prayer reached them. Barbara trembled with agitation. She went in for an instant, then drew back, holding Constance from entering, and said, in a low tone of distress,

"Too late! oh, too late!"

Constance tore herself away, and went in. There stood Edward Mordaunt and Elsie Roosevelt, just united in marriage. She stood speechless with amazement. A shock of intense pain went to her heart. She attempted to speak, but her voice refused to obey. She leaned dizzily against the wall, and then, lest she could not sustain herself, sank upon a chair. She looked again at Mordaunt, who, though the Domine was still praying, glanced up at the intruder. He turned his eyes away from the agonized face.

"Edward, Edward, what have you done?" she cried, regardless of the interruption. Mordaunt dropped the hand of his bride, and stood white and silent. The Domine ceased his invocation, and turned at the sound of that wailing voice.

"What is this?" he questioned sternly. "Is there any reason why I should not have united these two in marriage?"

Constance did not know what he said, or to whom he spoke. Her eyes were fastened upon Mordaunt as they might have been if he was dying. She was looking into the grave of their hopes, with nothing beyond it to soothe her despair. The Domine turned almost fiercely to Mordaunt.

"Is this the reason of your desired secrecy? I would not have officiated, had I suspected this." There was no reply, but a look of haughty defiance.

"Herr Roosevelt, will you explain it?" demanded

the agitated pastor, pushing back his huge wig and wiping his brow. But the Herr was quite as much astonished as he, and could give no reply. Meantime, Dame Roosevelt, seeing the pallor and the pain in Constance's face, went to offer aid, but she would have none. Summoning her utmost strength, she arose and without a word went away with Barbara, who wept as if her heart would break. When they reached home, Barbara threw herself into her mother's arms, exclaiming,

"Oh, mother! Mr. Mordaunt and Elsie are married. He was plighted to Constance. The betrothal would have happened long ago, but for the Lord Director keeping him here so long."

Dame Zwaller frowned till her eyebrows met. It was all too sudden to believe. She had long guessed at the betrothal.

"It cannot be a lawful marriage. They have not been published."

"Yes," said Barbara, "I knew from Baltazzar that His Highness the Director granted him a license as a high favor, but we believed he was to wed Constance in haste because of so many long delays." She burst into fresh tears on seeing again how white and unnatural Constance looked, and how strangely her voice sounded. Dame Zwaller went quickly for a glass of wine, and forbore asking any more questions. Mistress Primley sat in her chair, swaying herself back and forth in miserable uncertainty what to do or say. It was like a thunderbolt out of a clear sky, and it stunned her into silence.

Poor suffering Constance went restlessly from one place to another, now in this seat, now in that, and now to the doorway to catch the breeze. Dame Zwaller would have put her arms around her; Mistress Primley would have folded her to her bosom, but she was so cold and tearless, so proud in her struggle, that neither could console.

"You had better lie down and rest," suggested Dame Zwaller, not knowing what else to propose, and seeing her walking to and fro as if her very spirit was striving to escape out of its prison.

"No," answered Constance in a voice that was not hers, "I am well—quite well. I would only that I was in my little chamber at home. Can you not find Sir Henry?" Her pleading look could not be refused. Barbara sped with the summons herself, and it was not long before he came with great strides up the street. As soon as he saw Constance, he put his arms around her and folded her to his breast, laying his hand soothingly on her head.

"Dear Constance, he was not worthy of you!" said he, in a low voice.

"Will you take me home?" she entreated, withdrawing herself, as if no sympathy could dissolve her to tears.

"Go home to-night!" he exclaimed. Then looking steadfastly and troubled at her pallid face, he added, "You are not able to journey. Wait till to-morrow."

"Impossible! I must go alone, if you cannot take me. Oh, take me home!"

"You are a brave girl. You neither faint nor

8*

weep. You should have been a Roman maiden. What think you, Dame Zwaller? Can she bear the journey?"

"Better to-day than to-morrow," said the good dame. "She will not care to see all the gossipers, who will be at their wits end about this strange affair."

"Very well. I shall be ready in ten minutes," said Sir Henry, placing his hat lightly on the top of his huge periwig. "I wish to pay my respects to the groom and bride a moment," he added aside to Dame Zwaller. She looked after him with some fear as to what he might intend, for there was nothing gentle in his face or gait as he went. It did not take much time to reach the Roosevelt's at this pace. The door was still open. The mortified Domine had gone, and Mr. Mordaunt was alone, walking back and forth with his head bowed. He stopped at sight of Sir Henry, and straightened himself defiantly as if expecting an onset. But Sir Henry approached wearing the blandest of smiles, strangely out of keeping with the fire in his eyes. He bowed profoundly, and with a most cavalierly wave of the hand, said,

"Permit me to accord to you the highest pinnacle of your profession, since you have so ably outwitted the law and your best friends. Allow me also to offer you my most profound gratitude for saving my incomparable kinswoman from a life of petty tyranny by the generous sacrifice of yourself to-day! I beg you will give my heart-felt condolences to Madam Mordaunt. Farewell, sir."

Mr. Mordaunt was too confounded by this unexpected address to feel it as keenly at first as after Sir Henry had politely bowed himself out. It rankled as deeply then as his bitterest enemy could have wished.

XVI.

It was late when the travellers reached home. Lady Moody was much alarmed at their unexpected return, and not less so at its explanation. Constance refused aid, saying she required nothing but rest. The double journey of the day had greatly fatigued her. She assured her aunt that she would be in her usual spirits the next morning, and would then tell her all that had passed. So earnest was her desire to be alone, that, after assisting her to undress, Lady Moody left her to the loneliness of her own chamber, and descended to the Library to inquire more particularly of her son of the day's occurrences.

Once alone, Constance threw herself upon the bed, buried her face deep among the pillows, and gave vent in tearless sobs and moans to the pent-up agony of that endless day. It was as if her heart was clenched in the grasp of a strong hand, which tightened its pressure at every thought of Mordaunt, till she cried out in anguish. All the sweet interviews, his tender expressions that had thrilled her, his manly figure, his face, that was as an Apollo's in her loving eyes—each came vividly before her with the remembrance that they were hers no longer. She could not recall his faults. He had none now, any more than if he had been her precious dead. But she did recall her own acts that had offended him, magnified them, and reproached herself. She felt certain still that he loved her rather than Elsie, and then came again the remembrance of the great gulf he had fixed between them.

"All through this life — all through! I wonder how long it will be!" she moaned, tossing herself about. Then she sprang up, and threw herself upon her knees before the window. The stars were glimmering just as merrily as if her heart was not breaking. She looked into the far space, and reached out her arms, crying,

"Oh, my mother! oh, my father! If I could go to you!" But the heavens did not open; the stars glimmered coldly. If the sky had rolled away, and the stars had fallen, it would have offered the relief of terror. Any emotion seemed sweet, compared with this pressure of agony. She understood now how some poor souls were driven to suicide, and pitied them. But she had no thought of such a way of escape for herself; she was only measuring and weighting this heavy burden that she was to carry all her life. She resolved that none should know how heavy it was. The first moments of sharpest suffering were over; perhaps she might conquer the rest. Even now, as she sat there thinking, she felt more composed. She would seek rest, and be stronger to-morrow. Thinking thus, she went back to her tent-bed and laid herself down, calm and heavy-eyed, to sleep. It was as if decoyed into a fresh survey of all the charmed past and the dismal future. A smothered wailing cry burst from her lips, and she sprang again to her feet, shivering with the intensity of her emotion. Still she thought to come off conqueror. She summoned all her poor human strength, and quieted herself to rest, only to suffer again those overpowering surges of sorrow. Yet she shed no tears.

Lady Moody had made no effort to sleep. She talked with Sir Henry till after midnight, then prayed earnestly that this sorrow might not harden the young heart upon which it had fallen, but might turn it heavenward. She went several times to Constance's chamber door, but hearing no sound, returned pleased in the belief that sleep had brought a short respite. At early dawn, however, she heard footsteps upon the floor, and did not hesitate now to enter.

"Thee has slept a little?"

"No; I cannot. Shall I ever sleep again, Aunt Deborah?" Lady Moody approached, took both hands in hers, and felt them burning with fever.

"My precious child, this must not be. I thought thee sleeping all these hours," said she. "Why did thee not come to me?"

"I would not disturb you, dear aunt. You cannot help me. No one can."

"No one!" said Lady Moody, with sadness in her tone.. "Thee is looking only to thyself, poor heart, for support. Thy strength will fail thee. Even I am but a bruised reed to lean upon; but there is One who says, 'Come unto me, ye weary and heavy-laden.' He will be thy father, mother, friend. Tell him thy suffering. Go, lean upon his great heart of love."

"Why did He permit it? I cannot go to him."

"Ah, my beloved child, I do grieve for thee; for thou art in the furnace. But Christ sits as the refiner, and he will bring thee out purified like molten silver, if thee will but trust him. Trust him, Constance, without asking why."

Constance did not reply, but laid herself down and closed her eyes. The words soothed her. Lady Moody drew aside the soft folds of the blue drapery, that she might not be shut in wholly to herself, bathed her head and hands with cool water, and gave her an opiate. She did not go away, but rather busied herself gently about the room, as if to console Constance with the cheering presence of one loving human being, now and then telling her something cheery in a dreamy way, in spite of the heavy sighs and tearless sobs that would sometimes overwhelm her. At last, when the sun was high, and the sounds of full day diverted her ear from listening so much to those inner thoughts, she fell asleep. Then came Lady Moody's most anxious hours. She watched near her all that day, caring for her as the most skilful physician could have done, praying for her as only a mother can.

Constance awoke near evening. She wondered at first why she was there. Then full consciousness came back, and she wished she had not wakened. Her heart felt so like lead within her; and there was nothing to wake for. A robin, perched upon a tree near the window, was singing with all its might a rolicking little song. It was harshly out of tune with her soul.

"Aunt Deborah, I wish the bird would not sing," said she, plaintively. "Even the sunset glares to-night; its shining is doleful. Will it never seem beautiful to me again?"

"It is only because thy soul is down in the valley. Thou wilt reach the hill-tops soon, God willing." Lady Moody gently frightened away the innocent bird, and partly closed the heavy shutters while she was speaking. As she turned about, she saw Iyano standing in the doorway. His coming never startled her now. It was his habit to come at intervals since his first hearing of the Scriptures, both to listen to its reading and to learn to read it himself. Lady Moody had with great patience taught him the alphabet. She had grown accustomed to his sudden intrusions, and welcomed him gladly now; for might not his presence touch a chord of sympathy that would at least bring the relief of tears to Constance. He refused to enter, but stood looking wistfully at her.

"Me no hear the maiden's song. Her feet no find the forest. Iyano feel bad."

She could not but remember Omanee, and his revengeful looks at her loss. The change that had gradually been wrought in him, through this loss, also came to mind as she regarded him.

"I am glad to see you, Iyano," she said.

"The mother gave poor Indian medicine from the Great Book. Jesus Christ put his hand on Iyano's heart, and he no sick any more. Why no the maiden take the good medicine she gave Iyano?"

She could make no reply. It had been an easy task

to comfort him out of that source of Life, but it was strangely hard to seek the relief for herself.

"Me ask Jesus to come see the white maiden?"

"Yea, friend, do thou!" said Lady Moody, the tears rolling quickly over her cheeks at the childlike simplicity of his faith.

The once fierce savage knelt humbly and prayed:

"O Great Father, me only poor Indian. But when me heavy, good Jesus come and lift me up, and say, what for you bow down like bulrush? He love me, he shine on me, he take away stone and give me new heart. Me no sorry any more. Why no come see white maiden, and make her glad like Iyano? Great Father did let one make her sick to die, and now he send Jesus to shine on her and bless her very much. Yes; Jesus want much to speak to her heart. Tell her no hide her face so she see no shine. Great Manitou! hear poor Indian prayer, because he love Jesus!"

Constance's sympathy was touched. She knew what this humble friend had suffered. She felt her own weakness, and she well knew the strength of the proffered arm. She must lean upon it now, or reject the blessing. She attempted to speak as Iyano arose, but her lips trembled, tears that could not be repressed, stole over her cheeks, and she hid her face in the pillow and wept abundantly. What a luxury and a healing! What a relief to her burning head and aching heart!

"Let thy will be mine, O Christ, forever! Forgive

me, that I have doubted thy love in this misery. Keep me as thy child," she murmured.

Iyano went away as quietly as he came. Constance was left to the stillness of her own chamber, and soon sobbed herself to sleep like a soothed child upon its mother's bosom.

Several weeks passed before Constance recovered from the languor of a slow fever. Her old elasticity of spirits did not come back with returning health. Her occupations had lost their interest. She wandered about listlessly, looking into books only to shut them with a sigh, taking up her needle only to put it down wearily. Even the garden did not attract her. She had walked too often there with Mordaunt not to be reminded of him, and the seat at the end of the path under the palisades, draped with vines, had too many precious associations for her ever to rest there without tears. Had he not carved his initials here; and, while doing it, said, "You shall not forget me?" And was not every word and look of those sweet agitated days graven more deeply on her heart than his name on the rustic posts?

"It must not be so," said she to herself one day, after a paroxysm of tears, while shielded among the leaves of this shady retreat. "Have I not said to my Father, 'Let thy will be mine?' And is it thus I have accepted his appointment of my lot? No more repining, Constance! This place shall no longer remain sacred to that unhappy love. I will no longer shrink from coming hither, but will come till the pain grows dull. And yet, is it meet for me to look on those letters daily, from out of which I conjure his face and hear his voice?" She sat thoughtful and downcast. Suddenly a new energy possessed her. She arose and went to her aunt, who was occupied in the garden.

"Can the gardener serve me to-day, Aunt Deborah?"

"Truly he may, if it is thy pleasure," she replied.

"And can I do aught I please with the arbor?"

"Do with it as if all things here were thine own, my daughter."

"Thank you, my dear aunt. Lend me your pruning-knife, that I may first cut away some thorns that pierce me sorely, if I do but look at them." Tears were plainly glistening in her eyes, though she smiled while speaking. She turned back again through the path, reentered the little bower, and in a moment cut the initials smoothly away from the place where they had so long looked out at her from among the leaves. Then she untwisted some of the vines and trailed them across the spot, hiding it altogether. Summoning the gardener, she directed him to place the choicest potted plants near the entrance, made an embankment of grass around the sides, brought fresh moss from the woods to carpet it, old grey lichens for brackets, and a hanging nest to swing from the leafy roof. Then she helped him fashion a rustic stand of her own fanciful devising. Two cuts from a log of goodly diameter furnished seats. By night the transformation was complete, and Constance felt happier for the change and the day's abundant occupation. Here she intended to bring her work, to entice Aunt

Deborah into occasional rest, and Sir Henry to reading aloud his newest books. However it might be, she had succeeded in banishing the "Ghost of Love" from this retreat.

The next morning, Constance continued her new mode of warfare. She brought out from their hiding-places the treasured letters, an odd glove, a scrap of paper on which Mordaunt had printed her name with his in many fantastic ways, and a host of mementos, such as a loving heart treasures more than gold. All these she burned. "Not without mourning," said she afterward. "They did not writhe more upon the embers, than did my heart within me at sight of their vanishing." Still she persisted. She scanned the books which had passages underscored, or pages signalized by a pressed flower or leaf, and carefully erased the whole. She would commune no longer with this haunting shadow. But after it was all done, what then? Days went by, but the heavy, heavy heart remained.

"Give me work! Aunt Deborah, give me work! anything to escape from my sorrowful self!" she said one morning, bursting into tears.

"Thee has asked for the best happiness when thy desires go beyond thyself. God bless thee! Get thy hat, and go with me now to Patience Gordon's hovel."

Constance went. The sight of a pale, care-worn widow, homesick for her English home, striving to support a flock of little children, awoke feelings of shame and humiliation that she should repine while surrounded with so many blessings. Sympathy and pity filled her heart. She could go home now and take up her needle with active interest in behalf of that suffering woman. It would be such a pleasure to lighten her burdens thus. This was the beginning of a busy life for Constance. She was taking her first lessons in not "living to herself." There was Hihoudi too, the brother of Omanee, who came to learn his letters; and Rose, the maid of all work, who regarded her young mistress much as a princess in disguise, was eager to read like white people, and not be outdone by the dreaded savages. In this way, occupations multiplied. Sir Henry exerted himself also to provide cheerful company for Constance. He opened his doors hospitably to new cavaliers or to old friends, devised hunting and boating parties, went with her on horseback or in the chaise, read to her in the arbor; in fine, left nothing undone for her diversion. Yet, more than once, he had seen her turn away, in the midst of lively companions, to let tears fall unseen; and though she would return gentle and smiling as ever, he saw her hidden sadness. Twice he had marked her holding her hand against her heart, as if it pained her or throbbed too violently. At last a little incident occurred which broke his silence.

Hans and Lisbet came to Gravesend on a valorous steed from Herr Zwaller's stable, with cue and ribbons flying, to make a long-promised visit. The evening of their arrival was warm and moonlit, and there was no place so attractive and cool as the settle-bench under the front porch. Hans talked poetry to the moon and cast love-glances at Lisbet, but they were lost upon her, for her busy eyes were scanning the fashion of Constance's graceful dress, or Sir Henry's shining shoe-buckles, and her only reply to his quotations was, that he also should have a pair of silver buckles. He was charmed with the night sounds of the forest and meadows, but Lisbet said she loved better to talk than to listen to frogs gulping in muddy ponds, or birds peeping in the woods when they ought to be asleep. She seated herself then by Constance, and, in a confidential way, began her usual gossip.

"Do you know, they say Elsie is not happy with Mr. Mordaunt? It is quite right for all the mischief she has done. He is almost beside himself with grief, and they say his hair is turning white as his grandfather's!" Constance's face grew paler than the moonlight. She made no reply, but Sir Henry had caught the words, and saw the suffering spirit through the white face.

"Now, Lisbet," said he, bluntly, "you spun that bit of news out of your head, just as the spider winds its web out of its own body. If you were a man, I would say in plain Saxon, you lie!"

"My son!" exclaimed Lady Moody, "thou art not worthy of knighthood to speak in such wise to a woman, and thy guest!"

"Lisbet should better consider her words, lest possibly they might sting like arrows. As a woman, and my guest, I humbly crave her pardon. As a gossip I censure her," said Sir Henry, noisily pacing back and forth over the pebbled walk in front of them.

"I speak what is true," retorted Lisbet. "Carl

Steinbach went out in the ship with them to Virginia, and wrote back that saying."

"Fie! Fie!" cried Sir Henry, impatient at this testimony, which only made the matter worse. Determined to check her further words, he called out for Hans, who was climbing by the arbor to the top of the palisades. "He will break his neck, Lisbet, or get scalped if he tumbles over the other side." This brought her to her feet, and sent her into the garden.

"Stop!" called out Hans. "Hark, all of you; what is it?" All listened to soft, mournful notes, that swelled up from the depths of the forest.

"It is the lute of an Indian wooing his pretty squaw," said Sir Henry.

Constance buried her face in her hands. She had once heard that unearthly music when Mordaunt stood beside her. It recalled all the past, even more vividly than Lisbet's unthinking, cruel words.

"Oh, Edward! Edward!" she moaned, in a suppressed voice, dropping her hands, as if not knowing where to turn. Sir Henry shouted loudly,

"Don't listen to that tooting, Lisbet! it will bewitch you!" Her tongue was unloosed instantly, and she chattered like a magpie, under the palisades, scolding and entreating Hans to come down from his dangerous perch. Constance escaped to her quiet room. The melancholy notes still floated up to her, and filled her soul with a sense of loneliness unendurable. She bowed her head upon the window-seat, crying out,

"Oh, Jesus, my Saviour, do thou so take possession of my soul that I shall no longer suffer this despair. My poor resolves are unstable as the waves. Be thou my strength, for I am weak—oh, so weak. Do not let my heart question thy tenderness in dealing thus with me." She raised her head, leaned upon her hand, and thought aloud. "If Edward was happy with Elsie, it would be less hard to bear; but he grieves as I grieve. It is both sweet and bitter to know this. My heart, my heart, how it rolls and heaves within me." Faint with the violent palpitation, she unfastened her dress, rose feebly, dipped her hands in cool water and bathed her face, then sank back into the deep arm-chair.

"Why do I strive to arrest this? why not die? I would not live, yet when I feel my hold upon life loosing a little, I struggle to retain it. Strange contradiction!"

There was a rustling on the stairs, two little feet pit-patted across the hall, and a trim little figure stood tapping at Constance's open door. Lisbet was as irresistibly drawn to every event as the needle to the pole. It was impossible for her not to discover the absence of Constance, and just as impossible 'not to know the mischief she had done. Nobody in the world could be more sorry than she. She endeavored to repair it with kind words, with cologne and hot cordials, but Constance's pride and annoyance at being discovered enabled her to rally quickly, to put on a cheerful air, to descend again to the piazza, and even to smile at Hans' droll account of his school.

That night, when they separated for rest, Sir

Henry drew his mother aside, and held a long conversation about Constance's welfare. Lady Moody assured him that time alone would lessen her grief, and that constant occupation and interest in others were the best restorers of a healthy tone of mind and body. Above all, she was sustained by a trust which would presently give her entire peace and calmness.

"She will die under these slow processes," replied Sir Henry impatiently. "She must have change of scene. These people whom I would have only to amuse her, do but recall the past, and stab her with their silly words. The very flowers and birds fling doleful memories at her, and the great white oak on the highway is no better than a tombstone in her eyes. She must go to England."

"To whom can she go in England?" exclaimed Lady Moody, stirred at the thought of losing Constance.

"To her rightful guardian and kinsman, Lord Grey."

"Her father would not have it so. His sister is a church woman and a royalist, and lives gayly in London. Thee would not give our beloved Constance to such worldly keeping."

"Only for a short season; I will go thither myself, and convey her safely, and she shall return with me, if she wills it." Lady Moody could raise no objection to this proposal, and promised to lay the plan before Constance the next morning.

9

XVII.

Hans and Lisbet had just gone, the next morning, when Iyano stole into the garden, and stood in significant silence beside Lady Moody till she finished gathering a handful of flowers. Then he spoke a few words, and went immediately away. Lady Moody looked alarmed. All thoughts of the proposed voyage vanished, and she sent hastily for Sir Henry to come to her in the Library.

"Iyano tells me the Masapequas are preparing for an attack," said she. "Go quickly to George Baxter, and give intelligence. See that he sends out scouts to call in the scattered settlers, or prepare them for defence. Thee must not return till thine own eyes certify that every needful thing is done."

"What impudent vipers!" exclaimed Sir Henry. "Only two days ago a band of them came in to traffic, and, I doubt not, have well scanned the town. But half the battle is won, in being prepared for the cowardly dogs."

"I trusted the Masapequas were friends," said Lady Moody. "Some one has done them ill, else they would not break the peace. Do not tarry, my son; every hour lost may cost the lives of a family."

Sir Henry hurried away to the magistrate, leaving his mother to care for his own home. She immediately summoned the servants, and stated to them in so cheerful and calm a manner, what she required of each, that they obeyed with far less trepidation than might have been expected. Tobec gathered the cattle from the pastures, and put them safely in their enclosures. Lady Moody went herself with Mingo to examine every part of the palisades, to be certain of their soundness, and ordered tanks of water to be placed for convenient use, in case of the enemy's resort to fire. The shutters were closed and bolted; firearms and ammunition were brought into the hall and stacked. Before night those settlers who did not feel secure in their own houses, came with their valuables to Moody Hall, as being safer on account of its tiled roof. Some of the villagers came also, fearing to trust to the security of the palisades that enclosed the village. Others outside had failed to build their own, or had neglected to provide themselves with ladders to their roofs, as required by law. Lady Moody received them all with open arms, though reminding them they were every one like the foolish virgins without oil in their lamps.

By night preparations were everywhere completed, and sentinels posted about the village. All waited with nervous anxiety for what the night might bring forth, yet not without hope that the timely warning would ward off the blow.

Meantime, Iyano decked himself as became a chieftain; a long eagle's feather shot up from his shell-worked frontlet. From his waist hung dressed deer-skin, embroidered and fringed. A string of wampum and an English hatchet were fastened at his girdle; a quiver, from which dangled a fox's tail, was slung across his shoulder, and he carried an elastic bow, of dimensions that suggested a strong arm in battle. Thus equipped, he set out for the enemy's camp: as he approached, the howlings of the war-dance struck his ear. He surveyed the various groups from a leafy covert till satisfied, and then stalked forth into their midst, and stood in dignified silence. No regard was paid to the intruder at first. Some young warriors approached, but he scorned to confer with them. One tall, athletic Indian, whose features belied his disguise, looked fiercely upon him, but he was unmoved at the hostile menace; he still leaned indifferently on his huge bow, awaiting the pleasure of the chiefs to learn his mission.

Gradually the war-dance ceased; the chiefs and warriors withdrew to the council-lodge, and at length signified their readiness to hear him. As if to give time for the subsidence of the evil passions raised by the ceremonies of war, a long silence reigned. Iyano at last arose.

"My brothers, Iyano has not two tongues. He knows the Masapequas are brave. Many scalps have hung in the belts of the young warriors. But what does Iyano see! Do the braves go to fight great warriors? No, they go to kill squaws. The Englis you would kill do not carry thunder in their arms like the Englis of the Manhattas. No sachem sits in their council-lodge. The mother of the Englis sits there. She brings words from the Great Spirit. The God of the Englis will be angry if she is slain. He has sent Iyano to say it."

Iyano was silent for a few moments. He glanced over the swarthy host as if to fix every wandering eye, then broke forth with a fierceness that would have appalled Lady Moody, and made her doubt if indeed her pupil had felt the renewing power of the Holy Spirit. But the force of association and the glowering face that had been turned upon him since his first coming roused all his savage nature, and overshadowed the restraining precepts which his gentle friend had striven to bind as frontlets on his brow.

"It is the Evil-minded who has told the Masapequa braves to destroy the lodge of the good mother," said he. "Listen to Iyano. Eight moons ago, the White Swallow was in the lodge of her father; her eyes were as stars; her feet like the roe's; they were swift to obey the voice of the chief. A serpent crept in the forest and charmed the White Swallow. She followed him to the canoe that flies upon the water. The Great Spirit was angry. He sent her back in the arms of the waves. The stars are gone out. The White Swallow sleeps. The lodge is dark. The serpent is coiled by your council-fires. You take him to your heart. He is your son and your brother."

Iyano's voice and manner conveyed the utmost scorn. He paused amidst profound silence. Every warrior knew whom he meant, though not one looked toward the adopted pale-face—Lord Percy, who, escaped from an ocean grave, had taken refuge here. He did not cower before Iyano at his betrayal, but continued to fix his tiger-like eyes upon him, boldly waiting to know the end. Iyano resumed:

"This brave chief has a trophy in his belt. Is it a scalp? No. It is the white wings of the sleeping Swallow. Now he speaks. 'Let us slay the Englis!' Will he find scalps like the braves? No. There is a maiden pale and shining as the moon in the lodge of the mother of the Englis. The serpent would have her wings by the side of the White Swallow's. Will you follow him? Go! The nations will call you the slayers of squaws. Iyano is done."

He turned away from his silent auditors without waiting for a response, and disappeared in the woods. He disdained to linger in the council, but patiently watched with his scouts to know the result of his appeal. The discovery that Percy still lived, and the challenge in his fiery eyes and haughty mien, had aroused a storm of passion which hungered for an opportunity to vent itself. The intended attack upon Gravesend would afford it, and as night after night passed with no signs of a moving enemy, Iyano grew sullen. He had defeated himself as well as Percy, but he resolved to follow him and obtain revenge. Life for life. He should die for Omanee.

An Indian runner came at last with the news of a skirmish between the Masapequas and a band toward the east. Assured by this of the safety of Gravesend, Iyano went with slow steps to convey tidings of relief to Moody Hall.

All this time the villagers had suffered the misery of suspense. False alarms had twice filled them with terror, and given occasion to distinguish the cowardly from the brave. A sentinel, who had abandoned his post and hidden himself, was now doing duty in the public square on a wooden horse, with a sword in one hand and a pitcher of beer in the other, to denote that his courage was to be determined by the quantity drank. Some, doubting Iyano's truth, returned to their usual work, but not without loaded arms within reach. The villagers who had taken refuge at Moody Hall, seeing how multiplied were Lady Moody's cares, went back to their own homes and tried to quiet their fears, but those who had come in from scattered farms remained till Iyano's arrival.

The family were filled with new anxiety when Percy was known to be the plotter of the intended mischief. Although he had failed in this, what new plans might he not invent? He would scruple at nothing. Measures must be taken promptly to arrest him. During this discussion, Iyano's eyes glimmered so darkly and savagely that Lady Moody noted it. She attempted to draw from him the cause of the change in his countenance and manner since his last visit, but he was too morose and cunning to commit himself. He disliked to be questioned. He was in haste to depart. The more she regarded him, the more certain she became that he had either already harmed Percy or intended it. She knew enough of his savage code to believe that justice awarded by law would not satisfy; nothing but the blood of his enemy poured out by his own hand would appease him. As she thought of this, she remembered also that in her desire to inspire him with faith in the redeeming love of the Saviour, she had failed to impress him with the need of a forgiving spirit toward men. He was not prepared for temptation. This opportunity to enforce a hard and hated truth must not be lost.

"Friend Iyano," said she, "I perceive thy unwillingness to tell me what is in thy heart. Thee would fear to tell it to God. But thee cannot hide thy secret from him." Iyano turned to go. He had no desire to listen to his teacher.

"Stay, friend, till the Book holds a talk with thee." There was a power in her presence which he could not resist. He obeyed with sullen dignity.

"Thou hast done me a great service, Iyano. I cannot return thee a better, than to be faithful to thy soul." Saying this, she took from its shelf the great Bible with its iron clasp, and turning the thick leaves hither and thither for various passages, read in a slow, distinct voice.

"This is God's command: 'Thou shalt not kill.' If the commandment is broken, this is the punishment: 'Murderers * * shall have their part in the lake which burneth with fire and brimstone; which is the second death.' Iyano, thee must not dip thy hand in the blood of Edgardo Percy, to repay thy wrongs. Thee must leave that to God. Hear what he says: 'Vengeance is mine; I will repay, saith the Lord.'"

"Iyano has waited. Your God is asleep. The pale-face is yet free."

"Thou art wrong, friend. Our Father never sleeps, but he waits. Listen again. 'To me belongeth vengeance and recompense; their foot shall slide in due time.' The Almighty does not make haste to cut off the wicked. He is 'long-suffering to usward, not willing that any should perish, but that all should come to repentance.' Perhaps the Lord is waiting for Edgardo to repent. How does thee know, friend, but thine enemy may hear the voice of God, and receive mercy and forgiveness like thyself?"

This was a new thought to Iyano. He regarded Lady Moody with a strange, unsatisfied look, and doubtless marvelled in his heart, just as the disciples did when they heard a hard saying from the lips of their Lord. Constance, who had been a silent listener, wondered if a heart so full of evil intents could make room for Christ. "I should be filled with fear at the sight of Percy, even in heaven," she said.

"'Though your sins be as scarlet, they shall be white as snow; though they be red like crimson, they shall be as wool.' If Edgardo's sins were washed white in the blood of the Lamb, he would be no longer what he is, and therefore thee would rejoice to meet him. Iyano, if it please the High God to draw out his days and pardon him, thee can forgive also, and not use despite?"

"Iyano waits to see the white chief die," was the stony reply.

"Then thee must wait the pleasure of the Lord. All thee has to do in this matter is to forgive him with all thy heart. Jesus says, 'Love your enemies, bless them that curse you, do good to them that hate you, and pray for them which despitefully use you, and persecute you; that ye may be the children of your Father which is in heaven.'"

"The brave no love his enemy. He would have a squaw's heart."

"Satan tells thee that, friend. Thee must rather listen to Jesus. Hear how he would have thee use Edgardo. 'If thine enemy be hungry, feed him; if he be thirsty, give him drink; for in so doing thou shalt heap coals of fire upon his head.'"

This was too much for Iyano to receive stoically. He gave an ejaculation of dissent and disgust. He could not now meekly lay down his burden of vengeance. Like many another, he wished to roll this sweet morsel of sin under his tongue while he walked with Christ. Lady Moody felt that it was a crisis which might determine the triumph or the abandonment of his new-found faith.

"Iyano, I have but these words more to say to thee now. If thee does not forgive thy enemy, God will not forgive thee. Ask Jesus to help thee, or thou wilt perish." She closed the Book, and replaced it on the shelf. Iyano, understanding that the "talk" was done, went away, glad perhaps to escape from the dazzling light which this strange Book was pouring in upon his soul, revealing his unholy self. But the shining was there, and he could not put it out.

XVIII.

Elsie Mordaunt had neither the fine house " all of Holland brick," nor the "chairs with seats of bright russet leather bordered with gold lace," which she had once gayly said must be placed at her service, together with her lover's heart. Her air-castle had resolved itself into a simple cottage without external ornament, save a wild rose that had tried in vain to clamber without help up the side of the house, and had fallen back in sprawling helplessness on the uncut grass. The spinster, in whose charge Edward Mordaunt had left his bachelor domicile during his long absence, would have let it creep through the grass till it dragged itself back to its native woods if it chose, provided it kept out of her way. Experience Topping understood the use and value of a hop-vine, but a rose-creeper had no claims upon her.

Within the cottage, as without, there was no ornament. It was neat enough. Experience was devoted to the care of it. She was one of those methodical people who have a place for everything, and religiously send everything into place. She was a close economist too. She never walked over a pin. A bit of thread was not beneath her notice and use, scraps of lint slowly accumulated in a corner bag, and every garment she wore testified to her patient patching and darning. Her skill in converting apple-peelings into jelly, bread-crumbs into puddings, and making soup from bare bones, was marvellous. Yet she was a religious, not a miserly economist. She was conscientious in her stewardship, rendering exact accounts to her employer, and what she saved by her self-denials was freely bestowed upon the comfort of others. Her gifts were necessarily small, and her sphere narrow. Their very smallness gave rigidity to her thoughts and ways. The incoming of a new mistress like Elsie was a shock to all her notions and habits, and no wonder if she stood dismayed at the revolution in the affairs of the house on her arrival.

"Take away the joint-stools from the chimney-corner, and fill the gaping fireplace with holly branches. It looks like the grave of departed Yule-logs," said Elsie, frowning, when she had surveyed the chief apartment. "I will have silk hangings too, and not chintz."

Mordaunt was besieged for the alterations, and yielded. During a few weeks, every room was in a turmoil. No sooner was one at the point of completion than Elsie would suggest something new, pull down all she had done, and begin over again. To do this, she levied all the forces possible. She possessed the peculiar talent of impressing everybody who came near, into her service, and keeping every soul of them in nervous haste with their task. The task given was not often rightly appointed. She was quite sure to cut the tapestry too short, and summon her helper to take it down and lengthen it, or order a dresser too large for its place, and refuse to accept its clumsiness. After an apartment was duly settled, she was quite likely to feel its narrowness, and conceive the bright idea of tearing down a partition, or building an "addition." But it could not take forever to complete so small a dwelling. To keep it in order when finished, was quite another affair. For this, Elsie had no talent. She left it to Experience, and turned her energies to the entire remaking of the garden. And poor Experience strove in vain to keep the chairs in prim rows, sighed to see Mordaunt's costly books lying upon the floor precisely where Elsie had dropped them, or stood amazed to see her dresses tumbled on the chair, and her pretty boots flung across the room when they had happened to pinch. And who can imagine Experience's horror at seeing Elsie's spools of thread rolling hither and thither at the mercy of a playful kitten, or wound inextricably with tangled yarn, when she had stooped her lame back many a time to save a bit a few inches long? What could she do but grumble, and look after this spoiled child?

When Elsie had exhausted the garden and the temper of the gardener, she took a capricious whim to invade Experience's kingdom.

"Did you ever taste an oly-kock?" she asked, one day.

"No."

"Then I will make some this minute!"

"Not to-day," plead Experience. "I cannot serve you well to-day."

"But I feel precisely like it," returned Elsie. It was not possible to turn her from what she chose to undertake. So, in spite of the warm day, she caused a notable fire to be built and a kettle of fat to be swung on the crane. Without first bringing together all the articles needed, she began mixing the dough.

"Uh! how shall I get my hands out of this? Get some flour; do!" Experience brought it, smiling significantly.

"There! I have forgotten the salt. Pray get it."

"Oh, Experience, the spice! the spice! Where is it?"

"Not a grain in the house, mistress. And not a grain can you buy till the Dutch skipper comes up the river again."

"Ah well, I cannot wait till the skipper comes. I shall make the oly-koeks just the same, though they will never be oly-koeks without spice." By this time Elsie was well dusted with flour. Flour was over the table, and flour on the floor. She was too busy to perceive the burning of the waiting fat, and Experience was too provoked to hinder its spoiling.

"Take it off, Experience. Quick!" cried Elsie.

"Let the olys go. I have had enough already," grumbled the spinster while she marshalled forth the crane. Elsie, still bent on the work, dropped the cakes into the kettle, and stood watching them roll and tumble, and finally settle at the top in a benign sputter.

"Run for a fork, Experience. I must turn them." The fork was sullenly given.

"Do bring a pan! They are burning black!" cried Elsie, at the top of her voice. And thus, till the last cake crowned the dish, she kept Experience in active service, and in a state of mind not at all to be desired.

"These are costly cakes," Experience indignantly remonstrated when the hub-bub was over. "They have wasted more wood and flour than would have served to cook a feast. How many grains of wheat did it take to make the flour lying under your feet and upon your clothes?"

"Fie! What of an armful of wood, or a cup or two of flour? I can never worry my brains with saving scraps. Do you save, if you like."

"But a cup of flour and an armful of wood every day would almost keep poor Annice Hart through next winter," replied Experience, with warmth.

Who was Annice Hart, and what did she need, why did she need, and why should she not have all she wanted, were the questions that followed. Elsie immediately made large promises which she doubtless intended to perform, but beyond one gift of flour and wood they were never fulfilled. Her limited purse was always preëngaged for fine boots ordered from Holland, or had been emptied into the palm of the last pedlar. She could not forego a costly kerchief, a new bodice, or a dazzling brooch; at each pleading for help, she graciously promised herself and Annice Hart that another time she could better afford to be generous.

Mordaunt indulged all her whims and extravagances, but he paid her none of the pretty compliments that used to come so readily to his lips when she sat by him in his invalid hours. His eyes rarely rested upon her face. She was piqued and indifferent by turns, yet so long as he granted all her wishes she did not take it to heart seriously. Her life was too outward to permit even a doubt of her husband's love to stir her very deeply. She knew little of his inner life, nothing of his business, nothing of his ambitions or disappointments. He had no wish to intrust her with the knowledge. Sometimes, when in perplexity, his thoughts reverted to Constance. Had she stood at his side, her advice and sympathy would have been sought. Had she sat near while he pored over a book, he would have shared its thoughts with her. Not so with Elsie. She yawned at the sight of a book, and was very likely, in the midst of a proposed business plan, to scream with laughter at the gambols of the mischievous kitten, and go springing after it all the way into the garden. Then Mordaunt would fold up his papers and go away, sadly thinking of the incompleteness of his life, the void that his wife could never fill, the rich sympathy and love that might have been his if he had willed it; the adviser, the friend, the consoler, that he had madly thrust away. These thoughts never found voice, but they were written upon his face in plainer lines each miserable day. Elsie could not but perceive it, and one evening, after watching his clouded face as he sat busily writing, she reminded him of it.

"You have never looked the same, Edward, since Constance Aylmer stood at the door on our wedding day. If you loved her, why did you not make her your wife?"

"If I had not wished you to become my wife, I should not have asked you. A husband is not expected always to carry himself like a lover." To hide his emotion at the sudden mention of that prohibited name, Mordaunt spoke sternly. Elsie patted the floor with her little foot in vexation at the reply, and was silent. She sat looking at him again critically. Her eye rested upon the mass of hair that partly shaded his face as he leaned over the table.

"Edward," she exclaimed, "how gray your hair is! There was not a silver line in it when we were married. It grows whiter every day. How very strange!"

"I am growing old, I doubt not," he replied, without looking up.

"People do not grow old so fast. You are not old; you are not yet thirty."

"My grandfather may have been silver-headed at thirty, and the peculiarity have fallen to me," he suggested, with a calm sad smile.

"Ah me! Has that anything to do with it? I am glad my mother's hair is yellow yet—every thread of it; and my father's is jetty black. I shall not keep you company, you see."

"Yet your braids might bleach in a single night."

"How?" asked Elsie, leaning forward in surprise.

"Grief!"

"Edward, is that the reason your hair is whitening?" Her eyes were fixed earnestly upon him. He felt them. He did not wish her to know the silent anguish he had endured from the moment he had fixed his destiny apart from Constance Aylmer. He replied, with a careless air,

"You have forgotten my grandfather. Sorrow might bleach a woman's hair even white. A man should be too steel-hearted to let grief creep to the very tips of his locks. You must not boast, for you may yet outstrip me in growing old."

"I shall never spoil my hair or my eyes with grief. You used to praise both. You leave others to praise them now," said Elsie, pettishly.

"Who praises my wife?" asked Mordaunt.

"A gay cavalier in steel corslet, trunk hose, long boots, high-crowned beaver, and drooping feather," said Elsie, a bright smile breaking over her face.

"Chevalier Morton?"

"Yes. How I frightened him!" and she laughed gayly at the remembrance. Mordaunt's curiosity was awakened, and perhaps the faintest suggestion of jealousy moved him to question further.

"He was with our berrying party last week," she continued. "I sat warm and tired upon a mossy log, and he beside me, fanning me with a great leaf. He suddenly took my hand in his, and praised my eyes. 'Leave my hand,' I cried out, 'it belongs to my husband!' In spite of his brave-looking corslet, he blushed red as a maiden with shame and vexation, lest the rest heard me."

"What further said he?" asked Mordaunt, flushed with anger.

"That 'he might better clasp a thorn-bush than my hand.'"

"What more?"

"Nothing. I fled away, laughing at him."

"But you should not have laughed. You should have been angry."

"How could I help laughing at his rueful looks? You should have seen the wight in his corslet, and with his brave sword dangling, and how ill they became his frightened and astonished looks. I laugh now at the very remembrance."

"Have you seen him since that day?" said Mordaunt, rising and walking uneasily back and forth.

"No. But to-day came his little negro with a boquet of pretty wild-flowers, and 'massa's compliments.'"

"Where are they?" demanded Mordaunt, looking angrily about the room. Elsie sprang to her feet, clapped her hands, and laughed till she could hardly speak.

"I frightened the black sprite almost out of his wits. He had only left the gate, when I flung the flowers so hard after him that they struck his indolent heels. He turned the whites of his eyes full upon me, snatched the flowers out of the dust, and ran as if he believed me a wicked witch." Mordaunt could not help smiling.

"I doubt not you have quieted Chevalier Morton's gallantry, but do not trifle with those gay birds. Neither would I have you venture again for berries. The woods are never safe from prowling Indians," said Mordaunt. Elsie was full of vivacity and playfulness this evening, and the new thought of her suffering a hateful captivity, or the possibility of her love ever being won from him by the cunning arts of an admirer, awakened a tenderness toward her which he had not felt before. She had proved a true wife, in spite of his coldness and the wandering of his own heart. Yet without a single reproach for himself, he accepted her love and instituted a jealous watchfulness over it, that diverted his thoughts from Constance, and conduced to his own happiness, if not to Elsie's.

XIX.

All thoughts of the voyage to England were dismissed, after the threatened attack of the Masapequas. Sir Henry had not mentioned the subject to Constance, but in his own mind he postponed it only till the next season, when he trusted a better administration of government, and the increased strength of the colony, would allay all fears of the Indians. A proposal of a different nature was made to Lady Moody a few weeks afterward, which for some reasons met her approbation. George Baxter, an esteemed citizen and former magistrate, conferred with her upon the possibility of obtaining Constance's hand in marriage. He had served as secretary under Governor Keith, and acted as magistrate of Gravesend, till removed by the present Director for the bluntness of his criticisms on the administration. His abilities and learning gave him weighty influence. The countenance of this Quaker politician was pleasing, though slightly rayed with wrinkles. The plain adjustment of his hair perhaps added to his age, when compared with the bushy curls which mounted the head of the baronet. His costume too, deprived of the ribbons, laces, buttons, and jewels which entered so largely into the dress of the cavaliers of the day, suggested more staidness than he really possessed. This did not lessen him in the esteem of Lady Moody; and further, she regarded his sterling character, influential position, and easy means, as both desirable and suitable in the proposed alliance. In her desire to secure a protector, to retain Constance near, and to avoid for her the temptations of a frivolous life in London, she forgot the wants of a deep and loving nature, and the abhorrence Constance might feel at a business disposal of her heart, which had so lately learned, with painful acuteness, the height and depth of love. Lady Moody had the wisdom to advise Friend Baxter to wait patiently, and not spoil his suit by too hastily pressing it. In the meantime, she endeavored to prepare the way.

"Will thee go with me to meeting?" she asked, one sunny Sabbath. There was no house of worship in Gravesend, but the Quakers met at private dwellings, and occupied the hours in religious reading. Constance was often present. This brilliant autumn day she was not tempted to go.

"Will thee not go?"

"Not to-day. My dress displeases those plain people. I am loath to annoy them."

"Why does thee think it? None have complained of its unfitness."

"Last Lord's day, Mr. Baxter watched the long feather in my hat, till I was almost constrained to pull it out. I feared every moment he would reprove me aloud, and I drew back behind Mary Tilton; but she, unwilling to sit before me, moved herself away, so that I was covered with confusion at being unable to hide my offending hat."

"Art thou quite sure he was looking at thy feather, and not at thyself?" queried Lady Moody, with a smile so full of meaning that Constance's color was visibly heightened.

"Why should he look at me? He is fatherly in his kindness, and I feared would be too fatherly in his reproof."

"I do not think he intended to rebuke thee. I have heard him say he admired the excellent beauty of thy character, and holds thee an example for all the young people of the Manhattas."

"Mr. Baxter does not know me at all to say it. Neither do I like the saying, for it is an unpleasing constraint to hold me an example to any," she replied, with much warmth. Lady Moody did not think it prudent to approach the subject nearer, but a few days later ventured to express her wishes and plans. Constance was occupied in arranging a deep fall of lace upon a dress. She consulted her aunt as to the placing of it.

"Why does thee put so much fine lace upon thy dress, when it is pleasing without?" asked Aunt Deborah.

"Because the lace lends ease to the stiff stomacher. It finishes the sleeves gracefully too. Do you not see how soft and hazy are the cuffs, and how uncomely the sleeves would be, without them?"

"I see thy love for these luxurious belongings, but would thee not be willing to lay them aside, if one who loved thee desired it?"

"If it pains you to see me decked thus, I will lay aside the lace, dear Aunt Deborah. You never chided me before for the wearing of it," said Constance, much surprised.

"But if another desired to see thee wear plain apparel?"

"Who, my dear aunt?" replied Constance, still more perplexed.

"Suppose thy suitor a Quaker."

"You suppose an impossibility," was the laughing reply. "My high-heeled shoes, my trains, my huge fan, the brooches, bodkins, and jewels would frighten a soberminded Friend."

"They have not frighted George Baxter. He desires thy hand. Doubtless, seeing thy good sense, he believes thee able to loose thyself easily from the bonds of court fashions."

The elegant dress and costly lace fell from Constance's hand. She looked ready to cry, and ready to laugh. At length she gave indignant voice to her thoughts.

"Why does he not choose a wife whose age and opinions approach his? Tell him never to breathe the thought to me!"

"Thou knowest George Baxter is a citizen not to be despised. He is a noble-hearted man, and I think could make thee very happy."

"If he were Prince William, I should refuse his suit. I can never marry—never! never!" Constance could not trust her voice to say more, and took up the fallen dress, bending her head low to hide the dropping tears.

"Do not be hasty in thy decision. I would always have thee with me, but the day may soon come when I shall be removed hence, and it would be sore distress to leave thee in charge of thy London kinsman."

Whatever more Lady Moody would have added in Friend Baxter's behalf, was cut short by a summons from Rose, who said Iyano waited without, and would not be refused. A sick man was in his lodge and needed help. Such calls were in the ordinary routine of her duties. But it was unusual to go so far as the Indian encampment, and she sent for Sir Henry to accompany her. After preparing a basket of such articles as might be needed, they set out on horseback, following a narrow trail through the woods for two or three miles, then emerged upon the broad open space where the Indian village lay.

A flock of nude children sporting with arrows, squaws gathering corn, and a score or more of savages preparing for a hunt, met the sight of the comers. Bundles of flags and bulrushes for making mats lay near some of the wigwams, and squaws sat by them weaving mats or baskets of black and white rushes, or little baskets of crab-shells.

Apart from the rest was a wigwam built of saplings bent in a rounded form, and covered with thick-wrought mats. A long mat, brightly colored, served for a screen at the entrance. Within, eagles' claws, horns of deer, and bunches of feathers from the sea-drake or the eagle, hung against the handsome skins that lined the hut. A basket of roasted acorns was the only visible food. A rude bed of moss and leaves, over which was thrown a beautiful deer-skin, was on one side, and upon this lay the sick stranger.

When Lady Moody entered, she could not perceive the features of the sick man; but as her eyes became accustomed to the dim light, she saw that the face, emaciated and discolored with paint, had neither the mould nor the complexion of an Indian visage. His eyes were wild and restless, and his thin hands hot with fever. He refused the kind offices Lady Moody would have performed, and stared at her with an ugly glare. The sight of Sir Henry maddened him.

"Away with you!" he cried. "You come to gloat over my evil plight. You have hunted me down at last, but you will neither get me nor the Dutch boor's gold. The gold is in the sea. You are too late to serve your writ on me. I am mortgaged, soul and body, to the devil. Ah ha! you savage vagabond!" said he, shaking his fist feebly at Iyano, "is it for this you brought me here?"

Lady Moody and Sir Henry stood amazed at the sight of this fallen cavalier. His velvet, gold lace, corslet, and hose had given place to coarsely dressed skins; his massive periwig had disappeared, and his matted locks were tied in an ungainly knot upon his crown. His oily speech and courtier-like gallantries were dropped, as needless masks in his last extremity, and his true heart laid bare in confessions of the horrors of his guilty life, and in blasphemous reproaches against God. Lady Moody listened till she could endure no longer.

"I know, Edgardo Percy, that thou art a fugitive

from justice, a betrayer of thy friends, and a woful rebel against the Almighty," said she. "But thy sins can be washed white in the blood of the Lamb, if thou wilt believe in him. Even now, he is able to give thee a robe of righteousness in which to stand before him, if thou wilt take it. He died for such as thee."

"I cannot believe! I cannot believe! My soul is too full of horrors. All the evil deeds of my life crowd like grinning demons into my thoughts. There is no room for belief."

"But dost thou not grieve for all thy ill works? Canst thou not repent, and pray God for mercy?"

"Pray?" shouted Percy. "No. Pray to the rock that is even now crushing me? Judgment has come. I would fly from God; he is my judge. There is no mercy."

"Look to Christ, Edgardo. He is love and mercy. For his sake, the Father will receive thee."

"I have mocked Christ; he will not hear me. There is no time, no room for mercy and love. I am full of horror and hatred. Leave me! you do but taunt me. You come with your testimony, and your godly life, to condemn me. Why torment me before my time?" He cursed and blasphemed till the listeners were shocked. Tears poured like rain over the cheeks of Lady Moody.

"Come away, mother," urged Sir Henry. "His words are not fit for your ears. You do but 'cast pearls before swine.'"

"Let me at least better the pitiful condition of his

body, if I cannot help his soul," said she, preparing medicine, and attempting to cool his head and hands. Percy flung the potion from him, and warded off the bath. Her gentleness availed nothing. Seeing that her presence only aggravated his illness, she consented to withdraw and allow Iyano to serve him. She gave simple directions, and prepared such nourishment as she could over a fire of dry leaves and sticks. When she had finished, she called Iyano to sit beside her.

"How came Edgardo Percy in thy lodge?" she asked.

"His feet slide!" She remembered the verse read to him.

"Didst thou cause them to slide?"

"Me find him on cold ground, all sick. Me no want to touch him. The Evil-minded said, 'No help your enemy.' Me go away. Good Spirit come to Iyano's lodge and say, 'Give him drink.' The Bad Spirit say, 'Let him die; he kill the White Swallow.' Then Jesus said, 'Take him to your lodge, feed him; love your enemy, or I no love you.' Me feel very bad; me pray; me go bring serpent to my lodge. The mother sees him."

"Iyano, thou art a beloved disciple. God will reward thee. Thy end will be peace," said Lady Moody, much moved. Even Sir Henry was not an indifferent listener.

"This heathen has outstripped me!" he exclaimed. "I could in no wise do what Iyano has done."

"Unless Christ dwelt in thy heart," his mother

added. "Let us ask our Father to have mercy on poor Edgardo. I cannot go home without one plea," she said, as they arose to go. Sir Henry leaned against a tree, and waited silently and respectfully. Seeing Lady Moody kneel upon the ground, Iyano knelt also. She prayed fervently, as a woman with all her sympathies stirred could pray. The sick man in the cabin, only a little way removed from them, could hear her distinct utterance. It quieted him. Sir Henry wondered at the silence. He could hardly listen to his mother's words, for agitation and awe in thinking that perhaps the Spirit was moving upon that wicked heart, and casting out the legion of devils that had occupied it; or perhaps Percy had suddenly died. The suspense was painful. As soon as his mother had finished, he strode to the door of the wigwam; but before he could enter, there came forth a despairing cry, mingled with oaths, which arrested him as if they had taken visible shape.

"May the Lord spare me from such a death-bed," said he, turning away. He wished to escape from these terrible cries of remorse and despair, and hastened his mother's departure. She promised daily help and counsel to Iyano, and went away reluctant and oppressed. She had not prayed with faith. She was unbelieving now, and in all the homeward journey wearied herself with self-reproaches, because she could not approach nearer to the throne of grace with this great burden. She counselled with Constance; she searched the Bible for every passage that promised mercy to the erring; she prayed, fasted, went again with entreaties to Percy—all without once feeling the repose of faith that her prayers would be answered. This was a new and sorrowful experience.

"I fear that God is deaf to my poor intercessions. Can it be that this soul has persisted too long and wilfully against mercy?" said Lady Moody. "Oh, my son, thee can see how fearful it is to wait till the last day of life to make peace with God. Edgardo has no longer any power to look at the cross of Christ. The pains of an awakened conscience deprive him of reason. Alas! what can I do for him?"

Lady Moody labored in vain. There was no change except for the worse, in body and mind. Percy failed slowly. His iron frame resisted the progress of disease, and might have overcome it, but for the fiercer ravages of a remorseful mind. At times he refused to die, and, rising out of his bed, staggered from the hut, to the terror of all who beheld him, and fell exhausted, to be carried back again on the shoulders of faithful Iyano. Stories of witchcraft began to be whispered. This was an additional source of anxiety to Lady Moody. When Iyano came therefore one day and told her Percy was dead, she heard it with a sense of relief. Sir Henry made preparations to return with Iyano, to give him burial.

"Strange!" said he as he went. "This is a strange thing that I, who have spread so many nets to capture Percy, should go at last to give him a friendly rest in the grave."

"No law by which thou couldst have condemned him," replied his mother, "can equal that simple law under which he suffered: 'Whatsoever a man soweth, that shall he also reap.' His soul is in the hands of the living God. Do thou bury him with pity, remembering that thou also must reap either eternal death or eternal life."

Constance stood by with some late Autumn flowers in her hand, hesitating if she should send them forgivingly to repose with Percy. There was no mother, no sister, no kinsman to mourn him. She was touched by the utter forlornness of his death. She reached them toward Sir Henry as he was going, and then drew back.

"No," said she, "I cannot. They are too pure to lie upon his breast. It is not fit that he should wear flowers. I can weep for poor Percy, but I cannot honor him."

Many days passed before the family at Moody Hall could recover from the depressing influence of Percy's miserable death. New sympathies, interests, and plans at length diverted them from these sad thoughts. The days grew shorter, and the frosty evenings brought them in cheerful companionship about the fireside. Constance seemed herself again. Sir Henry told her of his purpose of going to England the next season, and amused her with his accounts of London and the gay Lady Grey. Oliver Cromwell's growing greatness was a topic of increasing interest. His successes at home and abroad, his boldness in all reformations, his piety, impressed them deeply. Constance was a hero-worshipper, and this kingly man, risen out of the common ranks by the force of his own character, and ruling men by the sole power of his own will, without the aid of royal prestige and pageants, was a sublime spectacle in her eyes. Had he been a less worthy ruler, she yet would have admired his grand strength. His godliness added a majesty which awakened all her enthusiasm. It was positive happiness to enthrone another human being in her imagination, and see him invested with all noble qualities. There would be less likelihood of his falling from the pedestal than that other, at whose feet she had laid the freshest emotions of her heart.

There was a frequenter of the family fireside who vied with her enthusiasm, though in a less lofty degree. This was Mr. Baxter. He could not perceive the singleness of purpose which she awarded Cromwell, nor would he consent that innate strength had any more to do with his reaching the throne than the force of circumstances. Yet he greatly admired the man and his work, and often expressed the wish that the Manhattas were under his rule, rather than subject to Holland.

Whenever a ship arrived with later news from England, or when any vague rumors of affairs over the ocean reached him, Mr. Baxter made it the occasion of a visit to Moody Hall. Yet, despite his frequent visits, he felt that he made little or no progress in Constance's interest. He had not ventured to express his wishes or his admiration, for she held him aloof. How, he could not have explained. Neither, perhaps, could she. It was simple aversion on her part to marriage without love, and the aversion unconsciously made itself apparent. He could not accept this subtle assurance of defeat like a wise man, and leave her, but seized the first opportunity to present himself as her suitor.

He found her alone one evening. She very soon discovered his intentions in coming, and her first impulse was to escape from the hateful interview. Then she reflected how very unquakerish was her toilet that evening. A bodkin set with rubies confined the bands of her hair, and a like cluster of stones glowed upon her bodice. Her dress was of the same rich dark hue, and lay in sweeping length upon the floor. The sleeves were slashed with silk of a delicate shade of amber. She hoped that Friend Baxter would be convinced at a glance of the unsuitableness of his choice. But the worthy citizen saw the beauty of her face and the grace of her figure, without noting if either owed anything to the choice of color or style of dress. He might have condemned the jewels apart from the wearer, but they seemed properly in place, without attracting his especial notice; the silk too, in so strong contrast with the dark folds against which it lay, might have offended his eye, had not the fairness of the arm which it half veiled made him forget to disapprove. If she had manifested a little vanity, or coquettish archness, or frolicsome gayety, in the entertainment of her guest, he might have criticised the worldliness of her attire; as it was, jewels, lace, and silk were forgotten in the repose of her manner and thoughtfulness of her countenance.

Friend Baxter adroitly led the conversation to the

verge of a declaration. Constance just as expertly diverted it. She hoped to convince him of the folly of his errand, and deter him from fulfilling it. Did he broach Quakerism? She showed herself churchly on all points. Did he speak kindly of his deceased wife? Most heartily she commended him to remain faithful to her memory. If he argued in favor of the union of youth and age, she almost scornfully condemned it. She was frightened at her own audacity in so opposing the opinions of one whom she regarded with respectful deference, yet was continually provoked to it by her perverse suitor. George Baxter was by nature a lawyer, though he had spent part of his youth as an officer in the British army. He gave a wonderful twist to all that Constance said, construed it favorably, or proved her contrary opinion to be one and the same with his. It was a useless strife. The more she placed herself beyond his reach, the more fixed was his purpose to woo. Ceasing his preliminary skirmish, he expressed himself distinctly.

"Constance," he asked, "hast thou set thy affections on any one with whom I should interfere unjustly, in seeking thy hand?" She hesitated, and trembled as if with cold.

"You would interfere only with myself," she replied. "Having no affection to bestow, your effort to seek it must bring disappointment." Friend Baxter did not dream, as he watched her white face and her seeming self-possession, what a storm of feeling he had awakened. The old love spurning the new, resentment at the thought of age asking the sacrifice of youth, dread of wounding by her frankness, and a struggle for courage to speak with decision, were like separate personalities conferring together so violently, that her mind's eye looked on in dismay. Mr. Baxter did not believe that she possessed no heart, and took courage.

"I do not expect to win thy love at once," he said. "Esteem is an excellent foundation whereon to build love. In time thou wouldst find thy affection awakened."

How matter-of-fact the voice sounded in her ear! What indignant thoughts were stirred by the cool suggestion that in time her love would awake, as if it had not already almost mastered her life! She was nerved to plain speech.

"Mr. Baxter, I honor you as a citizen and a friend of my aunt. The continuance of my esteem will depend upon the light in which you regard me. I shall hold myself free from any alliance—especially with one whose age would forbid a right sympathy."

"Thou art inexperienced, or thou wouldst think better of this. I request thee not to be hasty in thy decision." The calmness and the superior wisdom with which he received her agitated words annoyed her. She resolved to ridicule his purpose.

"Think of yourself with a wife in satin and pearls, feathers, lace, and jewels!"

"Thou wouldst not desire to dress in that showy fashion, when thou dost not already."

"Truly I do. Here is a jewelled bodkin in my hair. Color and ornament are not lacking in my dress, and, for needful state, I do not demur at satin and pearls."

"Hast thou forgotten what Paul says? 'Let women adorn themselves in modest apparel, with shamefacedness and sobriety; not with broidered hair, or gold, or pearls, or costly array, but, which becometh women professing godliness, with good works.' Knowing this, ought thou not to cast aside these needless ornaments?"

"My apparel is both modest and sober, compared with the reigning fashion. I would neither follow its fripperies, nor wrap myself in the uncomely garb of the Friends."

"Does thy aunt's apparel displease thee?"

"It becomes her age. It would disfigure mine, and its sombreness would fill my thoughts."

"But how dost thou reconcile the gold and pearls?"

"They accord with my station and means, and I give them useful disposal. If they cramped my purse, they would become me poorly, or if they had no end but display, I should not be above the squaw who decks herself with shining tin and copper."

"Most women set their hearts upon a fine show of jewels. Ought thou to favor their sinfulness by thy example in even a less display?"

"My example counsels moderation, not excess. Neither do I condemn myself for joy in the beauty of these things. See the superb color of these rubies!" said she, unfastening her brooch, and holding it before the light. "That delights me as does the excellent color and form of a flower. If you hold that sinful, it must be wrong also to glory in the splendors of the new Jerusalem."

"When we walk the streets of that city, we shall be free from sin. Here sin mingles in our best emotions. Thy harmless delight in these gems may grow to a vain pride in them before thou art aware."

"You would smother this joy just as monks and nuns smother all joys, lest they be sinful," said Constance.

"We should meddle with vanities as little as possible," returned Friend Baxter.

"You would put both soul and body in straightened durance," Constance replied. "I crave more freedom. I would never have these things stand between me and God, and I would have them bend always to the needs of a fellow-creature. But may my heart always bound at the sight of beauty, be it in a jewel, a flower, the plumage of a gentle bird, or the arches of a cathedral."

"Thou speakest indeed like a maiden unused to the world. When thou hast seen more of its vanity and temptations, thou wilt agree with me in this matter."

Thus Friend Baxter ended just where he commenced, with the argument of Constance's inexperience. Yet he began to perceive the hopelessness of his case, in the fact that more spirit lay under the guise of her gentle face than he had supposed. While continuing the conversation, he reflected that much of her expressed aversion was in regard to the strict plainness of the dress of his sect. Would it not be wise to humor a little the natural choice of a young girl? Age would modify her tastes. Why not please her now with less severity of costume, and return to it at some future time? He hesitated. He was thoughtful and embarrassed. But what would he not do to win this beautiful girl?

"Constance," he asked abruptly, at length, "if I should alter the attire which is so hateful in thine eyes, wouldst thou reconsider thy decision?"

"I fear if you escaped from under your wide hat for so small a reason, you would get under it again just as speedily," was the playful reply.

"I am not jesting. I desire to know, in case I were to conform less to the opinions of my people in this matter, if thy chief objections would not be removed?"

"No," said Constance, earnestly. "I should neither dare to mislead your conscience, nor should esteem you if you permitted it."

He saw immediately that he had gone too far, and felt humbled at her rebuke. After a painful silence, he arose to leave her.

"Thou art right," said he, "to bring me to a remembrance of the allegiance I owe to godly principle rather than to love. The fairness of thy countenance hath bewitched me, and lest I sin in laying more of my conscience at thy feet, I will leave thee altogether. Fare thee well."

XX.

The winter months passed unmarked at Moody Hall. Mr. Baxter spent some weeks in New England, so that he was missed from the lively disputations on English affairs still carried on. When he returned, he was absorbed in a new project, which he cautiously unfolded to such citizens as would probably favor it, but for some reason deferred making it known to Sir Henry or Lady Moody till his plans were nearly completed. One day he visited the Hall for the purpose of consulting with them.

"Friend Deborah," said he, after some hesitation, "I have come to tell thee of the important results of my visit to New England. Would thee not rejoice to see Gravesend brought under English rule?"

"Truly I would, if it could be done without dishonor."

"Cromwell has ordered the governors of New England to take possession of Long Island, and by force if necessary."

"Where didst thou get thy information?" asked Lady Moody, greatly surprised.

"Chiefly in Quinnipiac, now called New Haven. Governor Eaton does not despise the rumor, and when I related our grievances to John Davenport, the minister, and one of the 'seven pillars' of the new colony, he was filled with indignation that we should submit to so hard requirements. Others advised us to revolutionize the colony, and offered help."

"Were those offers of help from persons in authority?" asked Sir Henry, with an incredulous look.

"Thee knows my stay was too short to consult with many in authority. Two English captains tendered their ships and themselves to assist us."

"Adventurers!" said Sir Henry. "Doubtless they are fired by Cromwell's successes, and think to conquer the world in his name!"

"They promise the arrival of troops this spring," added Mr. Baxter.

"Friend Baxter," interrupted lady Moody, "what dost thou propose to do here, in preparations for these helps?"

"Renounce our allegiance to the Dutch authorities."

"Are any ready to venture so much?"

"John Grover, Sergeant Hubbard, and others of our townsmen uphold me."

"Friend, thou art engaging in a foolish rebellion."

"It is right to rebel against tyrants."

"But hadst thou stated our grievances to Oliver Cromwell, and were he our champion, it would still become thee not to cast thyself upon the Director single-handed. Rumors and two captains will never safely back thee, or frighten Petrus Stuyvesant."

"I hope to accomplish a peaceful revolution while the Director is absent in the West Indies, not doubting we shall have English troops here by the season of his return.

"I foresee your pitiful plight if they fail to arrive," remarked Sir Henry, who ridiculed the whole affair.

"But the cause is worthy of some risk. Gravesend can never become the fine city we planned, under Director Stuyvesant's rule. We are strictly an English colony, and should be under English rule. We are wearied with unjust restrictions upon our worship. Thou shouldst not consider the risks alone, but bear in mind the honors of success also."

"What honors?" questioned Sir Henry.

"Thee may receive the appointment of Governor of the Island."

"I decline the honor in advance. I would not stand in your way," returned Sir Henry, ironically. Crossing the room to the window, where Constance sat at her embroidery frame, he said in an undertone, "Do you comprehend this revolutionist? Are you dazzled by the governorship?"

"Pray do not jest," she entreated, and turned away lest Mr. Baxter should be wounded by the discovery of his ridicule.

"Friend Baxter," said Lady Moody, after a pause, "is thy heart fully set within thee to do this thing?"

"Yea, Deborah," was the earnest answer.

"And art thou sure that the interest of the colony alone moves thee?" His reply was less frank. He offered various reasons. Lady Moody put them aside.

"Friend Baxter," said she, "thee would use despite toward Petrus Stuyvesant, in that he deposed thee from office. I remember his anger and thine. Thee would throw off his yoke in retaliation."

"He had no right to interfere with the election. I was duly elected."

"It would please thee not only to take away part of his dominion, but to govern it also, and thus avenge thyself. Is this our rule of life?" said Lady Moody, fearlessly.

"Thou hast no right to impute to me these motives," was the reply. "If thou wilt be blind to thine own interests, thou shouldst not hinder others."

"George Baxter, thee knows I have the welfare of this colony near my heart. I warn thee not to disturb its peace foolishly. Thy plots will draw many people into sorrow. As for thee, the Director will send thee to Holland in chains."

Friend Baxter was offended, and arose to go. He was disappointed in not securing the approbation he sought, and not a little chagrined at so severe reproofs in the presence of Constance. There were many who would have been influenced by Lady Moody's and Sir Henry's endorsement of his schemes. Now he must continue his plans without them, trusting that success would quickly convert them to his views.

Rumors of disaffection began to reach New Amsterdam. Director Stuyvesant was absent on a peaceful expedition to the West Indies, having left the government in the hands of Councillor De Sille, who took no steps to arrest the promised revolution. The eventful day was already appointed, and so well known and so widely talked of, that Sir Henry Moody was amazed at the torpidity of the Dutch authorities, and shut himself up in vexation at all parties.

It was a bright morning in April when the townspeople gathered in the square before the Town House, some curious to watch the proceedings, and some full of enthusiasm at the prospect of pronouncing themselves once more subjects of England. Sergeant Hubbard harangued the crowd from the steps of the Town Hall, and was sustained by noisy acclamations. When his speech and the applause ended, Mr. Baxter stepped forth, and, after a few brief words, read a paper renouncing allegiance to Holland, and proclaiming the government of England. It was received with loud cheers, which grew almost frantic when the Prince's flag was lowered, and the British colors floated proudly at the head of the tall flagstaff.

At this moment a small party of horsemen galloped into town, and riding directly among the crowd, which scattered right and left, dismounted upon the steps of the Town Hall. In five minutes, George Baxter was under arrest by authority of the Council of New Amsterdam, the British colors were down, and the Prince's flag reinstated. The Fiscal ordered the crowd to disperse to their homes, which they were glad to do, congratulating themselves on so happy an escape, and leaving the village square as still as on "Lord's day." The Manhattan party swooped away with their prey. In a few hours, Mr. Baxter was safely immured in the "keep" of the Fort, to await the return of the valiant Governor.

Back of the Fort stood the school-house, in which was included the schoolmaster's dwelling. It was built by the Company in Holland that had planted the Dutch colony here, and was more expensive in finish than most of the houses in New Amsterdam. The red-tiled floor of the family room, and the blue and white pictured tiles of the fireplace, were a source of pride to the burghers, and of never-failing interest to the school urchins, who invented all manner of excuses to get access to this wonderful room. Hans was no longer its bachelor occupant. He had brought Lisbet to it as his bride one day. Her own bright pewter adorned the mantel now, in place of rusty nails, shoe roses, empty ink-bottles, birch-rods, and dusty manuscripts. The tiles had never shown half their beauty before. Even the stoop was more inviting, and the cleanly swept walk and trim flower-beds told every passer by that a good wife dwelt here. To keep the feet of unruly children from straying over the pet garden would have puzzled a wiser head than Lisbet's, but she administered oly-koeks and seed-cakes, and offered rewards of the brightest poppies that grew.

The noise of these children at play penetrated the solitary prison in the Fort, and was a pleasant sound to Mr. Baxter. He amused himself by divining their sports, by picturing characters from the tone of the voices, counted the hours by the alternate silence and noise, marked the holidays, and wrote hymns and sonnets on his wooden bench, suggested by the bubbling, careless life of these little ones. These sounds afforded the cheeriest moments of his imprisonment. Little else broke the monotony. A few who knew him when Secretary under Director Keith visited him, but for the most part he was regarded with aversion as a turbulent traitor, and avoided from fear of the disfavor of Governor Stuyvesant. Lady Moody was his most faithful friend. She had been severe when his monitor; now, in his distress, she had no words of reproach, but many for his comfort. Four months went slowly thus, when one day he missed the voices of the children at an unusual time, and wondered much at the reason of the holiday. May-day and Pinkster had gone long ago. It was not seventh day. Perhaps they were dismissed to the meadows. Perhaps the heat had awakened pity for their confinement. Was some official dead? Had an epidemic seized them? Thus Mr. Baxter teazed himself that long, still, warm afternoon, waiting uneasily for the hour of his evening meal to ask the question of his keeper. Before that time he learned in a pleasanter way.

Hans had granted a half holiday to his scholars, to give place to an entertainment. Lisbet had taken possession of the school-room for her guests' supper-room, and now, while poor Mr. Baxter was fretting over the unwonted silence, there sat in the tiled room Dame Zwaller and the Burgomaster, Barbara and Dame Roosevelt, and Constance Aylmer, who, for the first time in many months, was a guest under the Zwaller roof. Barbara told her how sleek the cows were at the bowery, how sweet the cream, how luscious the berries; described the pruning of the yew-trees into lions each side of the gate, and the successful growing of the prim box borders of the flower-beds. A roly-poly baby was plumped on the floor at Barbara's feet, the very embodiment of good-nature.

Lisbet stopped in her running to and fro to kiss its cheeks and shake it into laughter, and sometimes the Burgomaster lifted it on his knee, or passed it to its admiring grandmother. In any case, the baby was a model of patience, and endured all the pinching and tossing and praising without raising one cry in self-defence.

While Lisbet was preparing tea with deft hands and nimble feet, Constance and Barbara went out into the garden to enjoy its fragrant luxuriance. The morning-glories had clambered almost to the top of the wall of the Fort, which hemmed in the garden on one side. As Constance's eyes followed the vines, she thought they might some day mount the top, creep over the green esplanade, and toss their gay blossoms in sight of the forlorn prisoner, when he paced the yard below in his daily exercise.

"It must be very warm in the 'keep' to-day," said Constance. "Poor George Baxter is there yet. I wish I could see him."

"He is a wicked man!" exclaimed Barbara. "How can you wish to see him?"

"Not so badly minded as you think, Barbara. He believed himself a patriot."

"The Director will be angry with you, if you excuse his treason."

"He has not yet returned?" asked Constance, looking wistfully at the Fort.

"No."

"Let us go and visit George Baxter. It is but a step thither. Nicholas will admit us."

"I do not wish to see the monster!" returned Barbara.

"You need not look at him. Come, let us ask Nicholas. Or there is Mistress Bayard, at the Governor's house. You can ask her. She would not willingly refuse Baltazzar's wife."

"I will go to the house, but not to the keep," answered Barbara, trembling.

"Wait till I speak with Lisbet," said Constance, disappearing in the house, and returning again in a moment to gather a handful of choice fragrant blossoms.

"Here comes Baltazzar!" exclaimed Barbara, joyfully. "We may go without censure under his wing. His father will never be angry with him for admitting you." As Baltazzar opened the gate they met him, questioning.

"Go?" he answered, raising his eyebrows in his father's fashion. "Mistress Constance may go wherever she wishes, and see whoever she pleases."

"Thank you!" returned Constance, gratefully smiling. All three passed out of the gate, and walked toward the entrance of the Fort.

In a few moments they were within the keep, a strong inclosure for special offenders. An ill-ventilated apartment with a stone floor, a wooden bench, and a low pallet of straw, was apportioned to Friend Baxter. When Constance entered, his head was bowed upon his hands. She thought him asleep, and would have retreated, but he looked up and arose, astonished as if a vision had appeared before him.

"Is it possible that I behold thee, Constance Aylmer?" She took his extended hand.

"I was in Lisbet's garden, and wished to come and see you. I am sorry you are here. I would help you if I could."

"Thou art good to say as much; but thou canst not. The fool must suffer for his folly. How is Friend Deborah?"

"She is well. She has letters from England concerning George Fox, which she will bring when she comes. You will find solace in them." He smiled sadly.

"Friend Deborah told me of thy resolve to visit England," said he. "When dost thou go?"

"Three weeks hence."

"I shall miss thy face, if ever I return to Gravesend. But it will be happiness to remember thee did not forget me in prison."

"What message shall I bear to my aunt, from you?"

"Tell her I crave books. My thoughts devour me. Thou canst see that I suffer." Constance's eyes were suffused with tears as she saw his pale face and haggard looks, and thought how long he might yet remain a prisoner.

"Will you take these flowers?" she said. "They will bring freshness and fragrance to you a little while; let me put them in this cup. Perhaps Lisbet will bring you more from her garden when I am gone; I will ask her." Friend Baxter turned away to conceal his emotion.

"Thou art too tender in thy kindness, and the flowers remind me of the free air of heaven. God bless thee, Constance Aylmer."

"I must go now, else the friends at Lisbet's will miss us. Here is my fan; I will leave it for you, though it is gayer than you can approve. You must think only of its use, and not mind the gay feathers," said she, smiling gently, as she unfastened from her belt a large fan bordered with swaying white feathers, and laid it on the bench. "I would it were plainer, for your sake. Good-bye, Mr. Baxter."

"Farewell, beloved friend. I will not ask thee to keep me in mind; I am not worthy. May the Lord remember thee as thou hast remembered me in my sad strait. Farewell."

In a few moments Barbara and Constance were again in Lisbet's parlor. The lively chat oppressed her; she could not put away from her thoughts the gloomy room and its sorrowful occupant she had just left. Hans noted her abstraction, and the happy thought occurred to him to bring out some of his manuscript legends, since they owed their existence to her long-ago suggestions. He drew a chair out upon the platform before the door, where it was cool and quiet, and, giving her the papers, said,

"I would like you to read them; some sympathy would comfort me. Lisbet is a good wife, but she has no time to listen to ballads or legends, and is too light of soul to comprehend my yearnings. But I would not have her anything else than she is—my humming-bird."

Constance took the papers with real pleasure, read some of them, and talked enthusiastically with Hans of his plans till Lisbet called them to tea. Hans was a happy and proud host that night, and could not refrain from laying nets for the praises of his wife's matchless viands. And praises were not stinted, for even Dame Zwaller felt amiable. Dame Roosevelt grew unwontedly loquacious, and told what was uppermost in her heart. Elsie was coming home in a fortnight. Constance felt the deepening flush upon her cheeks, and tried to hide her agitation in some ordinary comments to Baltazzar. But her thoughts were busy with surmises if Edward Mordaunt was coming also. If she could escape to England before their arrival, she would be content. How could she meet Edward with composure? No, never this side of the grave!

After tea, when standing near Dame Roosevelt, she tried to summon courage to ask if Mordaunt was expected with Elsie; but her heart throbbed at the effort, her pride rebelled, and she turned away. The opportunity was gone now, for they were all saying good-night to Lisbet. She said good-night also, and walked home with the Zwallers, carrying the dread with her. The sun had set; laborers had finished their work, and the sound of clamorous voices, whips, wheels, tramping feet, and the echo of the hammer, the axe, and the noisy rat-tat of the drum in the fort, had all ceased. The Herrs sat on the "stoeps," smoking and meditating. Gabriel Carpsey, the herdsman, had just come in at the "land-gate" at the end of the street, with his long line of sleek cows, odorous of fresh grass and new milk. Gabriel blew his horn now and then, as he trolled along the street; and the dairy-maids came out to welcome the returning bossy, each one at its home-gate.

"I like the sound of Gabriel's horn," said Constance. "It wakes me early, and pleasantly."

"Pleasanter than to be waked by a hooting owl, as you were the first morning in New Amsterdam," laughed Dame Zwaller.

"You will hear enough of that music at the bowery to-morrow," said the Burgomaster. "One herdsman can no longer gather Baltazzar's flocks and herds. He reminds me of Jacob. His tenderness to Nicholas alone hinders his riches."

"Do not the misfortunes of Nicholas merit his tenderness?" asked Constance.

"Nicholas' misfortunes are of his own seeking. If he spends his time at races and cock-fights, or in smoking and sipping Metje Wessell's beer, he cannot long carry a full purse. An idle mill will not coin guilders."

"But the windmill is blown down. He cannot receive blame," said Constance.

"He should have had watchful eyes, and given it a stitch in time. Neither will it mend itself now. Baltazzar must come to the rescue."

"Ah, well, Baltazzar is a noble, helpful, patient brother. He will win Nicholas yet. I know Barbara would choose him to lose rather his guilders than his goodness."

The next day Constance made a farewell visit to the bowery, saw the famous lions at the gate, gratified Baltazzar with inspecting his fields and herds, permitted Barbara to row the boat for her up and down the river, and returned at sunset to the Zwaller's. Early the next morning, she went to see good Mistress Primley, who lamented that she could not chaperone her across the sea again, and gave her many charges for her safety during the voyage. Lisbet and Hans and Dame Zwaller went with her to the ferry. Dame Zwaller whispered, that when the "Hope" was ready to sail, she would send on board a box of delicacies, that she might not suffer from the coarse fare of the ship toward the end of the long voyage. Thus, with good wishes and tender embraces, they parted.

Two weeks afterward, the captain of the "Hope" sent a speedy message to Gravesend that he was in readiness, and wished to take advantage of wind and tide, as soon as Sir Henry and Constance arrived. This hastened the dreaded parting with Lady Moody. At almost the last moment, it was determined that Rose should go with Constance. She would have gone to the ends of the earth with her young mistress, for what did she not owe to her gentle goodness? She quickly gathered her little store of needs, filled with joy at the strange event, yet trembling with fear at venturing upon the vast sea.

It was no light thing for Constance and her aunt to part, even for a twelvemonth, when the Atlantic was to roll between them. It was as the separation of mother and daughter, so confiding had been the love of one, so tender had been the guidance of the other. And Lady Moody looked wistfully upon the sweet face, as she remembered it might light her dwelling no more, or that contact with the London world might change her artless uprightness. She prayed in her soul that God would keep this daughter from the falseness of life. She could not trust her voice to utter the words she would say in these last moments, and perhaps they were not needed. She only clasped Constance in her arms, and they parted with silent tears.

Old Cæsar, Pete, Mingo, and Chloe, conspicuous for her grief, were at the gate to say last words, and give God speed to the voyagers. Sir Henry laughingly bade them good-bye, and hurried Constance and Rose away. The quiet village was soon left behind, the bridge and the great white oak were passed, not without regrets, for they were associated with the saddest days of Constance's life. As she lost sight of one familiar object after another, she could not but think of the time when she first beheld them, and feel how different was the girl of to-day from the girl of two years ago. The spray of life wreathed her playfully then; now its surges had rolled over her. She had emerged from the double baptism of an earthly and a heavenly love, purified from selfishness —not wholly perhaps, for long and sorrowful discipline, even to the end of life, can hardly perfect such a work in any soul—yet she had learned what it was not to live to herself. She had come hither a passive, emotionless being, gathering the honey of life, and looking amazed at grief-stricken souls. Now she understood them, she had tears of pity for them, and yearned to see such cast themselves on Christ for solace. This rich sympathy was worth attaining, even through much suffering. She had learned, too, to trust her Father like a little child. She could place her hand in His, and say, "Lead me," gratefully kissing the rod that had brought her to Him.

Thinking these thoughts, Constance rode quietly beside Sir Henry, with Rose and Mingo following. Lightfoot would not carry her again, perhaps, and she stroked his mane, patted his neck, and talked as if the creature answered her. Arrived at Breuklyn, she dismounted, threw her arms over him, kissed the glossy neck of the dumb beast that had always borne her so gracefully and so well, and commended him to Mingo's gentlest care. Mingo wiped his eyes with his sleeves, and felt like kissing the ground whereon Constance stood, but he did better in kissing her hand with a profound obeisance, when she held it out to say good-bye. Cornelius Dirksen ferried the voyagers to the ship. In another hour the "Hope" sailed away, but not before they had a last glimpse of friends gathered at the landing in New Amsterdam. There was Dame Zwaller, the sincere and shrewd adviser, Barbara with her good heart, Mistress Primley, motherly and anxious to the last, bright and gossipy Lisbet, and poor wayward, jaunty Nicholas, straining their eyes to see Constance leaning over the bulwarks. They all disappeared from her sight in the misty distance; and soon with them the rows of houses, the Fort, the church tower, and last of all, the whirling wind-mills faded to a dark line, and sunk away to be seen only in her pleasant pictured memories of New Amsterdam.

XXI.

The voyage was unusually long and wearisome. Constance felt it had a happy ending when she stepped once more on firm earth, and forgot her fatigue in the strangeness and bustle of the port of Gravesend, England. She waited at the "Queen's Arms" with Rose, while Sir Henry went for a coach to convey them to London. Standing at the window and looking at the gray clouds overhead, or away at the wharf where the "Hope" was gently rocking, she did not notice two gay gallants who, just come down from London, were pacing the street beneath the window, till the words of one of them fell distinctly on her ear.

"By my troth," he exclaimed, "if Vandyke or Sir Peter Lely can find a sweeter face than that in all London to paint, I should like to behold it!"

Glancing at the speaker, she saw that both he and his companion were gazing boldly at herself. She instinctively drew back from the window, mortified and vexed.

"Do they count me a rustic? Am I so ancient in dress, after my long banishment, as not to seem a gentlewoman? But I ought not to stand dreaming at the window, as if I were in the simple Manhattas. I will not put myself in fault again."

The two voices, noisily discussing the beauty of

one Lady Cecil, still came in at the open window, and filled Constance with a vague fear. She rejoiced when Sir Henry came at last to assist her to the coach. The uncivil cavaliers stood gazing as she passed, and amused themselves with each other's wit at sight of Rose's black face. Sir Henry was too occupied to perceive them, and Constance kept silence, for she well knew his hot temper and the disturbance it would create. She quietly hid herself in shadow till the coach started for London.

Lord Grey's fine house was in the Strand, the then fashionable quarter of the nobility. It stood in the midst of spacious well-shaded grounds overlooking the river. Its solid look without was relieved by turrets and high-arched windows. Within, the cold aspect of the broad stone staircase heightened the magnificence of the rooms to which it led, and added softness and warmth to the rich carpets and hangings.

Lady Grey and her daughter were here, having lately returned from Bath. The mother was endowed with beauty, which she preserved with an assiduous care worthy of a better object. She was a thorough woman of the world, a spiteful royalist, and devoted to bishop's robes, rituals, pictures, painted windows, and other religious ornaments which the Puritans had sternly torn away. In this she was at war with her husband, an Independent, a member of Parliament, a close quiet watcher of Cromwell's acts, devoted to the reforms he would inaugurate, but distrustful and timid as to the means. The daughter, Lady Alice, inherited more of her mother's aristocratic spirit and love of gayety than of her beauty, though her face was by no means plain. For various reasons, she had speculated much on the coming of Constance, and had asked endless questions concerning her, which Lady Grey could hardly answer, not having seen her since her childhood. She could only assure her daughter that the Aylmer stock was noble, that the mother was an incomparable woman, and the father a true knight with but one fault—he was a Puritan. Whether Constance was a Puritan or a Papist, grave or gay, awkward or graceful, and, above all, if she would prove a rival in fairness, were questions that occupied her till the day of the arrival.

When Constance came, criticism was disarmed. Her unaffected grace and the purity of her accent took Lady Alice by surprise, and inspired her with a sudden affection which was certain to cool when closer acquaintance would discover how widely their notions of life differed. She devoted herself to her for several days after her coming, with great condescension, planning all manner of available amusements, lamenting with her mother over the graveness of society under the Protector's rule, laughing at the cleverness with which they and others managed to evade some of the prohibitions, and promising Constance that she should accompany them to the playhouse, in spite of grim Puritans.

"But you will not see the beautiful cathedrals as they were once," said Lady Alice. "St. Paul's is robbed of its altar and pictures and lovely image of the Virgin. The golden candlesticks, crucifixes and plate were sold for the service of the war, and the pretty pictures painted on the windows were broken out or defaced. Was it not wicked of those solemn saints to spoil everything? To demolish the organ too!"

"Was there not some good reason?" suggested Constance, secretly wounded by every thrust intended for the Protector.

"Oh, they feared we would turn naughty Papists."

"And does the Protector forbid music?" asked Constance surprised.

"He will not have it in the cathedrals, but he has enough at the cock-pit for the entertainment of his friends."

"What is the cock-pit?" asked Constance. Lady Alice laughed gently at the novice, and answered,

"A princely residence, once voted to the use of His Highness by Parliament. It is only called the cock-pit because it was King Henry Eighth's place of cock fighting."

"And does the Protector dwell there now?"

"No, he has right royal lodgings in Whitehall Palace, that which was once Cardinal Woolsey's house. You shall see it soon. We will drive thither when mamma calls the coach. I forget that you have not yet seen all London. How droll that you never came to London when you lived at Atherton Hall! But if you had once tasted London, you could never have endured two years among those Dutch fantastics, the other side of the sea."

"I love them very much," said Constance, coloring slightly. "They were exceeding gentle to me, and lacked no kindnesses to each other."

"And did you never fear that old sea-king, Petrus, who I have heard whips his burghers with his wooden leg when they do not please him? That is faintly like our lion, Oliver, who growls the members out of the Parliament House when they refuse to do his bidding," scornfully laughed Lady Alice.

"Governor Stuyvesant does nothing in that fashion," returned Constance, soberly. "You have heard only slanders to which his fiery temper gives some countenance."

"But truly, my cousin, was it not wearisome to dwell among those people with no cavaliers of gentle blood to attend you?"

"I was not ennuied in that wonderful New World. There are always some cavaliers seeking to repair fallen fortunes, whose learning does not come amiss."

"Had you no lovers there?"

"I have none," replied Constance, with downcast eyes.

"My mother must make for you a distinguished match," said Lady Alice.

"I do not wish to be betrothed to any," was Contance's reply.

"You would rather live in Lady Moody's nunnery?" asked Lady Alice, in amazement.

"Yes; it is heavenly there."

"And miss all the happiness of being a belle, and carrying off the prize of the season—always through my mother's help?" laughed Lady Alice. "My settlement is just completed, though it has gone hard enough between my father and Lord D'Arcy's father about the bestowment of certain lands upon him. You should see my Lord D'Arcy! He is of proud descent. He is handsome as the handsomest picture in his father's gallery of family portraits. And he dresses—not like those hateful Roundheads, but like a true courtier. Our betrothment is to be this day fortnight; the wedding not before next season. You shall see him. He dines with us to-morrow."

As Lady Alice ran on in her shallow way, Constance began to comprehend how little sympathy could ever exist between them. She held her life experiences in sacred silence, but Lady Alice was wont to pour them all out like a babbling brook. To her, love was a holy, deep emotion, not to be measured by words; to Lady Alice, it was an amusing phase of vanity, to end presently in a very convenient, desirable, and ambitious marriage. The greatest interest of the approaching betrothal was the elegant and becoming toilet to be provided, and the vexation that Lady So-and-so would feel at her failure in securing Lord D'Arcy for either of her daughters.

"Why do you look at me with such wonderment in your eyes?" asked Lady Alice, smiling, and abruptly ending her chat about her lover.

"You take life like a singing-bird. It seems to hold little for you that is serious."

"Happy that for me!" was the reply. "You would not have me look solemn as an owl, and repeat psalms apt to the occasion, would you?"

"No; not that," returned Constance.

"Here comes Sir Henry," exclaimed Lady Alice. "His merry countenance will not condemn me. And there is my father arrived from Oxford. He will dine with us to-day in honor of your coming. And you must esteem it an honor, for his time is much consumed at the Coffee House." Lady Alice went languidly to meet her father.

"Let me lead you to my cousin," said she, in a low tone. "She is fresh from a nunnery, and so naive and charming that I am captivated. She is such a sweet novelty!"

Lord Grey advanced toward Constance, and greeted her cordially.

"I honored your father," said he, "and for his sake, as well as your own, I am glad to welcome you. Choose this for a home, if you will. It would add greatly to our happiness, especially as we are to lose our daughter." After some courteous inquiries about Lady Moody, the voyage, and other matters, he resumed his conversation with Sir Henry upon the political state of England. Constance observed him while listening. He was a slender, plain-featured man, having an air of abstraction, as if meditating continually on painful and difficult subjects. That he should avoid the discussion of these with his wife, or that he should spend his time discussing politics at the Coffee House, was not marvellous to Constance when she listened to his sentiments, given in a low voice, but with intense feeling. The very atmosphere of his presence was totally different from his home, and she felt drawn to him with a daughterly interest which was manifest in her looks, and the close and quiet attention given to his words. Lord Grey was not unobserving. Lady Alice rallied Constance on her attention to politics.

"I wish to know of this expedition to Jamaica. It may bode something to the Manhattas," replied Constance. "Perhaps this is the 'help' George Baxter expected at Long Island." Lord Grey questioned about it, hummed his approbation, but shook his head and said nothing. Constance suffered herself to be drawn away by Lady Alice's importunities, and Cromwell and England were forgotten for a time, in the discussion of purchases for the approaching betrothal. In an interval of silence, the voices of the gentlemen in the next room fell distinctly upon the ear, though words could not be distinguished. A third person had joined them.

"Who is now talking with Lord Grey?" asked Constance. "Do you know the voice?"

"No. What of the voice?" replied Lady Alice. Constance hesitated, and then said, with a bright look of pleasure,

"It is a manly voice, tender and refined. The owner must be a prince by descent or by nature."

"Alas!" replied Lady Alice, "we have none of royal state with us now; only haberdashers and men of coarse stuff. The voice has nothing in it to me." But she summoned a servant, and inquired who had been admitted.

"Lord Huntington, my lady," said Maurice, retiring. "I ought to have recognized one so familiar to my father. He is of honorable estate, and a member of Parliament. This spoils him for me. It bespeaks him a lover of the Protector. He is a widower, young and distinguished, but not a marrying man, as many a fine dowager knows. His wife died in the first year of the Commonwealth, and since, he lives in his lordly forsaken house like an Oxford student, when not sitting in council. The most bewitching court beauty cannot draw him out of his seclusion."

Constance amused herself in picturing him while still listening to his fine round tones, in contrast with Sir Henry's brusque enunciation, and Lord Grey's faint voice.

"He must be broad-minded and broad-chested and tall. Neither could such a voice accompany narrow and mean features. Since he is a Cromwellian, his hair is not curled like a woman's, nor his dress in the gay fashion of the cavaliers. He is doubtless worthy to sit in Cromwell's Parliament." But these quiet speculations were presently dismissed, and, with the going out of the voice, Lord Huntington went out of her thoughts.

The next day, as promised, Lord D'Arcy was announced. Constance was dazzled by his costume before she saw his face. A velvet doublet, Flanders boots, and a sword-belt, worn sash-wise over his shoulders, from which hung a Spanish rapier, gave him a gallant air. The rapier and steel corslet were needful to balance the feminine effect of the lace tie and ruffles, and the mass of hair falling upon his shoulders. His features were classically handsome; lengthened somewhat in look by the pointed beard. The moment Constance glanced at his face, she remembered to have seen it before; and when Lord D'Arcy was presented to her, he also recognized her with confusion, as the young girl he had saluted at the Queen's Arms the week before. Constance did not betray by word or look that she had ever seen him, except by a cold reserve which passed unobserved by others than himself. He quickly recovered his nonchalance, and enlivened the whole party by his flowing conversation on society, art, literature, fashion, and the latest reports of the exiled Court, freely interspersing ridicule of the family at Whitehall.

"And now," said he, "I have a rare entertainment for your pleasure to-night. We have secured the play-house for two representations of a French play, which is to be so artfully supported by music that it shall be noised abroad as only a private concert."

"And if you are discovered in it?" questioned Lady Alice.

"The house will be closed, and we shall be fined. The fines we need not grudge, for Parliament is in woful need of money, and may better take it out of our merry entertainments than out of the estates of delinquents—poor royalist squires who have never yet compounded. You can go masked, as some other of the royalist ladies have in mind to do."

"My cousin," said Lady Alice, "you will see a stage-play sooner than we thought."

"But to go masked," said Constance, timidly, "will not be honorable."

"How droll!" laughed Lady Alice, turning to Lord D'Arcy. "She is so naive! She objects going to the play *en masque!*"

"I fear, if she appears without a mask, too many eyes will be withdrawn from the actors for their good encouragement," replied Lord D'Arcy.

"If I go with you," said Sir Henry, "you need have little scruple." And thus it was settled for Constance. Lady Grey had now some suggestions to make.

"You must not provide your coachman with a torch," said she, "else our rank will be proclaimed."

"No; we will display a lantern, if you are willing to appear in that plebeian fashion. Thus we shall pass for a merchant's family," replied Lord D'Arcy.

In this state they set out some hours later, the ladies disguised in black velvet masks with glass eyes, held to the face with a string and bead in the mouth. Uncomfortable enough, Constance thought, but not half as uncomfortable as were her self-questionings of the right and wrong of the whole proceedings. She sat quiet and observing in the play-house. The stage was strewed with rushes, and the walls richly hung. There was no stage-scenery in that day, and the only concealment afforded was by curtains, movable on an iron rod. In the background was an upper stage, or curtained balcony, from which parts of the play were given. Constance listened attentively to the very sweet music, and much of the dialogue. Seeing her so occupied, Lord D'Arcy came triumphantly to hear her praises of the entertainment. But first he had an apology to offer.

"I would humbly crave your pardon, my sweet cousin, for my rude liberty at the Queen's Arms. Seeing you unattended, I did not presume you to be a gentlewoman; which is the poor excuse I have to offer."

"It is well always to carry the manners of a true nobleman," said Constance. "If I had been none other than a peasant girl, I should have been equally affrighted. A true knight should shelter loneliness."

"Bravely said! You are plain of speech," returned Lord D'Arcy, "but do you deny me grace for my fault?"

"I gladly grant a pardon which you are generous enough to seek."

"Thank you. And now, how well does the play touch your fancy?"

"I am dazzled. Yet the play speaks falsely."

"How now! Those characters are to the life, if you will permit me to differ."

"They make a jest of all that is honest and sacred. I wonder no more that the Protector forbids the plays."

"You are a Puritan."

"Not knowingly. But I remember my father burned the writings of Shakspeare, and forbid my brother to go to the plays at Whitefriars when he came to London. Doubtless I inherit his prejudices."

"I blame none for burning Shakspeare's writings," replied Lord D'Arcy. "He was a dull fellow—too heavy for my liking. But this play, modelled equally after the Italian and French drama, pleases me well."

"I cannot choose, knowing nothing of either," said Constance. The curtains being now drawn for a new act, Lord D'Arcy resumed his place at Lady Alice's side. As the play proceeded, Constance listened with greater aversion, and at last with indignation, even to tears.

"Let us go hence," whispered she to Lady Grey.

"What! in tears?" was the reply. "Fie! Your delicacy should not be shocked at such foolish trifles. Alice does not regard it. See how merry she is over the actor's buffoonery! We should draw all eyes upon us in leaving. Take pleasure in the music, and close your ears to the rest, if it seems ill to you There is but one more act."

There was nothing to do but endure quietly to the end. Constance rejoiced to escape at last. But, again at home, she could not sleep, even in the stillness of her own chamber. The music bewildered her senses. Some of the sweetest airs plaintively repeated themselves in her imagination. She was eager for the morning, that she might reproduce them upon the organ. How could Aunt Deborah condemn such heavenly music apart from the play. But the play! The curtains swept back, and the actors reappeared. How vividly the words came back; the beautiful, the false, the mean and low vexing her spirit! The strangeness of the scene, the masked ladies, the showy cavaliers, the sense of danger and disobedience that had agitated her, came in rapid review; and last of all, Lord D'Arcy's self-congratulations that the Protector and the Roundheads had enough to divert them from discovering this infringement of an ordinance, filled her with self-reproach. Was not Cromwell wearying his burdened heart with efforts to raise England to purity, to greatness and godliness? And were not his efforts mocked to night? He was right to condemn the amusement. She had heard with her own ears, and seen with her own eyes, enough to know that noble men and women could not grow in such an atmosphere. But the music! Did the Lord Protector forbid that? She would ask to-morrow; and she began softly humming the sweet airs, and so fell asleep.

In the morning, when Rose came to assist her, she said,

"Rose, you may stay when I am dressed, and we will have our morning devotions together. I have no Aunt Deborah here to give me counsel, so I must ask my good Father in heaven to lead me all day."

"I 'specs you need him here, my lady."

"And you also, Rose."

When Constance, late in the morning, found her aunt in the boudoir, she was cheerfully saluted.

"I am pleased to see you so fully recovered from your ill mood last evening. You slept well?" asked Lady Grey.

"Sweetly, when once asleep, thank you."

"That is well. Sound sleep preserves youth. Let me caution you not to ruffle your face with sad tears, as yesterday evening. Weeping dims the eyes. Let me smooth your eyebrow, my dear. You should be watchful not to let them grow astray. They are prettily arched. You must cultivate your beauty."

"Thank you!" replied Constance, blushing slightly. "But it would seem to me odd and awkward to have a care of my eyebrows and wrinkles."

"My dear, the countenance grows awry from inattention, often. One eyebrow lifts itself beyond the other, or the mouth sometimes smiles unequally, without thought bestowed upon it."

"I fear I should never smile if I put my thoughts upon the doing of it," said Constance, laughing, and hiding her pretty mouth and pearly teeth behind her handkerchief, as if to shield herself from criticism.

"Did Lady Moody never recommend these important trifles to your notice?"

"She never told me how to carry my face, but I have often heard her say, 'Lord, keep the door of my mouth,' by which I am certain she thought more of the matter than the manner of her utterance."

"Is she grown old and withered?"

"I thought her face smooth and pure and gentle."

"So is my mother's," remarked Lady Alice.

"Yes," replied Constance, hesitating; "but—I think it was her soul that shone through. She never wore a frown, though her cares were sometimes heavy."

"Doubtless she learned to command her countenance when young," said Lady Grey.

"It seems to me rather the controlling of her

heart. She used to say, 'Out of the heart are the issues of life;' and I believe she kept it so well, that out of that came the heavenly content in her face."

"Your love is very dutiful to say so much," returned Lady Grey. "Yet I can teach you to carry such a face, be your soul ever so stormy."

"You need to begin soon, mamma," said Lady Alice. "It was only last night that Lord D'Arcy said my cousin's face was a telltale of all that goes on underneath it."

"What am I to do with my face?" asked Constance, embarrassed. "I would rather be condemned to put it under a mask, as last night, than to think continually how it ought to look."

"Society does not like to witness emotion, except it be a pretty vivacity," said Lady Grey. "You should cultivate perfect repose of countenance and manner. A little undercurrent of thought bestowed upon this need not interfere with one's ease." Constance drew a deep sigh.

"I thought it needful to forget one's self in order to be agreeable."

"To forget one's own comfort for others' sake is, doubtless, the essence of politeness. But it is another thing to sit a critic on your own countenance. Such a remembrance of yourself is harmless."

"You would take away a large pleasure from life," returned Constance. "It is sweet to read the countenance of a friend. But where would be the reading, if we become walking statues? I love rather the soulful faces of the Manhattas, than the counte-

jelly, bread-crumbs into puddings, and making soup from bare bones, was marvellous. Yet she was a religious, not a miserly economist. She was conscientious in her stewardship, rendering exact accounts to her employer, and what she saved by her self-denials was freely bestowed upon the comfort of others. Her gifts were necessarily small, and her sphere narrow. Their very smallness gave rigidity to her thoughts and ways. The incoming of a new mistress like Elsie was a shock to all her notions and habits, and no wonder if she stood dismayed at the revolution in the affairs of the house on her arrival.

"Take away the joint-stools from the chimney-corner, and fill the gaping fireplace with holly branches. It looks like the grave of departed Yule-logs," said Elsie, frowning, when she had surveyed the chief apartment. "I will have silk hangings too, and not chintz."

Mordaunt was besieged for the alterations, and yielded. During a few weeks, every room was in a turmoil. No sooner was one at the point of completion than Elsie would suggest something new, pull down all she had done, and begin over again. To do this, she levied all the forces possible. She possessed the peculiar talent of impressing everybody who came near, into her service, and keeping every soul of them in nervous haste with their task. The task given was not often rightly appointed. She was quite sure to cut the tapestry too short, and summon her helper to take it down and lengthen it, or order a dresser too large for its place, and refuse to accept its clumsiness. After an apartment was duly settled, she was quite likely to feel its narrowness, and conceive the bright idea of tearing down a partition, or building an "addition." But it could not take forever to complete so small a dwelling. To keep it in order when finished, was quite another affair. For this, Elsie had no talent. She left it to Experience, and turned her energies to the entire remaking of the garden. And poor Experience strove in vain to keep the chairs in prim rows, sighed to see Mordaunt's costly books lying upon the floor precisely where Elsie had dropped them, or stood amazed to see her dresses tumbled on the chair, and her pretty boots flung across the room when they had happened to pinch. And who can imagine Experience's horror at seeing Elsie's spools of thread rolling hither and thither at the mercy of a playful kitten, or wound inextricably with tangled yarn, when she had stooped her lame back many a time to save a bit a few inches long? What could she do but grumble, and look after this spoiled child?

When Elsie had exhausted the garden and the temper of the gardener, she took a capricious whim to invade Experience's kingdom.

"Did you ever taste an oly-koek?" she asked, one day.

"No."

"Then I will make some this minute!"

"Not to-day," plead Experience. "I cannot serve you well to-day."

"But I feel precisely like it," returned Elsie. It was not possible to turn her from what she chose to

like yourself, but she blesses all around her in quietness. Her works, not her words, speak for her."

"Does she not listen to the teachings of the Spirit?"

"Truly she does, but not in your fashion. You oppose yourself to the laws, and use your faith and strength to support yourself under the penalties. Why not rather use it in a gracious, lawful, womanly way, among those you naturally reach in your daily life; and your daily life would preach to witnesses better than your lips to strangers."

"Art thou an angel of light, or an angel of darkness?" asked Mary, tremulously.

"I love the same Jesus whom you desire so much to serve," said Constance, smiling. "I can give you no other proof of what manner of person I am, except that for His sake, and for the sake of her who is as my mother, I love you enough to lead you out of persecution. Come, let us go."

And Mary Collins suffered herself to be led away as one in a dream.

XXII.

"We were looking for you," said Lady Alice, when Constance returned. "My mother had ordered the coach for a drive, but it may please you better to see Hyde Park after we dine. Parliament sits till one of the clock, and later, you may meet some of the members riding or walking there with their families for recreation."

Accordingly, that afternoon Lord Grey's handsome coach was rolling toward Hyde Park, with a lively stream of other equipages and pedestrians. Some spectators who had assembled near the gates, and were unable to pay the high admission, consoled themselves with gaping at those who entered, or tormented themselves in contrasting their own hardships with the lolling ease of those who rode by, and their own poor garments with the delicate or showy luxuriance of the mounted cavaliers, or the occupants of the cushioned coaches: Levellers, some of them perhaps, whose hopes of distributing this world's goods equally among all men, had been extinguished in the bud by a prompt quietus from Cromwell. Lady Grey scarcely bestowed a glance upon these. Passing in, she bade the coachman drive along the wide avenue. He had not driven far, when forced to turn aside for the coming of the Lord Protector, at the head of his Life-Guards.

"He was so grand and bold a man at the head of his army, that I am glad to behold him first riding in gallant state with his Ironsides," said Constance, eagerly listening to the increasing sound of hoofs, and the warlike clatter and jingle of military accoutrements. In a moment the Lord Protector was in sight, and, in the intense gaze of a few seconds, Constance saw a massive, vigorous military figure, with stern, care-worn face dash by, and, after him, his eighty guards in grey.

"What think you of his escort in grim grey?" asked her ladyship.

"So plain habit is in keeping with his principles, and therefore in better taste than scarlet and gold lace," answered Constance. "But I supposed he appeared in public without state."

"He did formerly. The many plots against his life have persuaded him to more caution. He always rides now at the head of a body of horse or in a state coach, which better befits the ruler of England."

"Those soldiers love to attend their brave General, do they not?" said Constance, her face still glowing with enthusiasm for her hero.

"Doubtless they do," replied her aunt, scornfully. "Cromwell knows how to play upon the hearts of his soldiers."

"Do you count him a hypocrite?" asked Constance, amazed.

"Do not open your eyes so widely, my dear. You need to carry this morning's counsels with you. No; I will not venture to brand him a hypocrite, as some do, but he could never have climbed so high without skilful use of Puritanism."

"I shall appeal from you to Lord Grey," said Constance, half playfully, half in earnest.

"Or to Lord Huntington," replied her aunt with a bland smile of recognition, as the person named reined in his horse beside the yet waiting carriage.

"A fair day this, Lady Grey," said a full, manly voice. Constance instantly recognized it as that which had so charmed her ear a day or two before. She looked inquiringly at him, and was not disappointed to see a broad-chested, noble-faced man, habited in plain grey welted with black. He controlled the restless animal upon which he sat, with an easy horsemanship that signified a tranquil nature. He lifted his plumed hat slightly to Lady Alice, and bent his earnest eyes upon Constance, as he was told that she had lately arrived from the American settlements.

"Is it possible that you have performed that weary voyage? I shall wish to learn somewhat from you of New Amsterdam."

"She will likewise wish to learn much from you of the Protector, whose cause I wonder to see her espouse so determinedly. She but just threatened to appeal from me to Lord Grey. You will be a better champion."

"I should value the office, madam. But the wise deeds of such a man are better champions than the best of friends."

"His deeds need a friendly interpreter," said Constance. Lord Huntington smiled as he glanced from her to her aunt, and, after promising an early visit, bowed and left them, turning with an earnest look at Constance, as he rode away.

As the coach now rumbled along, Constance was diverted with the beauty of the Park, the deep shade of the trees, the silvery sheet of water, or was attracted by the lively passers or the approach of some distinguished friend.

"There is the Lady Protectress and her daughters," said Lady Alice, in time for Constance to perceive in a passing coach, a dignified, plain woman, and two young ladies elegantly dressed in a style not Puritanic; the one a solid English girl, the other slight, with firm lips and animated eyes.

"Mary is so cautious and reserved that I like her less than Frances," said Lady Alice.

"Which was Frances?" asked Constance.

"The slighter of the two. She has a pretty will of her own which becomes the daughter of Cromwell," continued Lady Alice, laughingly.

"It becomes no daughter to outwit her parents," said her mother quietly. "Mr. Rich, being the grandson of the Earl of Warwick, is a worthy match for any, and doubtless it was the cupidity of the Protector that hindered it."

"I heard the settlement was only hindered because her father thought Mr. Rich a worldly man and given to play. She resented it as false, and plighted herself to her lover in so solemn a vow, that the Protector dared not force her to break it. She is betrothed now with her father's consent. Darling Lady Frances!" said Lady Alice aside to Constance.

"Your father told me the Protector was not pleased with Lord Warwick's offer of the estate."

"Pray, my dear mother, do not spoil my praises of Frances' good spirit. Besides, if you will once let me defend our Ruler, he is too generous for his own gain, as I have heard it said. And that is all that I find pleasing in him. When Parliament voted him an annual income of £1,600, did he not give £1,000 yearly to provide for the war, and forgive all the debt they owed him for war service and for his governorship of the Isle of Ely?"

"A salve for his conscience, after the Irish massacre?" said Lady Grey, with compressed lips, and more fire in her eyes than she often permitted there.

"It happened before the Irish war, my dear mother," persisted Lady Alice.

"Drop the subject!" commanded the indignant mother. "Let me hear no more of the usurper, who holds the throne of our murdered king. Neither should you be so much a parvenu as to correct an elder; much more your mother." For once, Lady Grey's face was flushed with passion; but she quickly resumed her bland smile and calm voice, and bowed graciously to passing friends. Lady Alice did not recover from the rebuke till they left the Park and drove to the shops, where the merchant-men paced up and down, crying,

"What d'ye lack, madam? What d'ye lack?"

"These poor men must wax weary before they

sell all their wares," said Constance, laughing at the clamorous efforts of several to attract Lady Grey's notice. She, however, called one to the coach, and gave her orders for certain costly goods to be sent home for inspection.

The next morning these goods arrived, and were opened in the boudoir, where already a French modiste was fashioning some delicate materials for Alice's betrothal. Lady Grey unfolded a rich buff silk, which she commended strongly to Constance for purchase.

"It is the chosen color of the season," said she. "Even the gravest cavaliers sport it. At the presentation of the Swedish ambassador, Sir Thomas Fairfax wore a buff-coat, ornamented with silver lace; the sleeves slashed with white satin. The color would befit your complexion."

"Its splendor might well become a woman of state," said Constance, timidly. "I should feel better expressed in this quiet pearl-color."

"Delicate as a wood-violet," said Lady Alice.

"You should wear something more striking at your first appearance," said Lady Grey. "Pearls would contrast charmingly with this warm color." And she tossed the gay folds across the back of a chair, to deepen the shadows.

"I should feel ill at ease in anything that challenges the eye," returned Constance. "I am ashamed to combat your perfect taste, my dear aunt; but this gentle pearl-color wins my wishes."

"*Que pensez-vous*, Annette?"

"*Ah! Madame, les robes sont magnifiques l'une et l'autre!*" answered the frightened modiste, "*mais la modestie est aimable,*" she added. Lady Alice clapped her little hands.

"*Quand la Parisienne l'a dit, il faut que nous obéissions,*" she cried.

"Not so *brusque*, my dear," said her mother. "My dear," from her lips, always meant reproof. "The paler silk has less lustre, and therefore flatters the complexion. You chose wisely," she continued, turning to Constance. "A set of opals will complete a charming toilet. Here are some jewels Ashley sent this morning for my inspection. These opals are worthy of your possession. Only £50!" Constance looked at them, as her aunt laid the beautiful necklace and ear-rings against the silk. She shook her head slowly.

"I have well-set pearls which will serve me."

"Your purse is ample to supply these."

"I would limit my jewels in accordance with my estate, that other needs may not be cramped." Constance was thinking of Mary Collins when she said this.

"But many noble ladies," returned Lady Grey, "think it not ill to spend half-a-year's income on jewels!"

"Yet Aunt Deborah once told me that the possession of more jewels than my just need, is hiding the Lord's money; and that an honest and high taste should limit me to such as befit my estate. She thought that no queen ever made so sweet a use of her ornaments as Queen Isabella, when she yielded her crown-jewels to the poor, dejected Genoese, that he might have wherewith to search the unknown seas for a new world."

"Lady Moody's rules of life accord well with that new country in which she lives," remarked Lady Grey, with the blandest patience. "In London, one needs to loosen so pious restraints. A year with me will soften such austerities in you, my dear."

Constance was silent, and wondered when she returned to her own room why she so continually found herself in opposition to her aunt.

"Am I grown willful? I yielded always to Aunt Deborah. She appealed to something within me that ever approved her tender reproofs. Lady Grey appeals to another nature. Is it the outward? Does she desire to train my outer life, and so entice the inner life to conform to that? Does she mean thus to soften my austerities? Are these opinions austerities? Do not Aunt Deborah's gentle and noble teachings hold good in any land, among any people? *Any people?* Any *godly* people! Perhaps that is it." Constance felt perplexed, sad, distrustful of herself. She stood a long time looking from the broad window upon the winding Thames and the green meadows beyond, yet scarcely thinking of the pleasant scene.

"It is so difficult to know right and wrong," said she to herself. "At Moody Hall, I often felt myself a worldling; here, I am esteemed a bigot. Prejudice, custom, training, blind us so that none see clearly.

Why should I assume so fine a state as to make others believe I possess great riches? Should I wear a lie that I would scorn to speak? And be compelled to add another thereto when some sufferer appeals to my heart, and I must say, 'Go thy way, I have nothing to give thee?' Truly I am not wrong to limit myself for others' sake. Am I not safe also to follow those ways which seem to me upright and pure, even though one tells me I should renounce everything in this beautiful world and walk heavenward with solemn steps, while another ridicules me as a bigot and a Puritan because I weep at impure words, and do not delight in jewels? One learns here to distrust one's self. There are so many vigorous fighters of as many faiths! The Friends, the Levellers, the Presbyterians, Fifth-Monarchy men, the Papists, the Episcopalians, each clamorously condemning all the rest. I would that I understood them all. I crave some help to know even myself. There is one Friend whom I can ask, and his word will tell me how I can carry myself, yet it would be sweet to have a mother's counsels or a father's strong guidance besides."

Constance felt isolated. She might have found comfort in talking with Lord Grey, but he was rarely at home. Parliament had sat during the past two or three days from eight in the morning till eight at night, and when released from these long debatings, he seemed too painfully perplexed for her to intrude a question. On the Sabbath, she went with him and Sir Henry to the Abbey Church to hear Mr. Goodwin. Lady Grey had always remained at home since the rifling of the cathedrals, choosing to pay the fine for absence rather than worship without bishops, liturgy, or chants. As they passed Whitehall Palace, Lord Grey remarked to Sir Henry that the Council of State would sit to day, which boded some sharp events.

"Parliament," said he, "has debated furiously the entire week whether the government shall rest in a Single Person and Parliament, leaving rightful business untouched. His Highness is roused, and I doubt not prepared to dissolve so refractory a body."

"I thought the Protector would not permit state business on the Sabbath," said Constance.

"It is his maxim that, in extraordinary cases, something extraordinary may be done, and that the moral laws in such cases may be set aside," replied Lord Grey.

"He is less strict than I believed," said Constance. "Why does he countenance so formal observance of the day? My aunt calls it gloomy bigotry to force all to carry themselves with equal sobriety." Lord Grey turned and smiled at Constance in a fatherly way.

"You were not released from Atherton Hall, my child, before the Puritans had sway, else you would not ask it. As long as Kings and Queens and Bishops ruled, the Sabbath was no better observed than in a heathen country. Court balls and masquerades diverted the nobility, and the common people cried their goods or had morris-dances and church-ales."

"What are church-ales?"

"Pastimes and dances after sermon in the churchyard or at the ale-houses, where the people drank lustily and gave bountiful alms for the beautifying of the churches with pictures and images. These benevolent revelries were named church-ales. The ministers were compelled by King James and his bishops to read from the pulpits what was called the 'Book of Sports'—a declaration of His Majesty authorizing these Sabbath sports. If they refused, they were deposed from their sacred office and even imprisoned. Such as these found their way to New England for conscience' sake. These revelries, made lawful, took so strong hold upon the people that they could not afterward be restrained except by laws made continually more stringent. Now, all are compelled to remain at home in quietness, or listen to such preaching as they will on the Sabbath."

"Is there any other than Puritan preaching?"

"Yes. Various sects have their liberty, in so far as they do not disturb the peace or rant against the government. His Highness says it is his 'only wish that all would gather into one sheep-fold, under one shepherd, Jesus Christ, and love one another.' In this, he allows liberty of conscience to all."

"Except Papists," added Sir Henry.

"Yes," continued Lord Grey, "except Deists, Papists, and Episcopalians, who are now but Papists in the germ, and too hostile to the government to have liberty in any wise. Indeed, we were all Episcopalians once; the excesses of Archbishop Laud forcing us into popery and denying our liberty, caused us to rebound to the simplicities of the early Christians, as in Luther's day."

"Do the Friends, the Anabaptists, and Fifth-Monarchy men have all the liberty they desire in worship?"

"They all have liberty, so they do but keep the peace and not plant seditions. Such as will disturb the worship of others are justly imprisoned."

"The Lord Protector then is not the bigot his enemies cry him to be," said Constance, with animated interest.

"Far from it. The Friends promise him the wrath of God because he will not pull down the steeple-houses and silence ministers, and the Fifth-Monarchy men desire him to destroy all government and make way for King Jesus and his reign of a thousand years, while the Presbyterians would coerce him to forbid all sects but their own. He yields to the persuasion of none, but cries, 'Liberty of conscience to all.'"

They had arrived at the door of the church, and the conversation ceased; but Constance had learned enough to stir her thoughts into new life. This, with the beauty of the cathedral, so vast and unique to her novice eyes, absorbed her till nearly half the service had passed like a dream. Its length began to subdue her enthusiasm, and enabled her at last to listen to the severe rebukes and patriotic entreaties of the minister for the speedy settling of the affairs of the nation. Sir Henry sat restless, and wondered that the troubled members of Parliament bore so much. Lord Grey looked downcast, and sighed often and deeply.

At the end of the service, he told Constance he desired to speak to Mr. Goodwin, and she might await him in the aisle if she would. Lord Huntington lingered also after the people had gone out. He came to ask Constance if she had been within the cathedral before.

"I have not," she replied. "It seems to me too magnificent in itself to need the adornments of pictures and images, which Lady Grey mourns so plaintively."

"Yet some of those paintings might have well adorned a palace."

"Why were such destroyed?"

"There was no need. There should have been a more judicious destruction. But they were swept away with all decorations that courted idolatrous worship. Many ancient windows were defaced or destroyed also, because some ignorant people worshiped the representations of Deity painted thereon. Years ago, in one of the windows of St. Edmunds, in Salisbury, were seven pictures of God the Father in form of a little old man in a blue and red coat, with a pouch by his side; one represented him creating the sun, moon, and stars with a pair of compasses, and others as performing the remaining work of creation. In the last, he was seated in an elbow-chair at rest.[*] This window was broken when the Puritans were first struggling for power. They have but lately completed such breakings."

"I believed they broke such ancient windows because of the gay adornment only. I wonder now no longer," said Constance.

---

[*] Neal's Puritans. Vol. 1, p. 307.

"Then you will not at the destruction of the images," continued Lord Huntington. "In the Cathedral of Durham was a stone statue of Christ with a golden beard, a blue cap and sun-rays on his head, and in others were images of the Virgin. These had all been set up since the time of Queen Elizabeth, and it was in accordance with the spirit of the Reformation to cast them out as popish innovations."

"It was then more the spirit of reform than of intolerance that moved the decrees," said Constance, thoughtfully. "But," she added, looking up and blushing slightly as she found Lord H. studying her face, "but the music—why condemn that which calls up only heavenly emotion?"

"I cannot furnish you with so reasonable reasons against music. It was first proposed that 'music be framed with less curiosity, and that no anthems be used where ditties are framed by private men.' Later, the organs were taken down, and the singing-men dismissed, in order to return to the simple form used by the early churches."

"And does the Protector forbid instrumental music always, as do the Friends?"

"His Highness is fond of music," answered Lord Huntington, smiling. "He has furnished fine voices and instruments at the cock-pit, for the entertainment of his friends; and he does not refuse to go sometimes to Coleman's Music House."

"He is not then the austere man I had pictured. I shall mingle love with the profound reverence in which I hold him," said Constance with a bright smile and a feeling of pleasure in listening to his praises. There was something in the voice that spoke these praises, too, that touched her. She recalled it after they went out and parted at the church-door, and thought as she rode silently home that when she met him again, she would study what that was to which she listened as to a strain of music, although his tones were not musical.

The next evening it was rumored that the Protector had sent to the Lord Mayor to look to the peace of the city, and had summoned Parliament to attend him. The following day all London was moved at the *coup d'état* by which Cromwell brought turbulent members under his control.

"Parliament is dissolved, or somewhat like it!" exclaimed Sir Henry, coming in at evening from a drive with Lord D'Arcy.

"So our lion is roaring again," laughed Lady Alice.

"His Highness, as he has done once before, caused the mace to be taken away, the doors to be locked, a guard of soldiers to be stationed there—those Ironsides, ready always to do his bidding—and summoned the members to attend him in the Painted Chamber. He there delivered a speech most amazing for what it contained, and, above all, for that with which it ended."

Lady Grey waited with lip already curled with suppressed scorn. As Sir Henry teazingly withheld further information, she said,

"I wait to hear you say Cromwell has proclaimed himself king!"

"Not that, though his act was kingly," replied Sir Henry, stroking the long plumes of his hat still in his hand. At this moment Lord Huntington was announced. "Here is one, having been present, can make it known to you better than I," added Sir Henry.

Constance was happy at his timely arrival, and after Lady Grey had met him in her stately way, he turned to her and saw the bright flush of welcome in her face.

"You will interpret the Protector to us this evening, will you not?" she asked, in a low voice.

"Gladly. You have heard of his characteristic proceedings?" said he, taking a seat beside Lady Grey.

"Sir Henry has shadowed something," replied the latter. "We would know the ominous ending."

"Not ominous, but bright—promising the speedy settlement his Highness so much desires," returned Lord H., looking at Constance. "He claimed that Parliament had no right to discuss his authority, which came from the people. He quickly settled by a skilful stroke that which has been fiercely discussed since we assembled, with no promise of coming to an end. He summoned all to sign a writing recognizing him as Lord Protector, and promising not to alter the government as it stands in a single person and Parliament. Let me repeat what he said when he offered it. 'This,' said he, 'doth determine the controversy! I have caused a stop to be put to your entrance into the Parliament House. This only will let you in. I am sorry, sorry, sorry to the death, that there is cause for this. But there is cause.'"

"He will not permit the people to alter the government, then!" said Lady Grey, slightly elevating her eyebrows with amazement.

"He refuses to allow Parliament to do thus without consent of the people. 'I can sooner be willing to be rolled into my grave and buried with infamy, than I can give my consent unto,' he said. And you should have witnessed the metal of his frame while speaking. He stood nobler than a Roman before us, Madam."

"I see, in all that, only that he holds the authority of a king—he who was once but a country gentleman, and an ill-looking one at that!" exclaimed Lady Grey, indignantly. "It is the crown he looks to, and will yet put upon his own brow."

"You do not know the majestic soul of Oliver Cromwell," replied Lord Huntington, sadly. "He could have grasped the crown before this, if he had so chosen. You do not know the soul of his schemes for England."

"I believe it to be crafty ambition that moves him," said Lady Grey, bitterly.

"Ah, Madam, none so blind as they who will not see. His schemes do not admit of kingship. His efforts are against hereditary government, for 'who (he well says) can tell if he shall beget a wise man or a fool.' He has often said he 'would have men chosen for their love to God, and to Truth and Justice.' He would model our government after that form given by God to the Jews, and inclines to believe these are the last days which are to usher in the millennium. He says, most nobly, in justifying his acceptance of the Protectorship, thus: 'Concerning that promise in Isaiah that God would give Rulers as at the first, and Judges as at the beginning, I did not know but that God might now begin; and though at present with a most unworthy person, yet as to the future it might be after this manner; and I thought this' (his protectorship) 'might usher it in!'"*

"Fanaticism!" said Lady Grey, scornfully. "He is not far behind the Levellers, who would hasten the millennium by putting all the world to planting the earth with pulse. So he would sweep away the distinctions of high birth, and reduce all to a common level."

"It is quite true," returned Lord Huntington, "that he would not have hereditary distinctions, but those rather of a higher nature. He thinks, in due time, to govern this kingdom through godly magistrates."

"I see little prospect now of attaining so sublime an end," said Sir Henry.

"In due time order will arise out of so much warring. It is the hope of attaining this, that occasioned his high proceedings to-day. In watching events in detail close at hand, you do not discover the meaning of the confused picture of England. But beyond the seas, monarchs tremble and do homage to

---

* Carlyle's Cromwell. Speech IV.

Oliver Cromwell as they behold the grand outlines he has sketched, and is rapidly filling out with a firm and skilful touch."

"You speak truly, Lord Huntington, when you say we see the outline of his purpose better beyond the sea than near at hand. I confess that I do here but blindly understand the plans for settlement, and in all that which I have heard His Highness speak, he confesses that he walks much in the dark."

"He waits for Divine guidance," replied Lord Huntington. "Have you not heard him call that blasphemy which credits him or any man with the contrivances and production of those mighty things which God has wrought among us? 'Take heed,' he says, 'how you judge of His revolutions as the product of men's inventions!' He warns those who count these great events the result of the craft of statesmen or 'the cunning of the Lord Protector,' to have a care 'lest they vilify and lessen the works of God, and rob him of His glory!'"

"I have never before thought of Cromwell as waiting in uncertainty how to act," remarked Constance. "I believed he moved in the affairs of the nation as at the head of his army, with a clear head and quick will."

"True, Mistress Aylmer, when his decision is once reached. As did Luther, so Cromwell prostrates himself before God, with tears and striving of soul to know His will. Such souls do not walk easily to greatness, but step by step like little children; fearing and wavering till they feel the Rock underneath. It is the

unyielding firmness with which they stand when each
sure step is taken, that causes us to rejoice in their
strength and forget how they attained it."

During the conversation, Constance had seen the
scornful lips of her aunt, the flash of her vexed spirit,
the fire of her angry eyes repressed with courtesy, yet
not hidden. "Even she, then, cannot hide a stormy
soul under a calm face, as she promised me to do,"
thought Constance. But she forgot her in listening to
Lord Huntington, who spoke with enthusiastic warmth
after that morning scene in the Painted Chamber. It
gratified her to hear Cromwell's praises; to see him
pictured generous, godly, large-minded, and strong-
souled by the noble man who stood before her;
pictured in words rounded by the clearest and most
perfect pronunciation, and voiced with that refined
charm which she vividly felt, but had not yet analyzed.
And Lord Huntington was not unmoved by the trusting face that appealed to him at every sneer of Lady
Grey. Her sympathy and ardor inspired him too. It
was a pleasure to please her thus, a deep gratification
to teach one teachable, to satisfy her longings to discover what was just and true.

"But let us rest now from this discussion," said he;
"we each remain as strong in our own opinions as
when we began. I have no hope of making a Cromwellian of you, Madam; and you," he continued,
turning to Constance, "need no conversion, as I perceive. Let us speak of that country whence you have
lately come. I would know something of Governor
Stuyvesant, of whom I have heard quaint things.

Also of a former friend who went to Virginia, and lately was engaged by the Governor to settle an affair with our government. He was a cavalier of fine accomplishments, only too proud for his misfortunes; by name, Edward Mordaunt."

A sharp heart-throb tortured Constance for a moment, so that she could not speak at once. A deep color mounted to her temples and then receded, leaving her pale as a lily.

"My cousin, Sir Henry, knows him well," she answered at length, with a look of entreaty that he would reply for her. Happily she sat in shadow. Only the agitation of her voice and the frightened expression of her face betrayed her. Lord Huntington discovered it, and with generous tact received Sir Henry's reply without further question, and turned his inquiries upon Governor Stuyvesant. In the amusing conversation that followed, Constance quickly recovered her composure and reserved, for after reflection, the strangeness of this rencounter. But it brought Lord Huntington in unexpected and unwished comparison with Edward Mordaunt. She found herself persistently contrasting them—so like in some ways, so widely different in others. She remembered the pettish tone in which Mordaunt had sometimes chided her. She listened now and forgot every thing while listening to discover what seemed so sweet in this manly voice. And she found it! It was the tenderness in the falling intonations: an exquisite tenderness, lost in his louder speech, but most touching in natural tones. Constance was looking down, abstracted, her face all smiles with the enjoyment of her discovery, when rallied to consciousness by Lady Grey.

"I beg pardon, I was heeding your voice rather than your words," said she, in reply to Lord Huntington. He smiled and repeated an unimportant question, and after some other lively chat arose and went away. In going, he promised himself to see her again soon. She would wish to hear more of her hero. Besides, he owed it to Lord Grey's friendship to contribute to her enjoyment of the London season. Certainly!

After his departure, Sir Henry told Constance of his own intended return to America within a few days, and of a new proposal to remove to Virginia, if his mother could be so persuaded. Such prospects were held out to him as strongly inclined him to accept the change, as more favorable to his purse and to his ambition than his lifeless occupations at Gravesend. His speedy return was necessary to secure the offered position, and to win Lady Moody's consent to seek a new home. It only remained for Constance to decide if she would return with him or remain in London. Lord Grey laid his commands upon her at once. He should not allow her to leave his roof. He was her proper guardian, and she was not of age. It was needful that she should know something of her estates, but the road to Atherton Hall would be impassable in winter. A coach and six could not proceed much faster than one mile an hour, and it was a happy journey when such an equipage did not upset or stick fast in the mud. A pack-horse or the stage-wagon were safer modes of conveyance, but Constance would not care to mount a pack-saddle between two baskets, nor to crouch in the straw with a crowd of passengers in the back of the stage-wagon. She must wait till the next mid-summer.

Neither would Lady Grey permit her to go from England now. She secretly counted on the pleasure of transforming her into a London belle, and of manœuvering an estimable marriage. Now that Lady Alice was provided for, she needed such occupation to give zest to her enjoyment of the dulness of society. Constance acquiesced in the decision to remain, and, after weighing down Sir Henry's baggage with all manner of tokens of her love for dear Aunt Deborah, and not forgetting Chloe and Mingo, she allowed him to depart with her final message that there was no place on earth so sweet and peaceful as Moody Hall.

13

XXIII.

A SELECT dinner-party met at Lord Grey's on one of the pleasant autumn days, to celebrate the betrothal of Lady Alice. Mother and daughter were resolute to have a ceremonial use of the ring. For once, Lord Grey was equally resolute. He would have no papistical forms or symbols with which to insult his Puritan guests. Lord D'Arcy's family were there, stiff royalists, yielding outwardly to the inevitable course of events, crouching only till this regime should pass away. Flowing curls, lace ties and ruffles and diamonds distinguished these. Stanch Puritans were there also, in plain velvet hose, broad collars, and russet-leather boots. Lady Alice was exquisitely dressed in lace and silk, with flowing train and open sleeves, her hair laid in coquettish curls across her low forehead. She was full of pretty vivacity; easy and happy in being the observed of all eyes, and the envy of both mothers and daughters; thus publicly accepting Lord D'Arcy as her future husband in a graceful condescending way, much as if he offered her a costly bauble rather than the devotion of a full heart. Constance, in the midst of this aristocratic assemblage, was like a soft gleam of moonlight in her delicate robe, and in her reserved, slightly cold demeanor. If she often met admiring eyes bent upon her, she did not know it was for the sake of her winsome beauty, but believed they thought her that East Indiaman's daughter of whom she had been told, or a strange guest from across the sea. Unused to courtly ceremony, she was afraid of committing some mistake, and shrank from the criticisms of her aunt. She felt reassured, not flattered, when her aunt tapped her arm lightly with her fan and whispered,

"Do not fear. I am justly proud of your *entrée*."

After the simple ceremony of plighting, Lord Grey led the way to the sumptuous dinner with the mother of Lord D'Arcy, and, following this compliment to the royalists, Lady Grey, with delicate homage to learning, selected the Puritan, John Milton. Constance was consigned to Lord Huntington.

When the noisy discussion of the palatable viands sufficiently shielded her, she asked,

"Who is the gentleman of so solemn demeanor and so fine features, whom Lady Grey honored?"

"John Milton, the learned Secretary for foreign tongues. England owes much to him for the eloquence and dignity he gives to the political dispatches. He is blind and proceeds slowly, but the Lord Protector values him too highly to permit his retirement."

"I wonder that you say he is blind. His eyes are clear and serene."

"Yet moving among men, he lives in the solitude of blindness. But solitude ripens a great man's soul. He comforts himself with music and poetry. I have often, in passing through Petty France, where he lives, heard him accompany his organ with his own psalms, which Henry Laws, who belonged to King Charles' chapel, has set to flowing music."

"He is a poet, then!" said Constance. "He carries an austere air for a poet."

"But he writes with delicacy as well as strength. One never finds him coarse. He gives his ideal women a dignity and high purity beyond any writer I know. Witness even his drama, Comus."

"You speak in riddles," said Constance, timidly. "I know nothing of Comus."

"I will dispatch to you his volume of sonnets, plays, and psalms, written chiefly in his youth, and published these ten years."

"And has he written a stage-play?" asked Constance, as if she could not reconcile this with a good man's role.

"Lord Huntington!" laughingly exclaimed Lady Alice, who sat at his right and overheard the last inquiry, "Constance holds a horror for theatricals. She went with us once to the play and condemned it with tears. If you would possess her good will, you must not recommend an entertainment so unsaintly."

"The quality of the play, perhaps, distressed her," he replied. "Mistress Constance will not condemn Comus." Then seeing that she was sorry at having been betrayed, he called her attention to the dish set before them. It was a puff-paste hen, with wings spread over a nest of eggs of like composition.

"A pretty conceit," said he. "And every egg contains a fat nightingale, daintily cooked."

"These birds sing too sweetly to suffer so poor a fate," said Constance.

"Truly they do," replied Lord Huntington. "Mr. Milton loves the nightingale. He says in *Il Penseroso*, as you will see,

> "Sweet bied, that shunn'st the noise of folly,
> Most musical, most melancholy!"

He will be indignant at the sacrifice, if he discovers of what dish he partakes, and think it pitiful to bestow upon the lower sense that which is able to appeal with so much sweetness to the higher."

Constance made no reply, for general conversation had gradually ceased from interest in a topic discussed by two or three. The ladies at length withdrew and sipped coffee in the drawing-room. When the gentlemen rejoined them, Constance found Lord H. at her side, and when he sauntered away to others, could not fail to see that his eyes were sure to wander in search of her. Before taking leave, he returned again.

"I have just received a promise that Lady Gray will accompany you and Lady Alice to study some esteemed treasures of art which I brought from the continent. Also you will find some satisfaction in the flowers to which I have given up my garden-house," said he. Constance assented with both pleasure and surprise, for she knew that he lived almost a hermit, and that one rarely found entrance to his elegant home, except at some stately dinner.

The next day, Rose brought to her mistress two

volumes left for her inspection. One was Milton's poems; the other contained a few of Shakspeare's plays. This last took her unawares. Should she read it? Had not her father long ago condemned it? Would she not be like Eve tasting of the forbidden fruit? Yet Lord Huntington had sent it, and he a Puritan! He would not tempt her wrongly. She opened it and glanced over a page, then laid it down with fear, and took it up again resolutely, certain that she could trust his judgment. Once opened, the book was not closed till she had drank deeply all of Macbeth, all of Hamlet.

A week or two later, Lady Grey proposed to accept Lord Huntington's invitation. They found him at home, ordering the removal of some plants to his garden-house. He took them thither without ceremony. The sweet perfume of orange-flowers filled the rooms given up as a conservatory. Scentless japonicas, rose-tinted cactus, and gorgeous foreign flowers won exclamations from Lady Alice. Constance went from flower to flower in still ecstacy.

"These japonicas are cold, stiff and pale, like winter," said she at last; "and this scarlet cactus, with its ray-like stamens, well sets forth the warmth of the tropics."

"How unfortunate it is in its leaves!" said Lady Alice, languidly. "Without those I should esteem it *distingué*." Constance strolled further till she discovered a graceful-throated, delicate flower, rare and costly as the gem of a coronet.

"This should be worn by a princess only," said

she half-aloud, and then leaned forward to inhale the sweetness of a cluster of white tuberoses.

"How pure! how deliciously fragant!" she exclaimed. "Mary's precious box of alabaster must have given forth such sweetness. It is truly fit for an offering of the purest love." Turning, to call the attention of her cousin, she found Lord Huntington standing near, watching her enjoyment. As Lady Grey came to ask of the history and value of some plants, she passed on, not caring now for their history. The grace of form, the glow or the delicacy of color, the exquisite fragrance of the blossoms filled her with a dreamy happiness she could not express, and loved to enjoy in silence. In returning, she lingered again near the tuberoses, touched the long graceful foliage caressingly, inhaled the delicious perfume with a sigh, and followed the retiring party from the garden-house back to the portico of the stately mansion. Passing across the tessellated floor of a spacious hall, they entered a suite of rooms hung with silk, and frescoed with flowers. Here, they discoursed of statuary and pictures, of which Lady Grey was an enthusiastic connoisseur since forced to repress this taste. While she was studying a Holy Family, Lord Huntington led Constance to an alcove, to look over some rare books.

"I owe you an apology, Mistress Constance, for despatching to you a volume of Shakespeare without your consent. It is condemned, I know, but most unworthily. The plays I sent need not offend you. Have you read them?"

"Yes; with fear at first, but I believed I might rest in your approval."

"Did you find pleasure in them?"

"Indeed I did. Yet I am troubled that I could so profoundly admire wicked people. Lady Macbeth bears remorse with so amazing fortitude, and seeks so well to sustain, shield, and comfort, rather than reproach the weak Macbeth, that she wins my regard. She dissembles like an evil angel. She commands like a queen. I admire her, and feel condemned for it."

"It is her force of character that captivates your approval, not her evil influence. You have no need to condemn yourself."

"Was it for such reasons my father burned those plays?" asked Constance, earnestly.

"He may rather have been affronted at the coarseness of some scenes, and the harm which the picturing of vice may carry to some minds. Do you remember Hamlet with more satisfaction than Macbeth?"

"Truly I do not. Hamlet promised nobly in the first act. He proves aimless to my sense. Polonius, so wise at first, throws discredit on wisdom; and sweet Ophelia is weak. But I am ashamed to speak my unlearned thoughts of a great man's work. I am like the humble sparrow chirping its discontent with the glorious melody of the nightingale."

"No, Mistress Constance," replied Lord H. "It is pleasing to discover the impression made upon one not already fortified with borrowed opinions. But you will remember that Shakspeare offers no perfect characters. He took them as he found them in the world—bad men possessed of generous traits that win us; good men having foibles which lessen our esteem. He painted from nature."

"You help me," said Constance. "But I crave more than I find. His wicked people are magnificently bad. His good people are weak. Cannot a man be shown magnificently good? Is goodness always weak?"

"No. There are men who have as grandly lived unto truth, as Richard III. unto evil."

"Then why did Shakespeare withhold such?"

"Perhaps he had not that in his soul which loved to glorify the upright man. Knowing evil, he portrayed skilfully a large nature swayed by evil, but if he did not know the mystery of the strength of a heart moved upon by the Holy Ghost, how could he well picture it?"

"Then we can never behold a drama in which nobly good men may have a part, except it have birth in a godly mind?" asked Constance.

"That is my thought," returned Lord H. "I believe Mr. Milton might raise the drama if he were so minded."

"Whom could you find worthy to be his heroes?"

"Luther and Melancthon, as set forth against Charles V. and Rome's creatures, would surpass the fine contrasts in Shakespeare. Melancthon's delicate fineness of nature and high culture beside Luther with his strong convictions and his amazing boldness, defying from the Rock of Faith the artful oily-tongued plotters of Rome, at the Diet of Worms, is a nobler scene than any in our poet's volumes. I know another hero whom you would also approve," said Lord Huntington, looking at Constance as upon a beloved pupil. She gave back a smile as she questioned,

"Oliver Cromwell?"

"Yes," replied Lord H. warmly. "I should love to know him dramatized by a friendly interpreter. He accepted the leadership of this people with the fear and the faith of Moses. He once said to me, 'I consented to undertake the Protectorate only to save the nation from imminent evil, though I should altogether think any person fitter than I am.' And of late when the title of King was privately urged upon his thoughts, he said, 'I am ready to serve not as a King, but as a Constable. For truly, I have as before God often thought that I could not tell what my business was, nor what I was in the place I stood in, save comparing myself to a good Constable set to keep the peace of the parish.'"

"And he has refused the title of King?" asked Constance.

"Not publicly, but as urged in private."

"Does he excuse himself worthily?"

"Aye, he does. His reason ran thus. 'God hath seemed so to deal with the person and family of Charles that he blasted the very title of King. He hath laid it in the dust. I will not seek to set up that which Providence hath destroyed and laid in the dust; I would not build Jericho again!' he said."

"So good a thought could not come out of a mind full of artifice," said Constance with enthusiasm.

"Yet he is wise as a serpent," answered Lord H. "He moulds the army to his will, yet is careful not to betray it to the jealousy of Parliament. His Ironsides control men's passions. His eye is upon every conspiracy, but the arm of his power never falls upon the mere plotter, and herein is room for the dramatist's skill. He permits the utmost liberty of discontent till it is fully ripe for a blow. Behold then his grim soldiers at the final rendezvous, unasked, like Banquo at the feast. I am often amazed at his forbearance and tenderness to the last moment."

"Does he not then live in pitiful fear of his life?" Constance asked.

"No soldier would willingly die by an assassin. I believe these conspiracies grieve his soul most because they make darker the way in which he already gropes. He often says, Providence has dealt amazingly with him hitherto, and he knows not how he shall walk except as God directs. Think you Shakespeare would have rightly understood such form of faith and fortitude?"

"Cromwell! always Cromwell!" exclaimed Lady Grey, approaching them in her leisurely, idle way. "Lord Huntington, I fear you will plant so deep homage for the Protector in Constance's heart, that she will ill bear my loyalty to the royal house."

"I think it was well planted before she came hither," was the playful reply.

"Doubtless you are right," was the gracious assent. "But I must interrupt your further discourse since we are to drive in the Park before returning home."

Saying this, Lady Grey took leave and sailed away to her carriage with her *protégée*. After an hour in the Park, they arrived at home wearied. On entering her own room, Constance wondered at the fragrance with which it was filled.

"Can I have wafted hither in my garments, the perfume of those delicious flowers?" she questioned. Then her eye fell upon a vase in the deep window-seat, containing the tuberose she had admired at Lord Huntington's. A soft flush stole over her face at sight of it.

"What thoughtful kindness! How did he discover that my admiration centred upon this?" said Constance to herself. Then remembering that he stood near, she recalled his thoughtful attitude and his smile. "Did he hear my words? What did I utter? What?" she repeated, looking alarmed. "Oh —it was of Mary's offering I spoke. Did I not say too that this was fittest above all the others to express pure love? And so truly it is. Yet I would he had not heard so much. Perhaps it was not his thought. No! no! But it does set forth the sweetest friendship I ever knew." And Constance breathed the incense into her very soul, now looking with tenderness upon the pure flowers, and now, with a shade of sadness in her face, gazing at the distant meadows beyond the river, as was her habit when dreaming. There was reason for her dreaming; more than Lady Grey knew. She did not appreciate the delicate sympathy of Lord Huntington, the interchange of glances, unsought by either, yet happening often, to Constance's confusion. She did not know the charm to Constance of the noble tenderness in his voice and manner and how strongly it might appeal to a heart so lately bruised. Neither did it once occur to her that Lord Huntington could yield to the unconscious power of a simple girl, who, without coquetry, without the finished airs of a court belle, possessed only a graceful beauty, a pure soul, a mind that soared above the mimicries of fashion, and an ardent spirit always held in durance by womanly sweetness. All this Lady Grey counted admirable in country life, but as having little weight with a nobleman of a proud house, able to seek an important alliance. She believed what she had once told Constance, that he was not a "marrying man." He always had the freedom of the house, and if he came oftener now than formerly, it was because of the exciting state of public affairs; though it often happened when he came that he brought books for Constance, or rare flowers from his garden-house, or some of the wild blue bugloss from the dry ditches of Piccadilly, or other wayside flowers gathered when he walked or rode, as if he carried her always in his thoughts.

The months passed away into winter, Lady Grey still strangely oblivious; Lord Huntington daily more earnest in his devotion; Constance more conscious of beholding in him that ideal she had once worshipped mistakingly in another, and yet alarmed and shrinking from the conviction. She fought frequent battles with herself for betraying this in her agitation, for listening and recognizing his footstep, for being powerless to withhold the glad look of welcome, and for that heaviness of spirit that came when he was gone out of her presence. Sometimes she questioned, if he was amusing himself; for had not her aunt assured her that he would seek only a high prize, if any? Then her pride held her aloof from the family group when he came, till her doubts were forgotten in the sweet reception of some new token that she was supreme in his thoughts. How long this happy misery might have continued, perhaps Lord Huntington could not have told. But an unexpected incident put an end to it.

XXIV.

"St. Paul's Walk" was the fashionable promenade for loungers who vibrated between that and the Whitehall galleries. It was a stately portico, or covered ambulatory, at the west end of the cathedral, supported by pillars of the Corinthian order, and adorned with the statues of King James and King Charles. Driven from the leafless parks, the cavaliers and belles paced this walk, and, not unfrequently, the more staid parliamentarians found a pleasant rest here from the noisy discussion of politics at the Turkish coffee-house.

Constance, walking here one day with Lady Grey, lingered to listen to the musical twang of a harp played by a blind man. He, perceiving that some one stood near, began a plaintive ballad. Lady Grey passed on, and still Constance stood, forgetting the presence of any but the forlorn singer and his sweet instrument. Suddenly a hand touched her shoulder lightly, and a voice that had once been familiar said, hesitatingly, almost pleadingly,

"Constance Aylmer!"

She turned. Was it flesh and blood that presented itself to her sight, or a vision of Edward Mordaunt? She beheld him amazed. A quick, fiery flush mounted to her brow, and slowly rolled back, leaving her face cold and white as marble. Her hand rested in his, though she did not know that she had offered it. She no longer heard the tinkling of the music; the voices about her sounded far off; she knew not if she stood upon the marble pavement, or if the earth was moving away from beneath her. She only knew that Edward Mordaunt was there, and that a fluttering pain gathered about and grasped her heart. She made a strong effort to control herself, gently withdrew her hand and turned away without uttering one word, leaving him standing alone and perplexed. Not seeing Lady Grey, and conscious that curious eyes were bent upon her pale face, she went with slow and weak steps to the coach, entered it, and directed the coachman to drive home.

It was her old way to hide herself when she suffered. She admitted only Rose to her room, and told her how to help her. When the pain lessened and she rested languidly, she dismissed even Rose. Her thoughts were in stormy commotion.

"Why is Edward Mordaunt here? Why should he seek me?" she asked. "What right has he to call me Constance Aylmer in that old tender way, or to touch my hand when he is no more mine and I am no more his? Why did he summon a buried love, when no longer free to seek it? And why, why did the old enchantment fall upon me at sight of his face? Can a first-love never rest in its grave? Will its spectre always confront me? Can no other efface it? I thought yesterday it had been dead forever! I would that we had not met this side of heaven."

Constance lay quite still, with her eyes closed,

trying to understand herself and all that had happened. Two round, bright drops stole from under her eyelids, and rolled unheeded upon the white pillow. Just then a soft tap on the door admitted Rose. Her face was shining with pleasure.

"Here is good medicine, Missus Constance. I think the good Lord hisself sent it, to comfort you,' she whispered, displaying at the same time a packet having Sir Henry's seal, and the ship's post-marks. She received and opened it eagerly, while Rose withdrew. We will read it with her.

"To Constance Aylmer:
"Gravesend, 10*th* Dec., 1656.
"My Loving Cousin :—

"I have not sooner writ you since my exit from England, having nothing wherewith to delight your knowledge better than my mother was able to give you. No more should I honor you with my autograph at this time, but to remind you of one who was once false to you, yet whose repentance hath powdered his locks to such degree that I am able to forgive him.

"The ship in which Elsie sailed last autumn, was lost at sea, and only one sailor fetched himself safely from the wreck. My mother was moved to send you tidings sooner, had not many held hope that Elsie was picked up by some Dutch skipper going to traffic in the Virginias. But Dame Roosevelt mourns her as wholly dead, and Domine Megapolensis bewailed her in a set sermon two months gone.

"Mordaunt goes to England in the ship freighted

with these letters. I wait to know if your high spirit or your tenderness abide uppermost. He is a cavalierly fellow, and better fit for your notice since enduring with grieved patience his self-inflicted punishment. I wot not but he is tamed. I am loth to spare him from this country, to which he will no more return. I have stood his confessor and shrove him of his sins against you. *Errare est humanum.* Forgive him therefore.

"Send with dispatch the enclosed to my tailor. The dunce made my doublet half an ell too long. I would berate him soundly if he would lend his ear. Do you convey to him my good opinion of his skill in finding my height.

"*Vive vale,*
Henry Moody, Bart."

Constance dropped the letter in dismay.

"What have I done! Cruel, cruel girl!" she exclaimed, covering her face with her hands. Would Mordaunt go from London without seeking her further? Would he resent her conduct as of old? were questions that agitated her. What could she do? She longed for some one's wisdom beside her own. But where could she turn? To Lady Grey? No, she shrank from the cold, business-like way in which she would sit as judge upon the sacred history, and condemn with ridicule an affair of the heart which offered no worldly advantage. Could she ask Lord Grey? He was half a stranger yet, and always too absorbed for a quiet, fatherly talk. Who was there else but Lord Huntington? Who so reliable and so sympathizing? In remembering him, Constance felt an instinct to fly to him, to tell him all her perplexities, to rest implicitly in his judgment, certain to be met with interest and tenderness. The very thought of him quieted her emotion. She had been pacing the floor restlessly. She sat down to think.

"He knows Edward Mordaunt. But can I tell him all that sad history? Would I not betray Edward in thus unsealing my lips? Alas! I would not do that. Besides, why do I feel convinced at this moment that he loves me, and that therefore I cannot make this known to him. Is not this conviction sweet? Do I love both? What am I?" said she, rising in dismay, and walking back and forth greatly agitated. "Have I a double being? Does one heart look back longingly to the realization of girlish dreams, and fool me still with the trust that my hero was and is what my own fancy painted him? Have I outgrown that ideal? and does my other heart worship now a higher, nobler type? Can Edward Mordaunt satisfy that other heart?. Oh! what am I? How shall I know myself, and how shall I know to act rightly?"

She stopped before the window and looked away, away, from herself across the sea to beloved Aunt Deborah—at once her mother and her counsellor. Then she remembered what this best of earthly friends had once told her.

"There is none so wise to counsel thee as Jesus. Lay all thy perplexities before him, and he will guide thee gently out of them, in the best way."

"Yes. Why not?" said Constance, aloud. "Who knows my heart so well? Who can so rightly judge what is best in the future for me and for others? Who has such power to make 'all things work together for good to them that love God.' Yes, I will go to Him—my father, my mother, brother, friend—all in One." And with a glow of peace in her sweet face, Constance knelt.

XXV.

It was quite true that the schooner in which Elsie Mordaunt sailed for New Amsterdam was wrecked. Let us go back to the day of that event. It was not true that only one soul escaped. Elsie was not one to yield her life without a struggle, or to be overwhelmed with despair at the moment when her most composed sense was needed. She had one of those natures which cannot endure with calmness the little vexations of life, but which rises strong and self-possessed in important moments. While her companions were bewailing the inevitable death before them, she was deliberately calling to mind all the means of safety of which she had ever heard. The long, low shore of New Jersey was in sight. To die almost within hail of land was a thought she refused to entertain. She was too ignorant of the power of the great waves rolling in and breaking on the beach, to fear them with the ghastly terror that blanched the faces about her. Her very innocence of that awful power, secured calmness. She knew that it would be useless to cling to chance objects floating in the water, from the wreck. Any one of superior strength might clutch them from her, or she might lose her hold in a moment of exhaustion. She resolved therefore to tie herself firmly to some buoyant object. Remembering the light floating of the little pine canoes which she had many times sailed in a tub of water, to amuse Engle Zwaller, she dragged herself about the wet deck, till she obtained possession of two short boards, and then entreated a sailor to bind her arms upon them with small ropes cut from the sails. He served her well, shaking his head dolefully while he did it.

"You are a brave soul," said he, "but these will only help you into eternity. You will be sucked into the depths of the sea with the vessel. If you rise again before the last trump, you will be worthy to rule the stoutest skipper that ever sailed."

Thus equipped, and thus sadly condoled with, Elsie awaited her fate, pale and shivering at the stern possibilities of death. How many hours she waited, she never knew. A century of hours seemed to drag their heavy length, passing in review before her, as in a clear mirror, all the thoughts and acts of her life. How wasted and aimless it seemed now! They whose piety she had ridiculed, rose so lofty and pure, and worthy to possess life; they whose companionship she had chosen were but grovelling souls abased before their Maker. She prayed now, just as many around her prayed, even though yesterday they were scoffers. Then she remembered her mother's tenderness and sacrifices, and her own undutiful selfishness and neglects in return. Bitter tears fell for this. And now her thoughts went back to the little cottage at Jamestown, and rested with her husband. Had she been a loving helper and consoler? Had she not teazed, fretted and neglected him, seeking her own ease and comfort? Had she not wilfully left him when he desired her to delay the voyage a little longer? If his strong arm could shield her now, what happiness! She never loved him as at this moment, and yet it did not occur to her to rejoice that he was not sharing her suffering. But she promised herself that if she lived, she would be a tenderer wife.

And now came the dreadful last moments—moments filled with a giddy sense of descent, of whirling black waters, of appalling cries for help, when there was no help. With one long-drawn breath, a moment of instinctive resistance and of horror, and she was engulfed in the cold depths. In the midst of struggles, and but half conscious from intense suffering of soul and body, she still had thought and vigor enough to turn her arms in such way that the boards to which she was bound should not offer resistance to rising to the surface. Slowly, buoyantly, she felt herself ascending. What joy when she emerged struggling, and reached up, as if she would bound into the blessed light and air! But she discovered that these efforts would bring speedy death. She then rested quietly, suffering herself to float with her arms extended. She soon saw the shore growing firmer in outline, felt herself tossing nearer and nearer for hours, and at last, almost suffocated in the breaking surf, was flung upon the shore, dragged back by a retreating wave, then tossed again nearly lifeless on the beach. The boards caught against the stones, and anchored her. Still, dashed upon with fury by the thundering surf, she slowly but resolutely crept beyond its reach, and dropped exhausted and insensible.

When Elsie opened her eyes, the sun was shining in her face, and an Indian woman stooped beside her, endeavoring to loosen the pendant ear-rings from her ears.

"Thank God! Thank God! Saved! Saved!" she exclaimed, feebly. The woman started back from the reanimated body with affright, but Elsie entreated her not to leave her. The words had no meaning to the woman's ear, but the language of the pleading face could not be mistaken. She hesitated, and then, as if prompted by some thought of advantage, freed her arms from the cords, and wrapped her in her own mantle. Then swinging upon her back a basket partly filled with broken shells, she lifted Elsie in her stout arms, and carried her over a dreary waste of sand, made more dreary by the long, coarse grass waving in the wind. She followed an inlet, entered a forest fragrant of pine, and presently crossing a narrow stream, laid Elsie down in a wigwam, upon a pile of mats and skins.

Elsie yielded like a child to all that her rude nurse now prescribed, wearing a wolf-skin robe, and drinking a broth of which she neither dared nor cared to know the ingredients. A day or two sufficed to revive her, and by the time the master of the lodge came home, she had recovered her old vigor and elasticity of spirits.

Home occupied all her thoughts. To discover on what part of the coast she had been thrown, and the distance to Manhattan, and to persuade the silent old Indian to pilot her through the wilderness, was her daily effort, always baffled. To all her questions and gestures he replied with a puff of smoke or a low growl. She chattered persistently, determined to teach him her language by repetition, till he could answer. Sometimes, in her old capricious moods, she tied up a bundle, mounted it on her shoulder upon a stick, wrapped herself in mantle and moccasins, and shouting, "Home! Home! Manhattan! Manhattan!" strove to make her captors understand her wishes. But these stoics mildly refused to understand. She dared not venture away alone. It was of no avail to lose her temper and throw down her bundle, or to weep like a homesick child. She learned that to submit to her fate peaceably, was her wisest behavior. But to submit to serve, she would not. The squaw endeavored in vain to force her to bring water from the stream, or fagots for the fire. She resolutely refused, and commanded service in her turn with such tumultuous energy, that the solemn old guardian of the lodge verily laughed, and permitted her to rule.

Dreary weeks went by, and still Elsie was an unwilling prisoner. She found amusement in making a mantle of soft deer-skin for the approaching winter, and ornamenting it with quills and bright bird feathers, in Indian fashion. She was skilful in the use of the thorn-needles, and pleased the squaw, who patiently hunted them for her, by embroidering a pair of moccasins with fibres of bark twisted and stained with bright colors. She sometimes chose to prepare meats in a savory mode, or to string oysters to smoke and dry for winter use. She learned to weave mats too, varying and beautifying them to a degree that astonished her keepers. She had never been so industrious in her life, never so patient, so helpful. Food had never been so delicious, sleep never so sweet. Yet she yearned to take wings like a bird and fly over the space that divided her from her own people. Did they believe her lost? Would they mourn for her long? Would Mordaunt deeply grieve when he heard of her death? She wondered what the neighbors would say, and if the Domine would preach about her, and if they would weep, and if her mother would walk home talking mournfully of her. Wouldn't she frighten them all when she walked in some day! that happy day of escape that must come soon. How many miles lay between her and New Amsterdam? One hundred? sixty? thirty? Only thirty, perhaps only thirty! Could she not dare to try the distance alone?

Possibly, in her eager longings, she might have cast her fate in the attempt, had not an incident prevented. A band of Indians from the north arrived in the camp, and, as Elsie had done before at sight of every stranger, she went quickly among them and appealed, like a child, from one to another.

"Manhattan! Manhattan!" she cried, eagerly questioning in Dutch and English, if they would take her home. One nodded his head, replying,

"Iyano speaks Inglis." With a cry of joy, Elsie

almost threw herself in his arms. Would he rescue her? Might she travel with his band?

"She can go to the Manhattas. Iyano's lodge is there."

"Iyano!" exclaimed Elsie, in strong excitement, "I know the name. I have heard Lady Moody speak it."

"The good mother is the friend of Iyano."

"And do you know New Amsterdam? and my father and mother and the Director and them all?"

"Ugh! The white daughter may find them. She go with the Massapequas," replied Iyano. Elsie saw the talk was done. She fled to her hut, threw herself upon her bed of moss, and cried with frantic joy. Then she sprang up, danced around the astonished squaw, hugged her, and put in her ears the long-coveted ear-rings. And now she tied moccasins on her own feet, fastened on her half-finished mantle, and took her station in front of the lodge to watch the new-comers, lest by any chance they should move away without her knowledge. They remained all day and all night. She did not sleep. She lay down to rest, but at every sound sprang to her feet and parted the mats that hung at the opening of the hut, to peer out. At dawn, she saw them astir. Fearing lest she should be forcibly detained, she made haste to station herself near them.

A light snow covered the ground. The bare limbs of the oaks reached out among the green tufts of the pines as if for shelter and warmth. Curling wreaths of smoke went up from the camp-fire and sailed slowly among their tops. A rude kettle hung upon cross-sticks over the coals, and, hovering over this steaming caldron and dipping out portions of meat with a gourd, was an ancient witch-like woman in a gay calico kirtle and a necklace of copper triangles. Swarthy men gathered about the fire, sharpening arrow-flints or tearing hot venison with their fingers. No one noticed Elsie, who sat upon a log near by, too full of anxious fears and hopes to think of her need of food. Iyano, seeing her, brought a piece of venison on a clean piece of bark, reminding her that the Massapequas had "long moccasins," and would go far that day. Thus refreshed after her wakeful night, she was eager to go, and felt that she could bound like the roe in the path. When the band began to depart in single file, Elsie looked back at the lodge where she had spent the long weeks of autumn. The squaw stood there gazing at her and the departing guests. Elsie would have gone to her, had she dared. She waved her hand and cried out,

"Good Monitawa! You brought me home and gave me shelter. The white people will reward you." Then turned to Iyano with the sudden question,

"Will she believe I am cursing or blessing her?"

"Me say Good Spirit bless her for you," answered Iyano, motioning to the woman and repeating what he would say in her own language. And so Elsie turned away contented, and disappeared blithely between the black and scraggy trunks of the closest trees of the forest. She had vague notions of what this journey might be. The first day's vigor could not last well, but she had indomitable resolution, and so long as the hope of home was held before her, could suffer cold and hunger and weariness to the last degree. We will not follow her in the painful slowness of the tortuous journey, beaten upon by rain and sleet, torn by wayside thorns, her feet bruised and swollen, and her limbs aching from exertion beyond her strength. Iyano bound thick skins over her torn moccasins, and halted to give her rest, encouraging her with recounting the number of "sleeps" to Manhattan. While she is toiling toward home, we may go in advance and discover the events that precede her coming.

XXVI.

Before daybreak, on the morning when Elsie began her journey, a fleet of sixty canoes, filled with Indians, crossed the bay of Manhattan, floated noiselessly under the very walls of the Fort of New Amsterdam, and effected a landing without one signal of alarm. Director Stuyvesant had gone with his small army to subdue the Swedes at Fort Cassamir. The town was not in a state of defence. The cannon in the Fort were useless, the palisades broken, the gates open, the sentinels asleep at their posts. Many householders were gone with the Director, and those who remained, contented themselves with barring their doors, and slept in unsuspecting security.

The first knowledge of danger was in a noisy summons at the doors of many domicils for entrance, on pretence of searching for fugitive Indians. The occupants awoke out of sleep to find themselves surrounded by a dreaded enemy. The street was filled with these savages peering everywhere, to discover the weakness or know the strength of their victims, hoping to find men and guns gone, and the town secure for plunder. One gun was sufficient to put a dozen of these cruel cowards to flight. On the other hand, any sign of fear on the part of the inhabitants would invite an attack. Women summoned all their heroism and forbade entrance to their houses, and men sternly expelled those who had obtained admittance. The Vice-Director and the Council assembled as soon as possible in the Fort, and gave orders for such defence as could be stealthily prepared.

Herr Roosevelt had gone with the Director. Dame Roosevelt was alone with a slave woman, and returned to her bed sick with fright, after barring shutters and doors. The servant nursed her alarms with occasional reports of all that could be seen through the loop-holes in the shutters.

Burgomaster Zwaller was also away with the army. At daylight, old Mabel answered the thundering summons at the door, rolled up her eyes at sight of the visitors, dropped the latch and stood transfixed and helpless. Down the stairs and into the fire-lit room stalked Dame Zwaller. Masculine in her tread, straight and tall as the best of the warriors before her, carrying a gun in her hand and stern determination in her face, she was an object of fear to the intruders, though a woman. Striking the butt of the gun upon the floor, she pointed to the door and commanded them to go, with the air of an offended general marching out a clan of mutinous soldiers. One or two skulked away, others lingered, glancing with covetous eyes at the row of pewter shining on the shelf. The gun was lifted significantly. Dame Zwaller fearlessly came nearer, and her sharp eyes and sharper voice repeated the command. This time with effect. The room was cleared instantly and the door closed upon them with a vigorous sound that quickened the heels of the last goer, as if he believed it the report of the gun.

"My God! spare us from horrors this day!" she exclaimed, when she saw at sunrise a horde of war-painted Indians lounging in the street. "The Almighty alone holds them from springing upon us, Mabel. With His help we are our own defenders to-day."

Dame Zwaller meant to save her children and her house. She therefore put her house in order for defence, barricaded, provided water in every part, and caused Mabel to gather the marred pewter-plates and mugs, while she sat by the fire with poor little frightened Perle and Engle, moulding bullets. She had intense fears for Barbara. The marauders would attack the bowery before night, doubtless. Was Baltazzar on the alert? Their chance of escape was small. The Fort, the few soldiers, and the armed towns-people might intimidate the enemy; but the solitary farmers could offer less resistance. If the savages did not get blood here, they would seek it there. But who could give warning? Mabel was too old; Minxey would die with fright. Engle was a brave little fellow, who would not shrink from what his mother commanded; but how was she to spare this only son, this best of all her treasures. Then Barbara, murdered, rose before her eyes. Her heart leaped from one to the other. She trembled and gave great sighs, still busily casting the bullets. Suddenly her face lighted. She lifted herself from her work.

"Engle, you know how to use a gun."

"Yes, I do!" he answered proudly.

"This is too heavy for you," said she, thoughtfully, handling the one that had noiselessly helped her fight her first battle. She went into the loft, and after some search, found a carabine. Returning with it, she said,

"This you can use, and thus." Giving him a chair to mount, she taught him how to place the weapon in the crescent cut in each of the wooden shutters to admit light. She bade him fire from each window in succession, in case of attack, by which method a host would seem to resist.

"For," said she, "Engle, I shall leave you sole defender of your sister, of Mabel, and your father's property, while I go to the bowery and warn Baltazzar. Can you do this?"

"I can, mother!" said Engle, standing straight as an arrow, while his cheeks and lips blanched at the thought of acting the real soldier which he had so often played.

Dame Zwaller said no more, donned her wrappings, took the gun in her hand, bade Mabel bar the door behind her, and walked forth into the street. Engle's heart sank within him when he saw his mother go out among those cruel Indians. He looked a frozen image of terror, which the blazing fire had no power to melt, while he crouched on the hearth beside Perle, waiting for the dreaded yells which would signify the attack. Two endless hours those poor children sat listening to every sound. Would their mother ever come back?

The gate opened at last. Footsteps came nearer.

Was it the enemy? Engle stood up straight and brave and pale, and fixed his eyes on the loaded carabine. The tramp was near the door. Knock! knock! knock!

"Mabel, it is I!" Engle sprang forward with a glad cry, and helped let down the bar. As Dame Zwaller entered, he sprang into her arms, weeping because he had recovered his mother unharmed. She sat down exhausted and faint. As Mabel brought her a glass of wine, she whispered,

"Herr Van Spuyt is killed. I saw some arrows shot. They are getting bolder. I would not venture forth again with my life in my hand." Then speaking louder, she added, "But Baltazzar is warned, and I hope, saved. He is gathering in his flocks."

It was true that one citizen had lost his life, and that the Indians, becoming aware how poorly the town was defended, began to show signs of hostility. Within the Fort, secret preparations had been going on during the day. The citizens had determined to venture all in one strategic movement. There were several soldiers in the Fort, a few negroes, one or two prisoners, Nicholas Stuyvesant, the Vice-Director De Sille, and some members of the Council, besides a few citizens who had stolen in from time to time; in all a company of forty, to oppose to a band of three hundred Indians. To these was presently added little Lisbet, who, in a fit of uncontrollable terror, scaled the wall of the Fort that hemmed in her garden, and rolled over the parapet into the court-yard, with the agility and velocity of her own pet cat.

This mimic army, well provided with ammunition, hoped, with the aid of a big drum and fife, to save New Amsterdam. Councillor De Sille strove first to induce the Indians to leave the town, by friendly entreaties, then by commands, and, as the day wore away, by threats, which he presently put into execution. Attracting them near the Fort, he gave a signal, the gates were suddenly thrown open, and, with all possible noise of fife and drum and rapid firing, the little army sallied impetuously out of the Fort. The savages, believing a whole army pouring out upon them, turned and fled swiftly to the water's edge, pushed off the canoes, sprang in and plied their paddles with amazing vigor; while the soldiers, excited by success, continued noisily firing after the fugitives. The shouts of victory and the rolling of the drums sounded through all the town, till long after nightfall. Metje Wessell's inn was crowded with beer-drinking customers, congratulating themselves on escape, and applauding the Councillor's wonderful wisdom.

But before long, red flames began to light up all the regions about them—an awful sight to those who understood what horrors those lurid flames represented. Baltazzar Stuyvesant saw them and knew what cruel work had begun. At what moment the Indians might row up the river and lay his own home in ashes he did not know. Nicholas sent a message entreating him to abandon the bowery, and take refuge with his family in the Fort. Baltazzar sent back word to come and help him defend it. But this Nicholas had no thought of doing.

Baltazzar knew what orders his father would issue if at home. He was not willing to sacrifice his favorite bowery, and valuable imported stock, when by prompt and courageous measures all might be saved. He felt the responsibilities of his stewardship more than his personal danger, and determined to remain. But his wife and boy must be sheltered in the town, whither many were already flocking from their isolated homes. He went to seek Barbara.

"I cannot leave you, Baltazzar," was her reply.

"But you must!" said he, surprised at the unexpected opposition.

"If you are to die, I shall die with you," she said.

"But our boy, Barbara!"

"We will die together. I will not go to the Fort without you."

"What madness! You must go," he repeated, almost doubting if she was in her right senses to offer such disobedience—she, the ever dutiful wife.

"Go with me, then," she entreated. "Your life is worth more to me than land or house or gold."

"I cannot forsake what my father has committed to me. A hired servant is sometimes faithful to his post. How much more then will my father look for my dutiful service? I cannot fly like a coward, when I know that the bold action of a few may keep many savages at bay. I shall stay."

"Then I shall stay also," cried Barbara, throwing her arms around her husband's neck. "I will not cry or shrink from service. I can load the guns."

"But our child, Barbara! our child!" exclaimed

Baltazzar, vacillating between anger and love at the conduct of his wife. "My anxiety for you both will distract me when I need deliberate coolness."

"Is my love for you less than your duty to your father, that I should forsake you? No! Your choice is mine also. Send for soldiers! send for soldiers! The Councillor will not deny enough for the protection of the Director's bowery," said Barbara, parrying the debate with a woman's quickness.

"Send for soldiers?" repeated Baltazzar, revolving the thought. "I will try that," said he after a moment. "If they are refused me, do you promise then to take refuge in the Fort?"

"Yes," said Barbara, smiling through her tears. Baltazzar put his arms around her, kissed her tenderly, stooped to kiss their sleeping boy, and went out to send a messenger to De Sille.

Before midnight, seven French soldiers were performing picket duty on the Stuyvesant farm, and several negroes were stationed in or near the house. Baltazzar watched, from the highest point he could mount, the flames which marked the progress and direction taken by the Indians. The wretched bonfires of homes on Staten Island had faded out, and new lights shone on Long Island, in the direction of Gravesend and New Utrecht, so that hope grew strong that the bowery was exempt this night from attack. But Baltazzar groaned as he thought of the suffering friends there whom he had no power to help.

The next day, the Council of New Amsterdam sent a messenger to summon the Director home, and gave orders for the immediate strengthening of the fortifications, and the obtaining of serviceable cannon to replace that which had become useless, even for holiday service. No sentinel slept at his post now, no breaches were to be left in the palisades to tempt prowlers, and both land and water gate were faithfully secured at sunset.

One morning, while repairs were still going on, a slender canoe, containing an Indian and apparently a young squaw, shot over the water in front of the Fort, bent toward the landing. A French sentinel paced the parapet of the Fort. He believed it treason to the city to permit a red-skin to enter it. He had failed in his duty before, and he intended to obey the new regulations with military exactness. Besides, every savage ought to die after such outrages as had been perpetrated by them on the inhabitants of Long Island. He therefore shouted fiercely at the passing boatman.

"*Qui va là?*"

The Indian looked up, unable to understand.

"*Arrêtez!*" he shouted again, angrily. Iyano, for it was he, rested an instant on his oars, but still understanding nothing, lifted the paddles again and with a skilful sweep darted his canoe toward the shore.

"*Mourez! fils du diable!*" cried the soldier, lifting his gun. A bullet sped straight to Iyano. He fell back in the canoe with a groan.

"Jesus, I die! The Inglis kill his friend!" Elsie gave a shriek of pain and fear at the sight. She forgot to sieze the oars, and grasped the sides of the boat, uttering screams of horror. The canoe gently drifted away on the out-going tide. Iyano opened his eyes and looked mournfully at Elsie. He strove to rise, but could not.

"I die!" said he. "Tell my people no hurt the Inglis. Tell the good mother make the great book talk to my people. Iyano go see Jesus. He shine for me! He come!" His lips still moved, but Elsie could hear no more. Her heart-rending cries brought some frightened workmen to the shore. One kinder than the rest, put off in a boat, overtook the canoe, took it in tow and slowly rowed back to shore. By this time a crowd had gathered. Elsie sprang out of the canoe into the boat and from that bounded to the shore, unrecognized by any in her uncouth dress.

"You have killed Iyano!" she exclaimed, indignantly. "He was our good friend. He brought me home. He was tender as a brother—dear, kind Iyano! And you have killed him," she said, with streaming tears. The listeners heard with astonishment this young squaw speak to them in their own language.

"Do you not know me? I am Elsie Roosevelt. Where is my father?"

"Elsie Roosevelt! Elsie Roosevelt!" exclaimed many voices. Had not the Domine buried her with decent obsequies long ago? How had she arisen out of her watery grave? The news flew hither and thither while Elsie went with flying steps to her father's house. Dame Roosevelt stood looking from the window, wondering what all the stir was about down by the water-gate. Then she watched a squaw half running, followed by a troop of gazers. The squaw was coming toward the house. She stopped at the gate—opened, entered it, ran to the door.

"What can ail the poor creature?" said the frightened dame. Then seeing her nearer, cried, "How like Elsie she looks! Like my poor, lost Elsie!" This so touched her feelings that she went quickly and opened the door. Her heart almost leaped out of her frail body at the sight and the words that met her.

"Mother! mother!" cried Elsie, throwing her arms around her mother's neck and sobbing like a child. Thus we leave them to weep together in their joy and to recount all that had filled up those months of living burial.

The tidings quickly spread through the town. Many continually went to and fro to welcome and congratulate Elsie, to mourn over the tragedy, or to express fear of the consequences. At last, the Vice-Director caused the body of Iyano to be carried to the Stadt Huys and laid in state. He sent messengers to the Massapequas and to Lady Moody. Sir Henry came the next day, much excited by the events, and even more deeply agitated at Elsie's return than at Iyano's death. Why, no one knew but himself. He made eager inquiries as to when a ship would sail, and sought the captain of the earliest one outward bound, offering him a large reward to sail without waiting for a full cargo.

When he met Elsie, she asked him with a keen

look and nervous agitation if he knew Mordaunt's plans, or why he went to England so suddenly.

"Perhaps he would not have gone if I had arrived sooner," said she. "Will it be very long before he comes back?" There was a new, subdued air about Elsie that touched Sir Henry's feelings, knowing all that he did of her husband. But he replied vivaciously,

"Yes, I know his plans. He will return by the time the robins tune their throats. What a roundelay we shall have within and without!" Elsie smiled sadly and by and by asked about Constance Aylmer. Sir Henry divined her thought. He replied,

"I doubt me if she ever returns to America. My mother rejoiced but yesterday that she was removed hence, and that her tender heart did not suffer the horrors we have witnessed at Gravesend. I think, too," he continued in a confidential tone, "there is one who will never permit Constance to leave England, if my eyes saw aright while I abode there." Sir Henry may be forgiven this last remark, since he said it for the sake of lifting a load from Elsie's mind. And it did remove her fears, and helped her wait trustingly for her husband's return.

Sir Henry went back to Metje Wessell's inn, and, shutting himself up, penned two letters which he hoped would follow quickly in the wake of the ship in which Mordaunt had sailed two weeks before. We will glance at only one of them.

New Amsterdam, 24th Dec., 1656.

DEAR MORDAUNT.

May the winds that speed this to you, hold you in durance, and so quit you from the danger of the law to whose righteous clutches you are likely to innocently commit yourself, for polygamy. Even if you reach England prior to this, I trust in Constance's shyness and good sense to hinder a hasty betrothal or publishing of bans—*quod avertat Deus!*

Your wife, Elsie, hath arisen out of the grave to which she was consigned with many tears. I believe you will not reproach her for this, since the timeliness of her appearing will save you some sorrowful appeal to the courts. Her sufferings in passing through the wilderness must touch your pitiful love, and I think you will find her trained by her trials into such subdued and womanly spirit, as may make you a more pleased and willing prisoner to your marriage bonds.

As for me, I may soon pitch my tent beside you in Virginia. My mother is almost persuaded to go thither. We are now overwhelmed with guests whom she hath succored in the terrible scourge that hath fallen upon all about us. Many are without homes, and, though they draw largely upon our hospitality, my mother says, with the sweet patience that so well befits her, that "both her health and her purse being the gift of her Lord, she has naught to do, but spend both in His service." I believe her wishes may all be summed in this,—" *Ut prosim!* "

Your warning to me concerning George Baxter was owlishly wise. I had him removed to the debtor's room in the Stadt Huys. He hath forfeited bail and escaped to New England, whereby my purse suffers another leak, not so mildly borne as leaks to better use. But this writing must suffice. We await your return with impatient outlook.

Item. Mary Tilton is carried away prisoner by the Indians. A large ransom may recover her if she does not too quickly wilt, like a plucked heart's ease.

     Yours, Henry Moody, Bart.

XXVII.

There was a gentle tap at Constance's chamber door, a little while after we left her seeking heavenly direction. It was Lady Grey, just returned from St. Paul's Walk, where Lord D'Arcy had told her of Constance's illness and return home.

"My dear child, why did you not let me return with you?" she asked.

"I could not seek you without all eyes beholding my suffering," Constance replied.

"What caused it?"

"My heart doubtless," she answered, smiling.

"Have you suffered thus hitherto?" asked Lady Grey, alarmed.

"Twice, since I abode in England."

"Why then did you not make it known to me, that I might summon a physician?" was the reproachful question.

"Because I knew none had power to help me," she replied sadly. Lady Grey was silent. Then she spoke hesitatingly.

"Are you aware that heart-disease foretells sudden death?"

"Yes, I know it well," replied Constance, calmly.

"And you are unmoved! Does such a summons hold no fears for you?"

"I will not say--none. Life is very sweet. Yet

I seek to hold myself ready," said Constance. Tears were springing to her eyes, but she made a strong effort to repress them. There was a long silence.

"I confess I do not wholly understand you," said Lady Grey, rallying. "You are at once so gentle and so strong that you are a riddle to me, except I keep in mind that you combine father and mother in one. You face the possibilities of death, much as Sir Egbert Aylmer faced persecution, and I can no more mould you to my will than I could your Puritan mother, albeit you are as mild as she. What is this secret of your Puritan faith?"

"I know no secret but this; nor by what name it is truly signified. I desire to commit myself, and all of which I hold the stewardship, to my Saviour, and to live in such wise as not to offend him any more than I would offend a most loving father and mother."

"Love is your secret then!" said Lady Grey. "I wish such love moved all the Puritans who seem so filled with fear of God that they make life hatefully solemn and bleak. It is this which repels us, and causes such as Lord D'Arcy to delight in calling themselves 'Rattleheads and Impuritans.' This reminds me that Lord D'Arcy is offended that Alice does not smile of late upon his railleries. She came one day to your chamber door, to seek your help in working some lace, when she was hindered at hearing the voice of Rose within, pleading in such wise for her before God, that she was melted to tears, and has been troubled since."

"We were holding our morning devotions," Constance explained, "which we have done since we came hither."

"But," said Lady Grey, with some coldness, "I would not have you so disturb Alice as to hinder her happiness with her future husband. She is well enough—an obedient daughter—and I would not have any Puritan leanings thwart her marriage."

Constance was too surprised at this mother's evident wish to secure an advantageous marriage, rather than true peace of mind, to be able to make any reply. Lady Grey arose, and kissed her as if to heal any wounds she might have inflicted.

"Command me, or any thing in my house for your benefit or pleasure. I would there were more like you," said she.

In going, she met Maurice, who came to summon her below. She found Lord Huntington waiting for her. He, also, had heard of Constance's illness at St. Paul's Walk, and called to inquire how serious it might be. Lady Grey explained, adding that she would probably be in her usual strength to-morrow.

"But, madam, you shock me. Does she know that this may one day prove suddenly fatal?"

"Yes. She speaks as calmly as if the going out of this world into another was a thing to be happily endured."

Lord Huntington was indeed shocked. Such tidings were so unlooked for! So unwelcome, now! He arose and walked back and forth in silence, evidently agitated. Then suddenly stopping before Lady Grey, he spoke to her in a low tone, but with deliberate accent. It was her turn to show emotion.

"You do Constance a great honor," was her reply to the question we have not heard. "It would give us all happiness. But is not this sudden?"

"No, madam. It was my resolve the first time I saw her. This resolve has strengthened every hour that I have since spent in her sweet company. Will you be the bearer of my message?" said he.

"Most willingly, my lord."

While he wrote it, Lady Grey sat wondering at an event in which she had taken no part. That Constance, without her help, should have won the heart of a man whom the most ambitious London belle had not been able to compass, was more than she could yet comprehend. The supposed absurdity of it had utterly blinded her eyes, in all these months, to the progress of an affection which Sir Henry, with better appreciation, had perceived in the beginning.

"You will permit me to break these orange flowers?" said Lord Huntington, interrupting her thoughts.

"As many as please your purpose," she replied. She always kept her apartments perfumed with the choicest blossoms. The fragrance, if not the beauty or gracefulness of the flowers, pleased her senses.

Lord Huntington sealed his note by thrusting through it a stem laden with the significant blossoms. It contained but few words.

"Give to me so much of your precious life as remains. The balmy air of France or Italy may unite with my assiduous care to prolong a life more dear to me than any other that earth holds.

"HUNTINGTON."

He gave this to Lady Grey, and immediately returned home. Undoubtedly, he expected an early reply to a proposal made under such peculiar circumstances. He was disappointed in not hearing from Constance that night, and still more, when he returned the next day from the Parliament House and found no answer. He had invited a friend to dine with him that day, and gave himself as courteously to his entertainment as if no such disturbing weight was upon his mind. This friend was no other than Mr. Mordaunt, whose arrival he had early discovered.

After dinner, when the cloth was removed, and they sat together alone, Lord Huntington asked Mr. Mordaunt if it was his purpose to remain in England.

"The colonies do not attract me strongly," was the reply, "yet I may go thither again. Such a decision rests altogether with another."

"Indeed?" remarked Lord H., waiting for further explanation, if his friend chose to give it.

"You were once good enough to bestow an interest upon my affairs," continued Mr. Mordaunt. "Perhaps it may not be amiss to make known to you the reason of my voyage hither. I crave your help also."

"I am ever at your service," replied Lord H.

"I told you yesterday of the loss of my wife," he added. "Elsie was a sprightly girl whom I married in a fit of jealous passion. I loved one, of whom I can never speak with composure, knowing that, by my own act, I lost as gracious a woman as ever lived; whose beauty and whose purity of soul can be compared to none other, and whose heart was so wholly given to me that it well nigh folded her in the grave, when she discovered what a gulf I had, by my own will, fixed between us. My own sufferings when I beheld in my right senses what folly I had committed, were hardly less, as you may see in my bleached locks."

"Do you seek now to repair that folly?" asked Lord Huntington, with a keen pang of suspicion that this gracious person was no other than Constance Aylmer. He had not forgotten her agitation at the sudden discovery of his acquaintance with Mordaunt.

"I would repair it, but I was dismayed yesterday at the very beginning of my hopes," was the reply.

"That most sweet and gracious person is here then."

"Yes. I met her yesterday in St. Paul's Walk, for the first time since I saw her white face on my wedding-day. Her hand even rested in mine. But she withdrew it, not with scorn, but with so great pain in her countenance and so frightened an air, that I was transfixed while she disappeared. I sought her again, but could nowhere find her. I know not now how to proceed without a friend, lest I offend her."

Lord Huntington sat in thoughtful reverie. There was no longer any uncertainty. Constance's illness was explained. She owed to this man the sufferings which would shorten her life. She loved him still, doubtless. This was why no answer had yet been returned to his own pleadings.

"I will serve you in this if the power lies in me so to do," said he presently, rising and leading the way to another apartment, for the sake of concealing his own emotions. "I know of whom you speak. She is at Lord Grey's, where I have liberty to see her. I will prepare the way for you."

Mordaunt was overwhelmed at this discovery, at so much unexpected interest, and at the happy turn which events seemed taking. If he had not been so entirely occupied with his own excited feelings, he might have noticed the change which the countenance of his noble friend had undergone since his coming, and marked the rare thoughtfulness he bestowed upon a matter which concerned only others. When the latter added that he would see Constance to-day, and that Mordaunt might call upon him to-morrow and know her will in receiving him, he was more than satisfied, and went away rejoicing with fresh hope.

Lord Huntington was earnest and honorable in this arrangement. He believed now that Constance loved Mordaunt. Her happiness was above every other consideration. He was generous enough even to consent to intercede for his friend, though not without an inward struggle. Poignant as was his own disappointment, he was willing to withdraw all claims to her hand. With this intention, he went to Lord Grey's.

He doubted if he could see her. Perhaps she was

not recovered. He was surprised therefore upon entering the drawing-room to see her there as freshly beautiful as ever, and especially charming in a robe of silver-grey, slashed with blue. She received him with embarrassment, for she did not yet know how she could reply to his note of yesterday. She wished to undeceive him if he supposed her heart had never been given to another, and possibly this knowledge might alter his affection for her. But she had resolved to tell him all that had happened. He led her to a seat and took a chair opposite her.

"I have come," said he, "to plead for a friend before receiving your reply to my suit. I would in no wise stand in the way of your best happiness. You know that Mr. Mordaunt is come hither to seek you. He has told me all. He is free to offer you his hand once more, but, not understanding your emotion yesterday, he cannot present himself in your presence without permission."

Constance sat with downcast eyes.

"I did not then know that Elsie is no longer living. A letter from Sir Henry made every thing known to me, after my return from St. Paul's."

"You will receive him, then. Forget my note; not that I willingly yield my own hopes of most excellent happiness, but that I would do that which most perfectly promotes yours," said Lord Huntington, rising as if to end a painful interview. Constance looked up, beseechingly.

"Do not go, my lord, I wish to speak with you of this. Yesterday, I could have flown to you alone for counsel, but my fears hindered me. To-day, since you know all the sad history, I can unseal my lips. Sit, I pray you, and answer me." Lord Huntington needed no second appeal. He resumed his seat.

"Is it possible for one's being so to change that things which once gave happiness can satisfy no longer?"

"Yes," was the emphatic reply.

"Is it possible, then, for one's heart to retain its integrity if it plays false to that upon which it was once fixed, and attaches itself to an infinitely more satisfying object?"

"Yes. You cannot stay the growth of the soul. Its stronger needs may justly be supplied, if no laws of God or man forbid."

"Then, to forsake the love of undeveloped youth is not to be wholly condemned. You lighten my doubts to assent thus. I am no more that Constance who loved Edward Mordaunt, three years ago. I believe now, he was not the being that the magic of my fancy pictured him. That ideal which I loved so fervently, is filled out wholly by another."

"And that other?——" said Lord Huntington, bending his earnest eyes upon Constance's still downcast face.

"Is Lord Huntington!" she added in a trembling voice.

"Constance! My wife!" he exclaimed, rising suddenly and folding her in his arms.

And how was this to be told to Mr. Mordaunt? Constance wished to see him. Lord Huntington could not have the effrontery to keep the appointment the next day, however upright his motives had been. Constance resolved to address him a note herself, requesting an interview. She trusted that when he understood her frankly, he would suffer less keen disappointment than if she permitted him to return to America without seeing her. The visit was accordingly arranged for the next day.

When the hour arrived, she found herself much agitated. What could she say? She began to be alarmed at the difficulty and delicacy of the subject. She might have met it composedly without thought or plan; but the more she meditated what she ought to say and what he would probably reply, the more she shrank from the task. And to think it should ever become a dreaded task to speak to Edward Mordaunt! She felt there was something sad in this changefulness of one's nature.

He came at last. This was not like their first meeting at St. Paul's. Constance was tremulous, but open and cheerful. Mordaunt was graver than ever she had seen him, but he possessed all the old ease and nonchalance which had once so attracted her. His handsome face still carried its romantic dreaminess, his eyes still retained their habit of fixing upon her countenance or studying the arrangement of her dress, which had often been a source of so much confusion to her. Even now, she felt the discomfort of criticism, and almost expected him to find fault at once with her slippers, or comment whimsically upon the simplicity of her ornaments or the disposal of the coil of her hair. She could not even now prevail upon her eyes to meet his clearly, though remembering well how he used to chide her for this excessive shrinking. So there she sat before him frightened and trembling, not knowing what to say, although she had summoned him. It was a relief to her when he broke the silence.

"But for your note, Constance, I should not have trusted myself to come hither. I should have foreborne to see you, and sailed for America in a few days."

Constance looked up, her face full of timid inquiry. She wondered if Lord Huntington had spared her the necessity of explanation. He hesitated to continue. At length he added slowly, and in a voice betraying depression and almost despair,

"A letter, which seems to have pursued me on the wings of the wind, reached me this morning, and bids my speedy return. It kills all my hopes. It binds me an unwilling prisoner. It is no more possible for me to throw myself at your feet, and seek to repair that woeful wound I inflicted not only upon you, but upon myself, also. I am forced to abide by the destiny I chose in my madness."

Constance's eyes were fixed intently upon him. Mordaunt hardly dared to proceed. If she still loved him, might not this second trial break, altogether, the cord which had once almost snapped asunder through his cruelty? But seeing her suspense, he asked,

"Would it be sorrowful to you, still, to know that

Elsie—that my wife—is living?—was saved from the wreck?"

Surprise at this announcement, sympathy and pity for Mordaunt, relief from the unwilling task she had to perform, grateful joy that she had been saved from fixing her heart longer upon this man, all together crowded into Constance's thoughts and overcame her with tears. Mordaunt longed to shelter, to console her; but his honor bound him. He could say no more. He could only bow his head with a sense of humiliation and sorrow that was agonizing.

"I would not have you misunderstand my tears," said Constance. "It is well, it is happiest for us all, that you know that Elsie lives. That which I would say and know not how to speak will not so wound you, since your destiny is fixed without me. My love which you can no more seek, is flown so that you could not find it, even though you were free. I still feel tenderly toward you, remembering those sweet days at Moody Hall. You will always remain in my thoughts with a strange interest, unlike that I hold for others; yet my love is given to another."

"To Lord Huntington!" exclaimed Mordaunt. "Fool that I did not see it!"

"He interceded for you, Edward, believing truly that I might be so minded as not to forsake you for him." There was so much of the old uprising of a jealous spirit and wounded sensibility in Mordaunt, that Constance took his hand appealingly.

"I do not speak thus to wound you. I would not willingly do that. It is only that you may return with an eased and glad heart to Elsie, holding yourself forever free from regrets for me. Our sorrow thus healed, is not without some precious fruits. We have both grown into larger natures doubtless, through suffering. This world, at once so bright and so dark, may yet yield to us much sweet happiness—the more sweet for the hope of reaching a higher heaven, after this life."

Mordaunt made no reply. This silence was painful to both. At last he arose, and grasping her hand, kissed it fervently, and said with broken utterance,

"God bless you! precious Constance! Farewell, farewell on earth!" He turned, and without once looking back, left the room, and went quickly away to his inn.

Constance did not see him again. He sailed the following week in "The Hope" for New Amsterdam.

Lord Huntington was anxious to convey Constance to the Continent, both to enjoy the invigorating air, and with the hope that a calm, happy life might delay, and perhaps altogether arrest the progress of the dread disease, which she had so silently contemplated as fatal. At his wish—not to be disputed—the betrothment was celebrated immediately, and the marriage appointed for May. Lady Grey desired to give a magnificent wedding; Constance wished it to take place with quiet elegance, and she prevailed in her calm way.

"You will at least no longer refuse diamonds, as not befitting your estate," said Lady Grey, in deciding upon the important trousseau. Constance looked at her in dismay.

"I have nothing wherewith to buy them! Are they indeed needful? Will Lord Huntington think me poorly arrayed without them?"

"Your whole quarterly income lies untouched," replied her aunt with slight asperity. "That will not forbid a moderate purchase of jewels, beside a handsome wardrobe."

"It is wholly gone!" exclaimed Constance, not a little frightened at Lady Grey's expected displeasure.

"Gone? Whither?"

"Over the sea. I sent it all to those homeless people in Gravesend, who have not where to lay their heads, as Aunt Deborah wrote me. I did think I could well spare it for their sufferings, when I possessed so abundant happiness here."

"You did wisely not to consult me," said Lady Grey, vexed exceedingly. "I wonder that you ventured upon this alone."

"Lord Grey did not condemn me. He smiled upon me, and himself conveyed it to Mr. Mordaunt."

"It is altogether like him to permit so foolish an outlay."

"He thought, no more than I, that my needs would demand a large sum so speedily," said Constance, in reply. She sat thoughtful, and, Lady Grey hoped, penitent. But she added presently, "Even though I had known my need, I believe I could not have forborne to send wherewith to comfort those sorrowing people. I could not justly have kept it to spend upon baubles to shine for a day upon my bosom. I believe Lord Huntington will forgive my lack of jewels, for the sake of those people I love and pity."

"You are truly worthy of a republican court," said Lady Grey, scornfully. "But you shall not lack what is needful. You must submit these decisions to my better experience."

Thus it was settled. Lady Grey would permit nothing but the costliest raiment, and therefore Constance was not Puritanic in her bridal-dress. On the morning of the brilliant wedding, she found a package on her dressing-table, containing four-fold the sum which her aunt had condemned her for expending too generously. A note accompanied it, with only these words:

"Give, and it shall be given unto you; good measure, pressed down, and shaken together, and running over, shall men give into your bosom. For with the same measure that ye mete withal, it shall be measured to you again."

Constance knew that Lady Grey did not send it.

A few days afterward, Lord and Lady Huntington sailed for France. In parting, Lady Alice whispered some earnest words.

"I have loved and hated you, all at once, if that were possible," she said. "Your life, since you came hither, has preached more loudly to my conscience than any of Mr. Goodwin's sermons. I am sorely vexed in spirit."

"Say, 'my Savior, take me as I am, and mould me to thy will.'"

"Lord D'Arcy stands between!" replied Lady Alice.

"Let none stand between your soul and God," said Constance, turning to go. She turned back again, and added, "Alice, my cousin, speak your thoughts to your father."

"I cannot, I fear my mother!" she whispered, with tears filling her eyes. A kiss, a loving embrace, and Constance was gone.

Need we go again across the sea, and follow that stately file of mourners, conveying the body of Iyano to rest with his people? Need we look with Elsie for the coming of the ship which will bring back to her a more tender husband than when they parted at Jamestown, so long ago? We will leave them all; adding only that Lady Moody and Sir Henry sought a new home in Virginia, and that history records, later, the reception of Sir Henry as ambassador to New Amsterdam.

www.ingramcontent.com/pod-product-compliance
Lightning Source LLC
Chambersburg PA
CBHW030317240426
43673CB00040B/1196